PACIFISM

PACIFISM

An Historical and Sociological Study

by

DAVID A. MARTIN

SCHOCKEN BOOKS · NEW YORK

First published in U.S.A. 1966
by Schocken Books Inc.
67 Park Avenue, New York 10016

© *David A. Martin 1965*

Library of Congress Catalog Card Number 66-11368

Printed in Great Britain

CONTENTS

Contents

vi

PREFACE

IN a synthetic study such as this, one inevitably accumulates a large number of debts, only some of which can be acknowledged here. I owe a particular debt to Professor Donald MacRae, whose stimulation and confidence ensured that four years of painful gestation did not end in still-birth. I am also very grateful to Professor Ernest Gellner who cast a characteristically astringent eye over the new-born child.

I have had the benefit of correspondence and conversations with various people who should be named: Professor John MacMurray, Dr. A. R. Vidler, Dr. Geoffrey Nuttall, Dr. Keith Robbins, Mr. John Jackson, Dr. Bryan Wilson, Dr. Axel von Campenhausen and Dr. John Highet. I should like to mention the Manager of Pickering and Inglis, the Imam of Woking,— and the custodians of the Friends' Library, Euston Road, who extended a traditional Quaker kindness to me. Naturally none of the above is responsible for the rashness of my generalizations or the vigour of my prejudices: indeed they would specifically dissociate themselves from many of them.

I should also like to thank those who made my research possible without overmuch financial strain. The generosity of the Convocation Trust Fund under the custody of Dr. Dunsheath made it possible for me to take up the University Studentship in sociology in 1959. Miss Hunter and the External Registrar were likewise instrumental in this connection. I should say that this study was accepted for the Ph.D. degree in the University of London.

Very sincere thanks are due in various ways to Mrs. MacLeod and Mrs. Joan Mallison.

Some more particular obligations require acknowledgement. My obligations to Dr. W. A. Cole of Bristol University and to Dr. H. Barbour of Earlham College, Richmond, Indiana, are referred to in the text, but I am grateful to them for permission to use their material. The chapter on the Labour Party is heavily indebted to the work of Dr. S. Davis, while the section on the I.L.P. leans on research by A. J. B. Marwick of Edinburgh University. I have diffuse obligations to A. J. P. Taylor's *Dissent over Foreign Policy*, Herbert Butterfield's *Christianity and History*, F. A. Lea's *Life of Middleton Murry* and Julian Symons's *The Thirties*. Bryan Wilson's thesis—now *Sects and Society*—gave me considerable stimulation and I only regret that his distinguished work in the field of classification was not known to me until a late stage in my own formulations. The influence of Reinhold Niebuhr and Karl Mannheim pervades the whole of my argument.

I also owe something to the Non-Combatant Corps of which I was a member 1948–1950, to the Royal Pioneer Corps and to the Military Police—with which non-combatants are paradoxically associated. In the case of the Military Police they succeeded in converting my adolescent contempt for the psychology and institutions of militarism into a conviction never likely to leave me. I am entirely convinced that war and militarism are utterly repugnant to reason and religion. This book examines critically the mythologies of peace not in order to restore the mythologies of nationalism or any other form of 'reaction' but in order to root peace in realism.

Lastly, I am indebted to my parents and my wife in innumerable ways and I would like to take this opportunity of expressing my gratitude.

INTRODUCTION

THIS book is divided into two parts. The first part is concerned with expounding a broad framework and with illustrating it from a wide variety of historical examples. The second part narrows the focus to modern Britain, largely in the nineteenth and twentieth centuries, and has particular reference to the years covered by the world wars, 1914–1945. The aim of the second part is to exemplify the framework in detail within the specific context of British history. However, it would have been quite as feasible to select American history for this purpose.

The first and last chapters stand somewhat apart in their degree of concentration and they could present the reader with a certain amount of difficulty. As regards the last chapter it is largely a summary of conclusions and is comprehensible providing the previous argument has been understood. However, perhaps a little more needs to be said about the organization and purpose of the first chapter.

The object of the opening chapter is to combine two classical analytic frameworks which are crucial for an understanding of pacifism. These are Troeltsch's distinction between Church and sect and Weber's characterization of the attitudes which different religions adopt towards 'the world.' Clearly pacifism belongs to sectarian rather than ecclesiastical religion, and must be associated with religions which reject the world in some degree. Any difficulties for the reader arise because the logic of Church and sect is related to the logic of the world religions at a high level of abstraction.

The second chapter selects the phenomena of world rejection in various forms, particularly as these affect the practice of war. This can only be done by a further and more detailed analysis of the major world religions. On the one hand are different sorts of relationship between this or that degree of world rejection and war. On the other hand, there are the compromises at which religious beliefs must arrive between the logic of their position and the social realities of power and conflict. This tension between logic and social reality leads to the split between a sectarian religion which maintains that logic, and an ecclesiastical religion which enters into a compromising liaison with relationships of authority and coercion. This split is the theme of chapters three and four.

A second theme of these chapters is concerned with the particular logic of Judaeo–Christianity, which is identified as a *qualified* acceptance of the world and of meaning in history. This means that the element of rejection is subordinate. Withdrawal from the world is locked together with a far more fundamental acceptance of society and of God's creation. Hence, in a Christian context the sectarian refusal to compromise may take two forms, both of which upset the balance involved in the idea of a qualified acceptance. One version of sectarianism withdraws from power and from coercion altogether. Another version 'secularizes' God by bringing the attributes of omnipotence and absolute freedom into history. Both versions enter into permutations with each other, since the withdrawal from violence of the one and the total violence or omnipotence of the other coexist in a state of mutual ambivalence. This is the basic thesis: *an ambivalence between the rejection of power and the acceptance of revolutionary violence*. Each is an alternative way in which the Kingdom of God may come on earth as it is in heaven.

Withdrawal may either take the form of a communitarian enclave (analogous to the order), or it may be manifested in the sectarian refusal of all political participation. Otherwise, there remains Armageddon, waged by God Himself or by His Elect. Sections 3 and 4 of Chapter Four consider the various complex permutations of violence and pacifism and of related polar concepts as illustrated in the English Civil War. Section 5 of the same chapter concludes the first half of the whole study by suggesting certain *types* of relationship between pacifism and violence and by postulating a common causal background for both.

The second part of the study shifts from the contrast between sectarian absolutism and ecclesiastical compromise to the contrast between sectarianism and certain kinds of limited dissent, i.e. conflict which takes place within a broader agreement. Hence the fifth chapter characterizes 'The dissenting mind'.

Introduction

There is also a shift of scale. The argument remains the same but the broad categories previously laid down are now illustrated from detailed material in Britain. The natural focus for such material is the period of the two wars.

Dissent may be religious, political or intellectualist, or combinations of all three. A social group which embodies the religious or the political variety of dissent is given the name of 'denomination', a concept which provides an important key throughout the second part of the book, particularly as regards the Labour Party and the Free Churches. Dissent may also be rationalistic or emotional in tone and the contrast between the two is central to the development of the argument. Rational dissent is located predominantly in *bourgeois* commercialism and in the intelligentsia, but is also found in later developments of the Calvinist variant of religious nonconformity. Emotional dissent is located largely in the Free Churches, but also makes an appearance amongst the intelligentsia as a form of anarchist nostalgia. Every form of dissent makes its home in the Labour Party, which is accordingly given an extended discussion. Labour policies are the politics of the dissenting conscience, particularly so as regards the question of violence.

Each successive chapter (five to nine) attempts to illuminate the contrast between the absolute position of the sect and the limited disagreement of the denomination, showing how these positions belong to quite different types of social organization. Both the chapters on the Free Churches and on the Labour Party analyse the content of the term 'denomination' and try to illustrate how the wide range of internal opinion allowed in such types of organization permits sectarian and absolutist attitudes to be taken up by minorities acting as pressure groups within them. In the case of the I.L.P. the conversion from a denominational to a sectarian body is traced in some detail. An analogous type of development is also traced in the intelligentsia, whereby certain important groups evolve away from rational dissent and anarchist nostalgia towards acute sectarianism of a Marxist or pacifist variety.

The chapter on sectarianism develops the same contrast, but also utilizes the distinction between classical sectarianism, which simply withdraws from political participation, and the sort of communitarian sectarianism (or order) which attempts to build up the new Kingdom in a territorial enclave of its own. The second half of this chapter takes up the theme of individualistic life adjustment, in the form of modern quasi-scientific cults (such as scientology) and of psychological panaceas, to see how far these arouse any degree of tension with the realities of authority, coercion and violence.

PART ONE

The Framework

CHAPTER ONE

BASIC CATEGORIES:
TROELTSCH AND WEBER

THE basic categories required for the study of pacifism derive in the first place from the work of Troeltsch and Weber: the former with respect to the distinction between Church and sect and the latter with respect to his characterization of the world religions. Two analytical tasks present themselves: an expansion of Troeltsch's original distinction and an attempt to see how this expansion can be combined with the work of Weber.

Troeltsch proposed a basic distinction in Christian history between Church and sect, to which he added the concept of the mystical group. As regards the distinction between Church and sect he regarded the Church as a socially inclusive institution which adapted the absolute law of God to the relativities and necessities of politics as well as tempering its demands to average possibilities. The sect, however, regarded itself as an elect minority, proclaiming, or embodying the imminence of a new society and a judgement on the world. Troeltsch also noted, but did not develop, a contradiction within the category of sect between intense activity and passivity, between aggression and withdrawal. This contradiction is central to the present argument, which also aims to show that it is related to other contradictions, as for example between omnipotence and impotence, amorality and perfectionism, complete authoritarianism and total lack of authority. This means that the sect is a type of organization which polarizes at extremes. These extremes are not always associated in an entirely regular way: perfectionism for example may occur in conjunction with pacifism or with violence.

However, not all religious groups fall neatly into the division between Church and sect. Richard Niebuhr also focused attention on the denomination as constituting a developed stage of the sect when perfectionist demands have been ameliorated, the adventist hope dimmed and compromises made with the world. This process certainly occurs, although it can be argued that in the case of the historically most significant examples of the denomination (the Congregationalists, the Baptists and the Methodists) it begins as a type *sui generis* with characteristics which are only marginally sectarian. In general the denomination may be distinguished from the sect because it is a reformist body which only rejects the wider society within the more embracing terms of an overall agreement. It is not revolutionary, either in espousing revolutionary violence or engaging in pacifist withdrawal. However, although the denomination does not withdraw as a *body* from the enveloping society it does lay a stress on individual conscience which is important for the discussion of pacifism. Hence the importance of the concept for the analysis which follows.

There remain two further categories : the order and the 'cult'. The former can be viewed as an analogue, within the inclusive Church, of the spiritual élitism which finds expression in the sect. The order embodies only those polar extremes which are compatible with the wider society : a limited communism can can be admitted whereas revolutionary aggression cannot. Moreover, the acute eschatological expectations of the sect are felt to be already realized here and now in the communitarian enclave of those who have a vocation. The concept of a vocation open only to a minority is the kind of tacit acceptance of double standards which distinguishes bodies which remain within the Church from organizations like the sect and the denomination.

However, there is a certain type of sect which resembles the order in that it also adopts the principle of the communitarian enclave. Perhaps the best-known examples are provided by the various Russian and American experiments in communistic living. The resemblance to the monastic order is the more marked since such communities generally regard the eschatological event as already realized in their own organization rather than as remaining in the future. Since such groups are usually pacifistic they are briefly discussed under the heading of 'the order' in Chapter Eight.

4

The term 'cult' indicates the most radically individualistic forms of religious experience. To that extent the word is unfortunate since *cultus* implies the reverse of individualism. Troeltsch himself came close to the concept when he characterized mystical groups as being based merely on parallel spontaneities. Such groups lack the fellowship principle required to secure historical continuity. Naturally, some mystics remain within the social fellowship, moral disciplines and historical concerns of the Church. Others are possessed by an absorption in the absolute or in nature, enveloping them in a passivity which obliterates time and the knowledge of good and evil.

Radical individualism is not only to be found among mystics. The individualistic principle in Protestantism can undergo continuous extension to the point where it hardly requires a religious organization. It begins in the denomination but is there vigorously checked by an intimate sense of fellowship. While it is true that the denomination may progressively subjectivize worship in terms of what it does for the participant the element of divine service is still present. But in an organization like Christian Science, for example, worship is much more severely attenuated and subjectivity becomes a concern about personal ills. Thus the social psychology of the denomination develops into a religiously based psycho-therapy. The somewhat paradoxical result may be an interest in techniques of adjustment which is very unlikely to produce an ethos at odds with the wider society in any sort of major issue, including that of war.

So far then Troeltsch's original categories of Church, sect and mystical group have been expanded. The sect has been subdivided into activist and pacifist varieties, and the order has been viewed as a muted analogue of the sect within the bounds of the wider Church. Morover, certain connections between the order and the kind of religious organization which sets up a separatist communitarian enclave have been pointed out. Finally, the cult has been subdivided into its mystical form and a form of self-adjustment to society and to personal difficulties based on psychological techniques.

These categories are variously understood by different sociologists but they represent a fair consensus of work done in this field over the past half-century or so. The most complete and coherent exposition of them is to be found in the work of Bryan Wilson. Differences are largely over terminology rather than over criteria, although of course the criteria which one emphasizes vary with analytic purpose. In this case the purpose is to take different sociological types and examine their logical relationship to the quite crucial issues raised by political participation as it is focused in the question of war.

We now turn to a rather different intellectual task and one which, so far as I know, has not been seriously attempted. It has often been queried whether the categories of Troeltsch apply outside Christianity and it is this query which requires an attempt to link his categories with Weber's characterization of the world religions. Without this attempt it is impossible to set the issue of pacifism in a context wider than that of Christianity itself. Obviously, one wants to ask whether the pacifist variety of sect, and the denomination, with its emphasis on conscience, occur outside the ambit of Christian influence.

Two questions are involved here, each linked with the other. One is the *range* of categories implied by the basic logic of religions apart from Christianity: whether for example the logic of a particular religion implies only the Church, or only the pacifist sect. The other is the way in which this logic may alter to some extent the *content* of a category. For example the category of Church, in the sense of a socially inclusive religious institution, may contain a different content in (say) Christian, Confucian and Islamic societies. Of course, these relationships must be formulated at a rather high level of abstraction. The selection of types of religious logic lies along an analytic continuum, and the names of the actual historical religions are attached to these types for convenience of exposition.

The assumption is then that each type of religious logic (or basic attitude to the world) implies a certain *range* of sociological categories and also alters to some extent the *content* of those categories. The question of content is selected first for treatment, although it will be clear from the exposition that it cannot be separated from the question of range.

In order to exemplify varieties of content we may make a comparison between Christianity and Confucianism. Both Christianity and Confucianism imply the category of Church in the sense of an institution or pattern of institutions concerned with conservation and conformity. But there are degrees of conformity, and the content of the ecclesiastical category in Christian societies indicates a differing degree of conformity from its content in Confucian society. Confucianism more readily implies the category of Church in the sense of the formal definition relating to an institution rooted in conservation than does Christianity. There is, of course, no institution in Confucian society which can be described as a 'church' which exists *separately* from the pattern of conservative institutions. Just because Confucianism is the extreme case of simple conservation the 'church' is merged in the social pattern and becomes invisible.

This ready propriety of Confucianism to the ecclesiastical idea is the reverse side of its inability to imply another category beside it. Christianity views the world as sacred only in principle (and not in fact) whereas Confucianism views the world as an immanent sacred harmony maintained, with occasional abnormal divergences, by the Mandate of Heaven. Thus the Christian Church must embody some reserve towards the world and towards 'natural relations' (e.g. those of the family) whereas Confucianism sanctifies these social relationships without reservation. The element of Christian reserve, which is logically related to a sense of tension between body and spirit, implies a tension between Church and State. Christian societies tend therefore to achieve some distinction, however vestigial in some cases, between Church and State, the spiritual and the temporal. The monastic order is a permanent witness to these Christian reservations, which are maintained by those within the ecclesia who wish communally to rise above average possibilities. The closest analogy to Confucianism within Christian societies is the Erastian Anglicanism of the eighteenth century with its emphasis on the rite, its preoccupation with propriety and taste and its hatred of 'enthusiasm'.

So much for an example of differing content. We now turn to examples which bear more directly on the question of the range of categories. An appropriate example may be provided by Manichean dualism in the hope that the very extreme character of the instance may serve the more clearly to illuminate the situation. Manichean dualism regards the world as evil and conceives of God as standing in diametric opposition to the natural world. Believers must, therefore, set themselves aside from all activity in the world, including war and procreation. In this way religious ethics and social ethics are placed in almost total opposition, the only concession to social requirements being a distinction between inner and outer rings of initiates practising different degrees of detachment. Hence Manichean religion implies no sociological category apart from the passive sect. Its adherents must either constitute an ultimately parasitic minority or society as a whole must commit suicide.

In the discussion so far two religious attitudes have been described which imply only one category. Confucianism and the Church Manicheanism and the passive sect. Certain consequences follow from these limitations, either at one extreme or the other. Obviously, Confucianism can only be completely adequate in an entirely static situation. Equally obviously, so far as dualism is concerned there is the problem of continuing historical existence. These difficulties could be resolved in two ways: either the religion can develop another basic motif, somewhat analogous to the second subject in sonata form, in order to ensure continuity and to exercise a major influence, or other religions can provide the content of the vacant categories as need arises. As regards the two examples given the degree of extremism in terms of a continuum of acceptance and rejection is so great that the development of a second attitude is hardly possible. Dualism is too simply based on rejection and Confucianism on acceptance to be able to provide plausibly related alternative formulations. Hence they exemplify the type of situation where other religions provide the content of the vacant categories. For instance, in the case of Confucianism these categories are met by Buddhism and Taoism.

However, where some element of flexibility exists the religion itself provides an alternative formulation through organic development. An example of this process may be found in Buddhism in the course of its development from Hinayana to Mahayana. Because classical Buddhism does not envisage the world as evil but as neutral it possesses a margin of flexibility absent from dualism. Classical Buddhism, strictly interpreted, implies little beyond the category of the order, but Mahayana Buddhism can involve attitudes to the world more overtly positive and therefore including a wider range of categories. In

8

any case, the psychological cultivation of the monastic is conceived in such a way as to have positive cultural by-products, even though these are incidental rather than intended.

We come now to consider in turn three religions which include almost the complete range of sociological categories and are therefore capable of integrating whole societies: Islam, Hinduism and Christianity. Islam involves submission to the power of a God who is conceived as transcendent without qualification. The world is valueless in so far as it is compared with His majesty and man is the instrument of His will. Man does not share in the Being of God but can be the tool of the inscrutable divine purpose. Conceived in this way Islamic religion implies only the Church in the sense of a unitary theocratic society. The norms provided by Islam are not the norms of an absolute justice yet to be realized but social norms given an unqualified divine imprimatur. There is therefore no logical point of appeal for the perfectionist sect. However, there are elements within the Islamic deposit of faith which veer towards Christianity in stressing the justice of God and which therefore anticipate an eschatological event when that justice will be realized and incarnate in the world, through the agency of semi-divine Mahdi. Hence there is a historical point of attachment for sectarianism even though the logic of Islam's more central doctrines precludes it. However, sectarian developments are less pronounced than in Christianity, where they spring directly from the basic norm.

Hinduism can include all sociological categories since it does not possess any fundamental norm. It is a number of different religions: the only basic principle of Hinduism is syncretism. This syncretistic character not only gives it a wide range of categories but also involves relatively weak impulses towards sectarianism and Messianism. Aspirations towards absolute justice have no universally accepted point of reference. The various incarnations of Hinduism embody a whole range of principles none of which has undisputed supremacy. Because it includes so many varied principles Hinduism is an appropriate vehicle for a whole society but lacks the dynamism of a universal religion.

We have seen that Islam includes a range of sociological categories by virtue of a historical combination between principles which are logically incompatible and that Hinduism is ecumenical by virtue of a basic incoherence. Christianity, however, is sociologically inclusive through varied implications arising directly from its root principle. The Christian incarnation provides a unique point of reference, and is simultaneously capable of validating the world in principle and of proclaiming a judgement on the world. The judgement includes active and passive aspects: the proclamation of the ideal Kingdom and the passive suffering of the crucifixion. The validation of the world in principle implies the category of Church, while the form of the judgement implies both the active and the passive sect. The denomination stands in an intermediate position, both accepting the world in principle and endeavouring to realize the Kingdom progressively within it. This is to come about through the moralization of the individual will. The one category not possible as a logical extension of the Christian principle is the cult. A religion of brotherhood which acknowledges some tension between the Christian community and society and which celebrates an incarnation in history must be incompatible with schemes of self-cultivation which ignore history or with techniques of self-adjustment which accept society without qualification.

This completes the discussion of the range and content of the sociological categories implied by different types of religious logic. The argument in the following chapter will now try to set pacifism in the general context of religious development and to illustrate in more detail how the various relationships between this or that religion and the world do or do not include the possibility of a pacifist response.

CHAPTER TWO

THE BREAK WITH NATURE

A central theme of all religion is man's attempt to come to a working settlement with the condition in which he finds himself:

> a stranger and afraid
> In a world I never made.

Confronted by the primal chaos of experience, without form and void, he seeks a viable mode of ordering and understanding it. The agent of this purposeful activity is language: in the beginning was the word. Indeed, the word was God, because it was conceived as a source of power and because it was the means of differentiation, identification and categorization. As the Bible suggests in its description of Adam 'naming' the animals, it is by this activity that man brings the world into subjection. Such activity is both creative and teleological because meaningful order is imposed on pure flux and because that order serves as a basis for action.[1]

This order is imposed equally on the social and the natural environment. Nature and society form a working unity which finds its most striking illustration in totemistic conceptions and practices. Thus Radcliffe-Brown in his treatment of totemism lays emphasis on the process 'by which, in the fashioning of culture, external nature, so-called, comes to be incorporated in the social order as an essential part of it'.[2] This fusion of the natural into the social provides primitive man with a sense of being 'at home' in his environment.

This is not to say that nature is experienced as benevolent and

[1] A useful discussion of this may be found in Ernst Cassirer's *An Essay on Man* (New Haven, 1945), especially Chapter 4.

[2] A. R. Radcliffe-Brown: *Structure and Function in Primitive Society* (London, 1952), p. 131.

friendly: primitive man is well aware that his life is nasty and short. But the nastiness and the brevity, together with all the other ills which flesh is heir to, are endured as explicable. The framework of explanation is complete and provides for counter-measures against disaster and disease. Myth, magic and religion provide a system of conceptions covering not only the ills of life, but the origin of the world, the regional topography, the pro-cesses of growth, the mode of causation, the procession of the seasons and the source of tribal rules and rituals. Doubtless the 'powers' are mysterious, but they have a *modus operandi* and this is frequently capable of manipulation. Because evil is thus tied into a system which is complete, death and disaster create no problem, no sense of incongruity or feeling of outrage against the structure of things as such.

This sense of harmony within a 'closed' irrational framework persists well beyond the stage of religion normally regarded as primitive into the earlier developments of religion in Rome, Greece, India and China. Indeed the explanatory elements in this closed type of religion are frequently carried forward even into the higher religions.[3] Nevertheless the irrationality and in-consistency of these closed systems is increasingly perceived. Throughout the two millennia before Christ one can trace a tradition of maladjustment between man and his environment of which the Epic of Gilgamesh is one of the earliest witnesses. This tradition is perhaps particularly marked in the Hellenistic period when, for example, the plays of Euripides and the Book of Job equally arraign the justice of God. There appeared an attitude of 'reserve' towards nature which may be attributed to the perception of a problem.[4] The universe was now perceived as arbitrary and perplexing in a way which demanded an ex-planation.

The higher religions (in particular Judaism, Christianity, Islam and Buddhism), arise by way of answer to the problem of

[3] The explanatory systems are reinterpreted by higher religions in accordance with their basic attitude towards the world. For example Reinhold Niebuhr inter-prets the creation myth of Genesis as embodying a simultaneous affirmation of the goodness of creation and a refusal to identify the transcendent God with it. At the same time myths often continue to function as explanations and so tend to obscure the specific character of higher religions.

[4] *See* J. Wach: *The Sociology of Religion* (London, 1944), p. 110. Wach says that reserve towards nature is reflected in the concepts of conversion and rebirth. Such concepts are relatively infrequent in religions which lack this reserve.

injustice, disharmony and sheer inexplicable misery. It is important to stress that they do not *explain* evil: the explanatory content of Christianity, for example, is quite low, and in any case both derivative and peripheral. Higher religions are not systems of explanation (though a concept like *karma* may function as a partial explanation) but fundamental attempts to find viable *weltanschauungen*.[5] They are systems of interpretation, points of view, schemes of ultimate adjustment. Such points of view, considered as ideal types, are strictly limited in number. All of them are potentially universalistic, unlike the ethos of primitive religion which centres on the natural group. The principal division between these basic religious attitudes is that between the types of morality they imply. Certain religious attitudes imply what may be called a 'closed' morality, others an 'open' morality.

This difference, originally noted by Bergson,[6] refers to the tension between loyalty to particular groups and loyalty to humanity as such. It also covers a tension between reasonable moralities based on social utility and moralities which go beyond utility, and in going beyond it are frequently even at cross-purposes with social requirements. Charity may be seen as beginning at home and spreading outward like ripples in fainter and fainter circles, or all mankind may be regarded as 'the family', with the same claims as the most intimate relations. The former view will stress the 'platoon' into which we are born, with its particular rights and obligations, while the latter view will stress the idea that such obligations and loyalties are bars to universal love.[7] There will be a tendency for the partisans of closed morality to praise reciprocity, justice and the prudential aspects of conduct, while the partisans of open morality will praise a heroic disinterested virtue which rises beyond justice and sets legality on one side. Needless to say, systems of open morality give rise to dual standards within

---

[5] Wach (op. cit., pp 45–6) argues that we must pierce to 'the basic attitude conceived and nurtured by a decisive religious experience. . . .' In this way subsequent sociological and theological developments can be related to certain basic the matic materials.

[6] H. Bergson: *Les Deux Sources de la Morale et de la Religion* (Paris, 1932), p. 346.

[7] Buddha and Mahavira both attacked the claims of the family. Similarly Jesus declared that whoever loved father or mother more than Him was not worthy of Him. These attitudes can be contrasted with the Confucian approach to the family.

society and to monastic institutions specially designed for those who can practise heroic virtue. Closed morality by contrast tends to conventionality, pure ritualism, exteriority and the more reprehensible forms of calculation. In the categorizations which follow it is characteristic only of the first and last attitudes described, i.e. of cosmic pantheism and of 'arbitrary' mono-theism.

The first type of fundamental world-view to be considered replaces the irrational and arbitrary harmony of primitive religion with a rational harmony. Such a view is essentially pantheistic and monistic. It conceives of a cosmic principle, sometimes identifiable with reason, which equally informs man, society and nature. This principle is variously described as 'Li', the 'Tao' (or Way), Rita, the Law of Nature or the Logos. Happiness and even immortality is to be found by living according to nature or by absorption in the Tao. A man who does so will be inwardly at peace. Not to do so is less a question of radical evil than of intellectual error. Hence the Confucian stress on environment and education. Moreover, material evil is an illusion to which the good man is indifferent: the buffets of the temporal may be ignored by one who is rooted in a timeless reality.

To be rooted in this timeless cosmic reality[8] breeds an attitude not far removed from determinism. The deterministic tendency is increased by the identification of evil in intellectual error, since the concept of freedom must involve the identification of evil in the will. The cosmic principle is sometimes seen as determining all events: 'There's a divinity which shapes our ends rough-hew them as we will.' Such an attitude may well breed a form of quietism, so that the Taoist sage yields to the Tao believing it is best to let all things take their course and not to interfere. But this passivity, which is as close as cosmic pantheism can come to pacifism, is an extreme element in the spectrum of possibilities resulting from it. In general there is little or no tension between conformity to nature or to the Tao and the active performance of social duties, whether they be

[8] A useful comparison between Christian and Confucian concepts and an account of the intrusion of Christian eschatology into Chinese culture is available in J. Levenson: 'Confucian and Taiping Heaven: The Political Implications of Clashing Religious Concepts.' (*Comparative Studies in Society and History*, Vol. IV, No. 4, July 1962.)

those of the city state, the Roman Empire, the Chinese family or the caste. The only tension which can arise may occur in time of acute dislocation in which for one reason or another the course of nature is acutely disturbed, in which event both Stoicism and Taoism produce a mild primitivism.[9] On this view there was once a pure state of nature, a Golden Age. For the Taoist this Age has been lost because of civilization. Thus primitivism contains two ideas: the perfect state which preceded present imperfections, and the superiority of the simple life uncomplicated by civilization.

In religions embodying the idea of the cosmic principle man recovers his sense of being 'at home' in the world. But for Buddhism and Jainism the world is not a home but a prison. In a sense Buddhism and Jainism are more realistic than religions which see all apparent and partial evil as universal good. The discords are too strident to be glossed over, the particular realities of the empirical world too stark to be swallowed up and absorbed in the general principle. Material and moral evil are real and the lot of man compounded of disaster and misery. Yet the root of this misery may be found in desire they may render themselves secure from the pains of the phenomenal world and so eventually enter the peace of Nirvana.

Such a characterization, although grossly over-simplified, pinpoints world denial as the fundamental Buddhist attitude. Attachments of all kinds are a source of pain because they involve the inevitability of loss: therefore one must cultivate non-attachment. To do so means that the ties which bind one to family and to society must be loosened in the individual's search for his own salvation. The root of this ethic must be in a high, disinterested love which rises above the claims of caste and family. Any self-assertion or aggression militates against this passionless love: even the lowliest creatures should be safe from the assertive appetite arising from the will to live and the will to have.

Plainly such an ethic cuts sharply across any rational social

[9] Some forms of Taoism advocate the practice of *wu-wei*, which may be defined as non-aggression or non-meddlesome action. Politically this is associated with a form of *laissez-faire* and an idealization of the small village. As regards foreign politics it is claimed that '... if a great kingdom humbles itself before a small kingdom it shall make that small kingdom its prize'. See J. R. Noss: *Man's Religions* (New York, 1956), pp. 315–27.

ethic. Moreover, it implies either that its followers should remain a small minority[10] or that a double standard should exist expressed in monastic institutions. Thus Buddhism, and to an even greater extent Jainism, are extreme religious adjustments to the problem of evil, which in so far as they are consistent[11] run directly contrary to culture, its rights and particular duties. Religion and society are placed in acute tension, but the tension is not revolutionary since the religion, having no positive doctrine of creation makes no claim *over* society : it merely abandons it. Buddhism has its pacifism therefore, but no revolutionary eschatological communism such as is historically associated with pacifism within the cultural area affected by Christianity. This kind of eschatological communism is rendered doubly impossible by the rejection of society and by the fact that history is not regarded as meaningful.

Buddhism is not the only religion to see the world as a prison. Such a view is found in religions which embrace a thoroughgoing dualism. By dualism one means, of course, not the familiar Cartesian dualism between mind and body, but a metphysical dualism in which the principle of evil is exalted to the pinnacle of power where it confronts the principle of good on more or less equal terms. With a large number of variations one finds conceptions of this type in the Babylonian religion,[12] in the later Avesta, in Manicheanism, in Marcionism, in Gnosticism, in Bogomilism and Albigensianism. Generally the world is regarded as being under demonic or satanic domination and the goal of life is therefore to escape from the darkness of the material into the world of light. All that chains man to the material must be rejected, sexual activity being particularly reprehensible since it brings more beings into the prison.

Dualism has affinities with Buddhism so far as fundamental attitudes are concerned, but whereas in Buddhism the individual achieves his salvation by psychological self-discipline (an

[10] The Jain community, in a sense, constitutes an order within the wider society.

[11] Buddhism has a rich relation to culture but this is due partly to the incidental products of monasticism and self-discipline and partly to the rarity of complete consistency. Classical Buddhism tends to remain a minority faith while Mahayana Buddhism (the 'Pure Land' sects for example) illustrates how 'cheerfulness keeps breaking in'.

[12] *See* H. Frankfort: *Kingship and the Gods* (Chicago, 1948). Frankfort relates this type of conception to the uncertainties of life in the basin of the Tigris-Euphrates.

activity which has positive cultural by-products) in dualism salvation is by divine deliverance. In 'Christian' versions a heavenly 'Man' appears in apparent flesh and delivers the saving message. Once the particles of light imprisoned in the darkness of the body have been released the material world returns to chaos. This return to chaos constitutes the judgement.

Now this union of the world-denying impulse with the redemptive idea is not really culturally viable at all. Because God is defined in terms of pure negative transcendence the material world is deprived of all element of divinity and religion of all relevance to real life. Whereas Buddhism regards the world rather more as indifferent than as a positively satanic creation and so views society in a somewhat similar light, dualism tends to take a stance directly opposed to the world and to society. The dualist ethic exists in a state of tension with culture which is almost absolute and consequently uncreative. Indeed in some versions it does not even produce a *cultus*. It is not surprising that a religion which combines a pacifist ethic with such a complete form of world denial is culturally evanescent. The religious adjustment is complete, the social adjustment is non-existent.

With Judaeo-Christianity[13] we encounter a version of the redemptive idea such as has been noted in dualism, but in alliance with ethical monotheism. Redemption in such a context possesses a radically different character. Because God made the world it is potentially divine[14] and redemption is therefore not from the world but of the world. And yet man is not 'at home' in the world as he is in religions of the cosmic principle. God indeed made the world, but He remains transcendent over it, so that the spiritual realm and the natural order overlap but are never coincident. Man is a creature of two worlds existing in creative tension. The world of the spirit strives actively through history in the world of nature, completing it, not denying it except in so far as there exists a recalcitrant resistance to good. Man has an appropriate reserve towards nature because it is not identical with God and may therefore furnish some sort of contrast with Him, and yet he may claim the world for God

[13] Treated here as one religion, although early Judaism with its emphasis on the purely numinous non-rational character of Yahweh has close affinities with Islam. *See* R. Otto: *The Idea of the Holy* (London, 1923), p. 90.

[14] Hence the sacramental idea, which selects bread and wine to symbolize and particularize the potentially sacred character of the material world.

since ultimately, 'the earth is the Lord's and the fullness thereof'. Man may not be at home in the world but he is a hardworking tenant with a decent lease from the landlord. As the landlord worked on the 'material' world so also man works on it. In this conception we see the germ of the psychological activism, of the gospel of work, and even of the scientific curiosity found in the Judaeo-Christian tradition.

Since God is Lord He is supreme not only over nature but over history. Indeed history is peculiarly the realm of His activity and of His righteous judgements. Yet the concept of a just God as transcendent both over nature and history raises the problem of evil in a specially acute form. The sun shines on both evil and good, and historical experience underlines fundamental injustices in the whole disposition of affairs. The godless triumph and the righteous are put to shame and suffering.[15] Both the Psalms and the Book of Job raise the question of justice in relation to suffering. This setting over of a just and righteous God against historical realities produces a vivid contrast between ideal and actual, the importance of the which can hardly be exaggerated. The problem could be solved by rejecting God's transcendence, thus destroying the tension and returning to pantheistic naturalism. But the prophets were above all else aware of precisely this, that before the earth was brought forth, from everlasting to everlasting, God is God. The problem must be solved otherwise.

It is in fact solved in two ways which are woven together. Deutero-Isaiah conceives of the suffering of Israel as a redemptive spectacle which shall usher in the ideal Kingdom : a conception itself born out of the suffering of the Babylonish captivity. Good was to be victorious in an encounter with evil at its worst, in the fact of death itself. Suffering and death were to be deprived of their negative character and power, and made into victory of love. The core of Judaeo-Christian religion thus became a creative tragedy, not as in Aeschylus the tragedy of ineluctable fate, but the tragedy of freedom. Yet the Kingdom does not come, and the will of God is not done in earth as it is

---

[15] A summary of these developments is provided in H. Butterfield: *Christianity and History* (London, 1944). It is perhaps important to add that the problem of suffering relates to the suffering of Israel more than to suffering in general. To that extent the idea of eschatology develops from the Covenant of God with His Elect.

in heaven. It remains constantly in the future, so retaining its dialectic tension with the present and constituting a constant challenge to actuality.

Such a tension is potentially revolutionary, so that whenever religion begins merely to luxuriate in natural harmonies or carries its compromises with actuality to the point of complacent acceptance of whatever is, then the ideal vision rises up in judgement. So a dichotomy is created in culture between the compromises and relativities of the terrestrial city as set over against the city of God. The prophetic tradition is thus written into Judaeo-Christianity from Isaiah to Karl Marx. The Kingdom to be proclaimed is free from 'mine' and 'thine' and from the wars which are its consequence. It is of course natural for the Church, as deeply involved in the social nexus to emphasize the necessity of compromise, and for the sects, as the organizations of the socially deprived, to attempt to set up the ideal Kingdom of peace, equality and Communism, or to await its foundation by God's intervention. Thus the cultural area of Christianity is always potentially dynamic and present-day Communism shewn as directly derived from it.

With Islam we appear to return to a simple social morality without any grave tensions between religion and culture except in so far as certain negative tensions are derived from Indian religion and certain positive tensions from Christianity.[16] In common with Judaism and Christianity Islam is monotheistic. By contrast with the negative transcendence of dualism Islam presents a doctrine of pure positive transcendence. Pure transcendence also differentiates it from Christianity which sees God as working through humanity, uniquely so in Jesus Christ. A further mark of differentiation from Christianity is found in the stress upon the arbitrary power of the Deity.[17] His justice completely transcends human canons of justice and He predestines men either to salvation or damnation. To such power the only attitude is submission. This enables Islam to present a simple challenge to the non-Muslim, even if it is lacking in richness.

The activity of the Deity in creating the visible material

[16] Sufism has affinities with Vedanta, and the Shi'ite division has affinities with Christianity.

[17] As in Judaism the contrast between nature and God's power renders the former not so much corrupt as valueless.

world produces an active attitude to which the conception of unlimited power adds fanatical militancy. Hence the idea of the Holy War and the general military attitude of Islam. The unqualified character of the Deity (at least in orthodox Islam) and this absolute differentiation from His creation means that the ideal is not seen as a contrast to the injustices of the real world and also that it is raised above actuality beyond the possibility of dialectic tension. The only conceivable eschatology is entirely beyond this world in the traditional heaven and hell:[18] submission in any case inhibits revolution in the sense of an attempt to inaugurate a kingdom of justice on earth. At the same time it makes possible an ethic relatively adjusted to social needs. This is true even today where, as in West Africa, Islamic codes are more adjusted to social needs than are Christian. As in Confucianism the social and the religious ethic are roughly coincidental, except that whereas in the one the social element dominates the religious, in the other the religious dominates the social. Thus Islamic society has no concept of secular law: law and theology are synonymous. Naturally with such a socially integrated ethic and with such an unqualified concept of God's power the possibility of pacifism is remote, except where alien elements intrude.

The foregoing survey of the major types of relation between religion and culture, although very much over-simplified by the employment of somewhat arbitrary measures of central tendency does enable us nevertheless to formulate certain sociological consequences of these different relationships.[19] To make such consequences clear it may be worth while representing these relationships diagrammatically. In the accompanying diagram the circles drawn with a thick line represent the religious sphere and the circles drawn with a thin line the social.

The tension between society and religion which exists in Buddhism, Judaeo-Christianity and dualism is here clearly illustrated. It follows therefore that each of these world religion-cultures should possess institutions embodying dual standards,

[18] Heaven and hell arise with the idea of the 'last things' in logical association with monotheism. They should be distinguished from notions of survival (such as Sheol) based on dreams, ancestor worship, etc.

[19] Since Hinduism is syncretistic it embodies elements from almost all the types discussed, although the conception of Brahman-Atman perhaps brings it closest to cosmic pantheism.

one for virtuosi of the religious life, the other for the laity; and that such dual standards should be absent from Islam and from cosmic pantheism. This is in fact the case. Christianity has its monastic institutions, indicating a certain tension between religious and social goals; Buddhism is peculiarly the religion of the monk, indicating a high degree of such tension; while the tension in dualism is so great that the whole 'Church' consists of monks. Islam by contrast is a lay religion[20] which frowns upon religious orders, while Confucianism lacks the concept of laity as contrasted with religious virtuosi altogether.

Cosmic pantheism does not produce the idea of a Church standing in a specific relation to society. Rather it lays stress on performing the 'rites' as an aspect of social duty. As has been

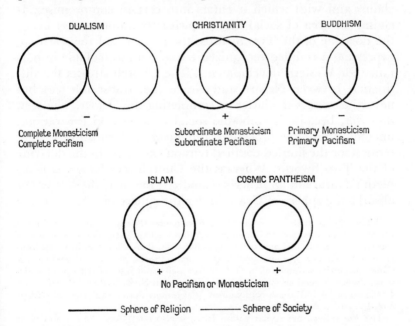

suggested, it is perhaps faintly echoed within Christianity by Erastian Anglicanism. Nor does Buddhism produce the idea of the church since its relation to society is negative. Rather it expresses itself in schools and pre-eminently in the Order. Dualism is a 'Church' which is really a sect or order: its

[20] Comparisons with Calvinism are instructive, in this, as in other respects.

'Church' is completely cut off from society and can enter into no fruitful relations with it. Islam is a Church which absorbs society and produces no 'sects', only *divisions*. There are largely territorial divisions in Islam (e.g. as between Sunnis and Shi'-ites), there are schools of interpretation of the law, and there are reform movements like the Wahhabi, but there are few confrontations of a compromising 'Church' with an idealistic revolutionary sectarianism. [21] Indeed the idea of Church and sect, the former standing in a specific positive relation to society, neither absorbing it nor absorbed by it, is a peculiar sociological consequence of Christianity.

The Christian Church, as a socially inclusive institution enters into relations with society upon which it makes certain claims and with which it enters into certain compromises. It claims an area of social life as spiritually autonomous: hence the doctrine of the Two Swords, the secular and the spiritual, expressing a codified recognized tension of incalculable importance for Western developments. The Church stresses the distinction between Nature and Grace (i.e. transcendence) but nevertheless sees the latter as completing the former. The sect, however, because it embodies social tensions and frustrations, uncompromisingly proclaims the ideal and substitutes total tension for the limited codified tension expressed in the doctrine of the Two Swords. Whereas the Church sees Grace as completing Nature in an orderly, canalized manner, the sect either absorbs the sphere of Grace under the sphere of Nature or the

[21] The whole complex of Shi'ite ideas, in particular the expectation of the Mahdi (or Messiah), is very close to Christianity. A movement of particular interest, and of special relevance to this present study, is Bahaism. Bahaism began in nineteenth-century Persia as a proto-nationalist movement of social protest. Originally, messianic, revolutionary and millenarian, it eventually split into a pacifist wing and a violent wing. A good account of Bahaism is given in N. R. Keddie: 'Religion and Irreligion in Early Iranian Nationalism' (*Comparative Studies in Society and History*, Vol. IV, No. 3, April 1962).

The Ahmadiyya movement within Islam is also interesting. An account of its attitude to war can be found in *The Religion of Islam* (Lahore, 1950), by Mohammad Ali, a representative of the Conservatives within the movement. This writer accepts defensive war as having Quranic sanction but rejects the idea of propagating Islam by force. It seems that Ghulam Ahmad, the founder, claimed to be the Messiah in a Second Coming, the Mahdi, and an avatar of Krishna. Conceivably his insistence on the peaceful character of the Mahdi was intended to allay the fears of the British Government just as the apolitical attitude of the original Ahmadiyyah movement may have reflected a reliance on the British to maintain a communal balance against the Hindus.

sphere of Nature under the sphere of Grace. Thus, while it proclaims a total tension between ideal and actual it aims at the total elimination of that tension. It aims to make the spheres of religion and society coincident, either by absolute immanence or absolute transcendence. The protagonists of absolute immanence, notably the Communist Party, make the divine coincident with history, while the protagonists of absolute transcendence, such as the Witnesses[22] proclaim an immediate end to history as it is swallowed up in the power of God. Both Communists and Witnesses find the distinction between Nature and Grace intolerable, but they attempt to eliminate it in diametrically opposed ways.

The dichotomy of Church and sect (as will be further argued in later chapters) does not exhaust the typical sociological consequences of Christianity.[23] Whereas the sects seek in one way or another to eliminate the tension between Nature and Grace, and whereas the Church sees this tension in static terms, it is always possible to conceive the relation between Nature and Grace dynamically. The denomination, as the eventual sociological realization of the impulses of the Reformation, does not destroy the distinction between Nature and Grace but allows the sphere of Grace to act dynamically on the sphere of Nature. This gives a certain affinity with the idea of progress and also makes it an important agent of democracy. It makes it an agent of democracy since it substitutes a democracy of the spirit for an aristocracy of the spirit. Whereas the static conception of Grace and Nature in the Church is associated with a rather pessimistic view of their interrelation, so that the sphere of the former is *in principle* restricted to special orders, in the denomination the sphere of Grace is seen as *in principle* open to all. Such spiritual democracy has organizational consequences (in the substitution of ministry for priesthood) which are sociologically democratic. What is particularly important for our argument is that a dynamic conception of Grace is inclined to overestimate its possibilities in overcoming Nature within the ordinary man, so that there arises a misplaced optimism about

[22] The persecution of Witnesses in the Soviet Union expresses Soviet awareness of this polar opposition and possibly also of psychological identity.

[23] I am presupposing the typology of Church, sect and mystical group as proposed by E. Troeltsch: *The Social Teachings of the Christian Churches* (London, 1931), pp. 991 ff.

the degree of moralization to which man in society is susceptible. The denomination never, as an organization, adopts pacifism, which belongs to the sects and to their complete absorption of Nature in Grace, but it does adopt a pacific optimism which becomes an important political factor in those countries where denominationalism is widely disseminated.

Finally, one may bring together a few comments on the types of pacifism which have been noted in the major religious traditions. Firstly we have noted a passive tendency marginally related to absorption in the cosmic principle. Secondly we have noted the doctrine of *ahimsa* or non-attachment in classical Buddhism and Jainism in connection with the impulse of world denial. This same impulse, with similar pacifist consequences is found in dualism. Finally we have noted pacifism with Communism in the ideal aspect of Christianity as espoused by the sects. This is contrasted with the relative compromises of the Church as well as with a pacific tradition associated with a type of organization midway between Church and sect viz. the denomination.[24]

A CONCLUDING NOTE ON COMMUNISM

Whereas dualism produces a Church which is really a sect, Communism turns a sect into a Church, thus attempting to close the gap between ideal and actual and so eliminate the historic dialectic of Christianity. Hence the function of the party, still operating as a kind of monastic order of virtuosi in Communist society, is to remain only for the interim: when the circles of religion and culture are made absolutely coincident the Party as an order will disappear because it includes everybody. It will then be a Church, but not in the Christian sense of the word because it will function as a simple theocracy with no sects set over against it. The Kingdom of Freedom, as Engels called it, will have arrived, and so sects will be sociologically impossible.

To make the spheres of religion and culture coincident the Party must eliminate religion, more especially Christianity. Cosmic pantheism is less dangerous because, like Communism, it is monistic. The Chinese Communists may rehabilitate

[24] The conception of the denomination is worked out in the Appendix to the present study.

Confucius without fear, knowing that there is a fairly easy transition from pantheism to Communism. Antagonism must necessarily be concentrated against the priest, because the separation of his order symbolizes the specifically Christian tension.

The fundamental antagonism of Communism to the Christian religion is necessary because the latter questions the idea that the sectarian ideal once 'up above' has now been actualized, or is in course of actualization. The more surely Communist society appears as something decidedly less than heaven on earth, the more violently must the idea of heaven or the spiritual realm be rooted out, otherwise religiously motivated tensions will upset the supposed sectarian paradise by 'judge-ing' it. Moreover, the established Churches, on the basis of their long historical experience, mock at the Communist Utopia, although their own failure (itself theologically under-standable in view of the inevitable corruption of human affairs) to attack those injustices which *were* organizationally capable of elimination, gives Communism much of its psychological vigour.

Of course, there is a sense in which a certain type of Liberal democracy shares Communist illusions: in that it believes that the ideal is gradually being realized and that history is 'its own redeemer'. This is because it fails to distinguish the senses in which progress is possible and those in which it is not. Neverthe-less, Liberal democracy may be the best illusion we have.

CHAPTER THREE

CATHOLIC COMPROMISE AND SECTARIAN REJECTION

THIS chapter is concerned with the association between pacifism and eschatology in those forms of sectarianism which spring logically from the central religious attitudes of Christianity.

Questions relating to the form of that association are largely held over to Chapter 4. However, it is worth briefly indicating that eschatological expectation either anticipates God's action in renovating the present world or in replacing it by a better: in which activity He may or may not require human co-operation or the help of the Messianic agent. Pacifism may arise during the period of increasing expectation, perhaps by way of preparation, or it may be found in the period following the failure of such hopes. These hopes are then transferred to the self-selecting community, which constitutes a special form of what theologians call 'realized eschatology'.

The relation of pacifism to eschatology within Christian sectarianism requires to be set against an immediate background and a wider background. The immediate background is that of the inter-testamental period and the gospels. The broader background is that of the Catholic compromise with nature (which developed as the Jewish sect of Christianity grew into a Church), and of the social movements which protested in various ways against any accommodation of the primitive vision with actualities and social requirements. These protests were variously those of an intrusive dualism and of revolutionary sectarianism. We begin with the immediate background.

A sociologist approaches the subject of Old Testament history and of the theological and social background of the gospels with necessary caution. Only the most expert higher critics can hope to pick their way through the field without danger to academic life and limb. Nevertheless, the sociologist, in this as in other spheres, must take his life in his hands. Moreover, there are general surveys of the material which at least command widespread respect if not universal agreement. The origins of eschatology and Messianism are the subject of a magisterial study by Mowinckel entitled *He that Cometh*, and Martin Noth has recently provided a standard history of Israel. Another standard work of the previous generation is to be found in *A History of Israel* by Oesterley and Robinson.

The eschatological hope, in the sense of a sudden change in the world order by the activity of God, originally lay embedded in hopes of Jewish national restoration. Whereas the first pro-phets, such as Amos, announced the destruction of Israel and of Judah, by the time of Proto-Isaiah there was renewed hope that God would not forget His covenant and that a remnant might be saved. During the period of the Babylonian exile this hope was maintained and in Deutero-Isaiah it appears in a drama of cosmic proportions. Deutero-Isaiah takes the details of the drama from very much earlier materials belonging to the period of the monarchy and associated with the major festivals at Jerusalem, in particular the New Year celebration of God's victory over chaos. In this victory the themes of paradisal renewal of nature and of Israel's national restoration are com-bined. Thus Jewish nationalism remains a part of the universal hope even in the writings of Deutero-Isaiah. As Mowinckel points out the underlying presupposition of these conceptions is the rule of God and the victory of His purpose, however much political reality may seem to contradict it.

After the return from exile the emphasis of Jewish religion turns on social integration around the priesthood and the con-cept of the law. 'The organic unity of the old Israel was replaced by the circle of those who acknowledged the law.'[1] It would seem that the future hope lay in partial abeyance during suc-ceeding centuries, even when the Persian overlords were ex-changed for Greek and Egyptian ones. Indeed there was some danger of Judaism succumbing to Hellenic influences, a danger which remained in being until the period when Palestine passed under the rule of Syria in 198 B.C. However, soon after this had

[1] M. Noth: *The History of Israel* (London, 1958), p. 333.

occurred the Syrian King Antiochus Epiphanes attempted to prohibit Jewish religious observances and in this way occasioned a revival of piety, notably among those known as the Hasidim (or 'the Pious').

The sacrilegious activities of Antiochus not only revived religion but also revived the sense of Jewish national identity. Hence the armed revolt of the Maccabees. But while the Maccabees were interested in national independence as well as in the restoration of the religious order the Hasidim were interested only in the latter. The Hasidim anticipated that the restoration of the *cultus* at Jerusalem would usher in the new age and were inclined to see the actual fighting as only a 'little help'[2] compared with the victory which was to come from God. Some of these quietists were drawn into the fighting once the situation became critical, though it seems that others maintained their attitude of passive eschatological expectation.[3]

The new age did not appear with the restoration of the Jerusalem *cultus* and the Hasidim were in any case content to achieve religious freedom without pursuing national independence. Otherwise, the ultimate triumph might be left to divine intervention. Moreover, even their religious aims seem to have diverged from those of the nationalists as soon as the latter had achieved their major political object with the foundation of the Hasmonean dynasty. Once in power the Hasmoneans proceeded to support the Sadducees, who were the priests of the liberal aristocracy and who not only rejected the apocalyptic hope and belief in the resurrection but wished to continue the Hellenizing tendencies of the previous period.

At this point the Hasidim seem to have divided into a variety of parties and groups, pre-eminent amongst which were the Pharisees and the Essenes. The former to some extent allowed the apocalyptic expectation to fade and concentrated their attention on the law and the organization of local worship around the synagogues. As regards politics they were disposed to quietism. The Essenes, however, combined apparent political pacifism with an aggressive warlike symbolism rooted in a resurgent eschatology. A further party which emerged some-

[2] *See* Daniel xi. 34.

[3] According to W. O. E. Oesterley and T. H. Robinson: *A History of Israel* (2 Vols· Oxford, 1932), p. 316.

what later, known as the Zealots, united eschatology to explicit violence. Moreover, it is important to note that all these variations on the eschatological theme acquired a strong Messianic component during the first century B.C., particularly after the Roman occupation in the year 63. This concept of the Messiah originally grew out of an idealization of the oriental ideology of kingship, but as the situation of Israel grew more difficult the Messianic figure came to possess correspondingly greater potency.

The thinking of the Essenes merits some further examination, partly because they provide a clear instance of the way in which acute symbolic aggression can be combined with political pacifism. Our main sources of information derive from the community at Qumran, which existed from *c.* 120 B.C. to A.D. 68. It was organized into a monastic group, which was Communistic in basis, and a non-monastic group which probably possessed some private property and did not reject procreation in principle. Essenes held that God was responsible for the whole creation, but that the creation is 'fulfilled' in that the powers of darkness and light are both at work in it until the end of the world. Such conceptions, together with the attitude towards sex, indicate the presence of dualistic influences. As regards their Jewish inheritance they looked back to the doctrines of Proto-Isaiah concerning the elect remnant and envisaged themselves as the only true heirs of the patriarchs and of the new covenant proclaimed in Jeremiah.[4]

The moral standards of the community regarded worldly riches and unchastity as the most deadly of sins. Poverty was important because it represented a voluntary and charismatic preparation for the Messianic liberation. Not that the poor were the redeemed of God merely in a passive sense; they also had the task of waging God's war of vengeance, although ultimate victory naturally belonged to God.

The Messianic event would be ushered in by a period of 'woes': the more terrible these became the nearer the end. Eventually there would be a new creation and a re-ordering of the cosmos. The community expected a Prophet, a Priest-Messiah and a Lay-Messiah. The Priest-Messiah was to be supreme in matters of ritual, the Lay-Messiah in military

[4] Jeremiah xxxi. 31.

matters. Although these particular Essenes were clearly military in attitude the evidence from Philo and Josephus suggests that other Essenes or Essenes of a different period were pacifist.[5] If this is the case then the association of eschatology and pacifism in the same social milieu is clear. The pacifism of many of the Pharisees, which followed on their loss of the more immediate eschatological hope, illustrates the same association in a different form.

The Essenes constituted only a part of the general eschatological movement, distinguished from its other elements mainly by the priestly emphasis. Besides the Essenes there were those who awaited 'the Man'. This particular conception would appear to combine the Messiah of Jewish nationalism with a cosmic archetypal 'Man' derived from Zoroastrian eschatology.[6] There were also many, amongst them the circle of John the Baptist, who in a more general manner 'waited for the Kingdom of God'.

In a sense Jesus fulfilled these various expectations, giving each of them a different content. 'Son of Man' was His favourite description of Himself. His Messiahship He interpreted with reference to the Suffering Servant poems, not to the Davidic kingdom. He even fulfilled the legalism of the Essenes and the Pharisaic sect by declaring that He had not come to destroy the law, and that far from taking one jot or tittle from it He desired a righteousness which exceeded it. Yet at the same time He reduced the law in essence to one positive precept. He completed John the Baptist's proclamation of the Coming Kingdom, but renounced the asceticism which had been so marked a characteristic of His forerunner. The Son of Man came 'eating and drinking'.

The gospels are not history nor are they a blueprint for Utopia. They are not philosophy or ethics. They illustrate neither a 'Liberal' nor even a 'Socialist' Jesus. Rather they are

[5] K. Schubert in his *The Dead Sea Community* (London, 1959), argues this was because their accounts were doctored for Hellenic consumption. E. Wilson in *The Scrolls from the Dead Sea* (London, 1958), believes the movement developed in successive phases. He says, 'One can, in any case, plausibly explain the defiance of the Teacher of Righteousness, the pacifism of Philo's Essenes, and the turning of the other cheek of Jesus as marking successive phases of the adjustment of the Jews to defeat.' (p. 102)

[6] There is a brief discussion in R. Bultmann: *Primitive Christianity* (Edinburgh 1960), pp. 85–6. Further material may be found in Mowinckel op. cit.

witnesses of and witnesses to the redemption of the world and the coming of the Kingdom. They affirm the absolute and radical character of the moral claim and the all-sufficiency of the Divine Compassion. All is required and all is forgiven: except pride and hardness of heart, which will not allow itself to be forgiven and therefore retains the wrath of God. On this account the publicans enter into the Kingdom before the Pharisees. The majesty of the law and God's righteousness remains, and not only obedience is required but interior assent. Yet in another sense, the law is totally abrogated, so that nothing whatever is required except a simple childlike trust in the love of the Father.

Thus the Christian life is set within the poles of a dialectic at once heroic and humane, for while the unlimited liabilities of love stretch out beyond the requirements of law, or convention, of ritual or social expediency, yet the heart of the matter is no more than a simple renewal of trust and the act of turning one's face in the direction of good. By this act alone the sinner is completely 'justified': and supremely so through the manner in which God Himself enters this dialectic in a loving and sacrificial activity whereby He not only fulfils the law but goes beyond it and so proclaims a forgiveness which is conditional only on its acceptance. In the Passion of Christ the law is confirmed in so far as it is life and freedom; destroyed in so far as it is tyranny and death. And the act whereby this is achieved converts death, the last defeat of man, into an eternal victory.

The Epistles of Paul are a tremendous series of variations on this theme: their supposed disagreement with the gospels is a myth which recent scholarship more and more dispels. Paul, a Pharisee of the Pharisees, knows the tyranny of the Law but he suddenly realizes that the grace of God in Christ has in principle destroyed this tyranny along with all other tyrannies. Grace is sufficient for him. *Solâ fide, solâ gratia.*

Within the dialectic of love the gospels are pervaded by a sense of limitless freedom. But so dynamic a concept is necessarily open to many and grave dangers: Grace may be conceived mechanically, a new ritualism may develop, the gospels may themselves become a new legalism, and even the dialectic itself may become a routinized and lifeless religious psychology. It is in connection with a new legalism that pacifism develops, because while the gospels are neither pacifist nor non-pacifist, yet there remains a sense in which the Sermon on the Mount is the law of the 'Kingdom' and this sense is readily misunderstood. It is misunderstood because every articulation of freedom is easy to misunderstand : freedom is always balanced and poised on a knife-edge, in process of discovery or loss. It is literally true that to call another man a fool is to stand in danger of 'the judgement' and to realize this is a potential gain in moral sensitivity. But the consequence is not a legalistic fear but confidence, since the law lays all men under condemnation in order that all men may be under Grace. Thus the gospels are not only radical freedom but radical equality : equality before God. Both the freedom and the equality are such *in principle* : taken as facts they are self-destructive, because the contrast and the tension between actual and ideal is not arbitrary but constitutional and inherent.

The key to any analysis of sectarianism, and therefore to any analysis of pacifism, must be found in the fact that sectarianism does not comprehend the paradox of Nature and Grace. Take, for instance, the sectarian reaction to the teaching of Jesus on adultery, which stresses the fact that the heart is often guilty of adultery when the body is not. This teaching may either be turned into an intense Puritanism, struggling to eliminate desire itself, so creating a fresh legalism ; or alternatively it may be argued that since the adulterous heart incurs condemnation along with adultery itself, then there is no difference of degree, and, since Grace is sufficient, one might as well commit adultery. The Sermon on the Mount can thus be turned into a new law (including its pacifist injunctions) or the concomitant doctrine of Grace may be exaggerated to the point of amorality. So, while with regard to the material world sectarians absorb Nature into Grace, or Grace into Nature, with regard to morality they allow the law to eliminate Grace or Grace to destroy the law.

The Church, however, is enmeshed in social requirements and cannot embrace either an impossible legalism or an antisocial amoralism. Like all institutions it embodies legalistic tendencies but these have to be adjusted to average capacities rather than to ideal requirements. The more the Church expands to include the average man the more it becomes aware

of a need to compromise, even while maintaining some reference to a higher law. It therefore elaborates, on the one hand, a
relative law, which regulates a long-term compromise with the
world, and on the other hand an absolute law which serves as a
point of reference providing a formal distinction between sacred
and secular. Obedience to this absolute law is in principle restricted to the Orders which are to that extent analogues of the
perfectionist sect within the institutional boundaries of the
Church. With regard to Grace the Church canalizes, mecha-
nizes and regulates the whole conception through an apparatus
of confession, absolution, indulgence, etc., without, however,
necessarily destroying the inner meaning of Grace for the
genuine believer.

The period from the apostolic age to the age of Constantine
was one in which Christianity developed from a Jewish sect into
the heir of Roman civilization. As it did so the Church assimilated alien influences, such as the philosophy of the Stoics,
which assisted it in the formulation of norms which should
regulate its relation to society. The attempts to find such
norms and the compromises mentioned above inevitably
brought the question of the Church and its attitude to war into
focus.

In the early years of the immediate post-apostolic age nothing
occurred to bring the problem of war sharply before the minds
of Christians. Indeed, when objections did arise they concerned
the sacrifice to the Emperor involved in military service as well
as the shedding of blood. Cadoux put the matter in this way:
'No Christian . . . would voluntarily become a soldier after
conversion: he would be deterred from doing so not only by
fear of contamination from idolatry but also by natural reluc-
tance—and doubtless in many cases a conscientious objection—
to carrying arms.'[7] Round about the year 180 this attitude was
sufficiently widespread for Celsus to complain that if all men
were Christians the Empire would become a prey to barbarians.
In a similar way Origen's answer to Celsus some seventy years
later suggests a continuance of conscientious objection.

These first three centuries of Church life were therefore
marked by a continuous protest against military service from
substantial groups of Christians. These same centuries were also

[7] C. J. Cadoux: *The Early Church and the World* (Edinburgh, 1925), p. 190.

those in which hope of the Last Day played a large, though diminishing part, in the minds of Christians. To what extent pacifism and eschatology were directly related during this time it is difficult to say. However, it is clear that towards the end, objections to military service were becoming less frequent and that after the Church became the official religion of the Roman Empire they diminished still further. It wasn't long before reservations about war became the special and rather formal preserve of the clergy and the monastic orders.

The Church recognized war as an institution belonging to the relative natural law which existed as a scourge for sin. This recognition was given more precision by St. Augustine when he elaborated a doctrine of the just war. In his view wars of defence are just in principle, whereas wars of offence can only be justified if they conform to a number of strict conditions. These conditions were crystallized by later writers into three criteria: a 'just' cause, a declaration of war by the recognized sovereign, and a 'right' intention. A right intention meant that the good which was aimed at should manifestly outweigh the evil involved.

The doctrine of the just war remained the basic position of the Church throughout its subsequent history, except that the criterion of a good intention was given relatively greater weight by the neo-scholastic jurist Francis de Victoria, while his contemporary St. Alphonsus de Liguori further stressed that the results of war were *generally* evil. According to him a war is 'hardly ever just if declared on probable reasons of justice alone and not certain reasons'. This position has actually given scope for a modern form of Catholic pacifism which regards all contemporary wars as inevitably bringing about more evil than good.[8]

The compromises of the Church gave rise to protests of various kinds. The first of these to be considered is based on the type of dualism which the medieval Church labelled 'Manichean'.[9] Manichean dualism is a form of adjustment to the problem of evil which denies the responsibility of God for the creation. The material universe is regarded as dominated by

[8] References are drawn from A. C. F. Beales: *The Catholic Church and the International Order* (Harmondsworth, 1941).
[9] Information concerning dualism is largely based on S. Runciman: *The Medieval Manichee* (Cambridge, 1947).

Satan and the believer therefore abstains from participation in it as far as possible, particularly as regards the process of procreation and the institution of war.

Although the logical consequences for society of this doctrine involve universal monasticism, it is almost impossible to adhere consistently to the implications of such a position over a long period. Thus the heresiarch Mani (martyred in A.D. 276) organized his 'Church' into the Elect and the Hearers. The Elect had to pass through strict initiation ceremonies, after which they were held to be full of light. They were not to allow the light to mingle again with earthly things by marrying, holding property, engaging in agriculture or even breaking bread for themselves. They were also total abstainers and vegetarians. The code of the Hearers was less strict, although it included vegetarianism and a period of fifty days fasting during the year.

Naturally such a creed aroused opposition and persecution from Christians, Zoroastrians and (later) Muslims alike, since the ultimate logic of its position was race suicide. Responsible authorities were unable to approve of a faith in which all killing, even of animals was forbidden. What is more, considerable numbers of believers wandered about refusing to work or to recognize secular regulations, living on the charity of others and exercising a vast influence on the whole community.

The roots of the doctrine probably lay in later Zoroastrianism, but even before Mani it appeared within Christianity in the form of Marcionism. Its influence on early Christianity can be traced through a whole series of heresies, for example the Montanists, the Adoptionists, and the Messalians. It is quite unnecessary to chart the varieties and permutations of dualism and semi-dualism in these heresies except to note that they formed the beginning of a long tradition of opposition to the Catholic Church extending through the Middle Ages and eventually working itself out within Eastern and Russian Orthodoxy right up to very recent times. Certain particularly interesting movements within this tradition are worthy of separate attention.

The Paulicians,[10] who flourished during the ninth century in

[10] Collectors of theological curiosities may be interested in their discovery by Lady Mary Wortley Montagu and their eventual conversion to Roman Catholicism. They now exist as a small community of Bulgarian Uniates in the neighbourhood of Phillipopolis.

the Eastern Empire and on its borders, are of interest in being an exception to the pacifist rule. In fact, as Orthodox Emperors knew only too well, they were amongst the finest soldiers of the day. Unfortunately the materials available for their study are scanty and in some respects uncertain. It may be that part of the explanation of their militarism lies in their marginal divergence from complete dualism. If we assume a natural psychological ambivalence between aggression and passivity, the former alternative would be precluded by the logic of the completely dualist position. The presence of a deviation from complete dualism could conceivably allow this ambivalence to come into play. Perhaps the deviation can be located in the fact that while they distinguished in the usual dualist manner between a Heavenly Being and a creative Demiurge who made the world, they nevertheless held that the Heavenly Being would eventually take control. Most dualist doctrines held, on the contrary, that the world would eventually disintegrate or be consumed with fire. Thus there were positive elements in Paulician doctrine which differed from the purer forms of dualist religion. Moreover, their iconoclasm linked them to a very much wider movement within the Orthodox Church itself and gave them some affinities with Western Puritanism.

Whatever may be the truth about this obscure group it seems likely that they were the channel whereby dualism took root in Europe. Dualism succeeded in finding lodgements wherever strains in the social structure allowed. For example, in Bulgaria during the tenth century the country not only suffered foreign oppressions but was also sharply divided between a wealthy aristocracy and higher ecclesiastics on the one hand, and the lower ecclesiastics and the peasantry on the other. It was to the latter group that dualism (or Bogomilism as it was known) made its appeal. When Bulgaria was conquered by the Byzantines in 1018 the heresy made an unexpected appeal to the philosophically minded amongst the higher Byzantine nobility. These organized themselves as the 'Dragovitsan Church' to distinguish themselves from the 'Church of the Bulgars'. They were eventually ejected from Byzantium in successive purges.

In Bosnia, wedged between Eastern and Western Christendom, the Bogomil heresy became the State religion. During the twelfth century it provided an ideological mainstay against the expansionist designs of Catholic Hungary. Bogomilism survived until the Turkish invasions during the fifteenth century, when Bosnia became almost the only European country to adopt the Islamic faith of their conquerors. Even this was not the end. Friedrich Heer sums up the subsequent history of the Bogomils in a way peculiarly apt as regards the theme of this study.

> As an underground movement Bogomilism divided into two branches: one was a radical and militant secret society . . . the other branch was a pacifist brotherhood, equally radical, which from the sixteenth century joined forces with idealists in Western Europe in Transylvania, Poland and Moravia, and from there penetrated into Russia.[11]

The dualist heresy achieved its most spectacular successes in Southern France in the form of the Albigensian (or Catharist) movement. Catharism included a rich *mélange* of theological materials derived from the gospels as well as from Gnosticism and Manicheanism. It gained momentum partly from disgust at ecclesiastical corruption, partly from the incipient break up of feudalism by commercialism, and partly from a growing feeling of local independence. Just as Bosnia eventually became Muslim so the Catharist areas eventually proved hospitable to Protestantism. The Cathars were also numerous in Italy amongst the 'meditative trades', (scriveners and weavers) who formed the intelligentsia of the proletariat. But in Italy they were partially countered by a Christian sectarianism of a revolutionary kind and by the newly formed Catholic orders.

A wide variety of dissatisfactions seem to have assisted the progress of dualist religion, but it is worth noting that one function of dualism seems to have been to differentiate a national culture which was on the point of achieving self-consciousness from oppressive neighbours, Orthodox or Catholic. Dualism had the advantage over specifically Christian sectarianism in that it did not share basic presuppositions with the wider universalistic whole. It was also able to give expression to conditions of acute political difficulty since it embodied 'a negative, defeatist reaction'.[12] The position of Bosnia between

---

[11] F. Heer; *The Medieval World-Europe* 1100–1350 (London, 1962), p. 165.

[12] Runciman, op. cit., p. 68.

two major universalist cultures is interesting since it is oddly paralleled by the position of the Sikhs between Hinduism and Islam. The birth of the Sikh religion, like Bogomilism, served to express the growing self-consciousness of a nation. The parallel is made more striking in that the original pacifism of the Sikhs developed into marked militarism, just as the pacifistic Bogomils were converted to the military religion of Islam.[13]

In Russia dualist tendencies mingled with the genuinely Christian sectarianism which is to be considered below. A summary of the Russian situation therefore provides a useful link between the two traditions.[14] The story begins with the development of a radical wing within the schismatic body known as the 'Old Believers'. This wing comprised the 'priestless' who, as their name indicates, employed lay elders. As is common in such sects a major role was played by women. All the sacraments apart from baptism were rejected. As regards the sacrament of marriage some of the polar extremes of sectarian development are plainly evident. Many of the 'priestless' repudiated marriage altogether, while others were in favour of celibacy. Moreover, it is interesting to observe an alternation between these two extremes in that some of those in favour of celibacy reverted to total licence, which in turn provoked a reaction so extreme as to include ritual castration. The 'priestless' rejected both the established order and the State and even embraced the notion of redemption by suicide. In this suicidal tendency the logic of pacifism and the psychology of introverted aggression is carried to its furthest extent.

Sects of this type constantly proliferated in response to the intense strains imposed by social conditions in Russia. In most of these sects the alternation between asceticism and licence continued to be a notable feature. Many interesting and significant features of earlier sectarianism faithfully reproduced themselves. The extremist sect of the 'Runners' (or 'Wanderers') for example resembled the followers of Mani and the Cathars in dividing adherents up into two classes. The second class of 'Residents' was to assist the first class of 'holy tramps'. One variant of the Wanderers, called the 'Mutes', resembled the

---

[13] *See* J. Noss, op. cit., Chapter 8 for a short account of the Sikh religion.

[14] There are several available sources. A short account is given in J. Hecker: *Religion and Communism* (London, 1933), Chapter 4.

Essenes in demanding vows of silence. A quite typical mutation was provided by those who accepted a serf-Messiah whom they believed to be a reincarnation of the Tsar Peter III. Perhaps most interesting of all are the Doukhobors who so impressed Tolstoy. The Doukhobors obliterated the distinction between God and Man, regarding each initiate as a 'Christ'. At an early period the women were also regarded as 'Mothers of God'. In common with the Diggers during the English Civil War they rationalized and psychologized Christian dogma, converting the Trinity into Reason, Memory and Will, and writing the law on their own hearts. As is well known they were both pacifist and communistic.

The dualist opposition to the Catholic and Orthodox Churches really represented a threat from a rival religion rather than from a Christian heresy. Where pure dualism was followed through to its logical conclusion it constituted a withdrawal from the material world so complete as to make death the supreme object of life. Christian sectarianism by contrast sought to claim the material and social worlds for God. The Christian sects continued the traditions of prophetism and eschatological expectation within Judaism and combined them with a primitivism which drew on the Stoic conception of nature as well as on the conception of an original Paradise.

This primitivism deserves some attention since it is a constant source of mythological inspiration from as far back as Deutero-Isaiah to the romantic anarchism of the late nineteenth and early twentieth centuries.[15] The early Church succeeded in marrying off the Judaic and Stoic forms of primitivism into a potent unity. It was, of course, impossible to adapt the Judaic idea of creation to the Stoic conception of recurrent cycles in which the Golden Age periodically returned, but it was comparatively easy to assimilate the state of Adam in Eden to the state of nature.

The conclusions drawn from this common theme of an original perfection to which all things might one day return were various and flexible. Philo, the Hellenizing Jew, put forward what Boas calls a 'hard' version of primitivism in which contempt for luxury and civilization passed over into the Cynic

---

[15] Information drawn from G. Boas: *Essays on Primitivism and Related Ideas in the Middle Ages* (Baltimore, 1948).

gospel of work. Others felt more drawn to a 'soft' primitivism. Theophilus, for example, in his Ad Autolycum described the first pair as living in conditions of abundance. Lactantius similarly, except that he believed stalwart virtue more worth while than infantile innocence. Ambrose and other Fathers regarded Eden as egalitarian and communistic, in accordance with God's original intentions, providing in this way an easy link with revolutionary ideologies. The idea that Adam fell because of his curiosity even produced a certain amount of Christian anti-intellectualism.[16]

The best-known and most widely ranging survey of the theological underground from the period of the early Church to the English Civil War is Norman Cohn's *The Pursuit of the Millennium*.[17] Cohn describes the social situations which produced millenarian movements as remarkably uniform. Perhaps of primary importance was a situation of rapid social change, particularly where the process of industrialization and urbanization led to a rapidly increasing population whose traditional bonds with the manor or the paternal master were weakened. The perception of new horizons was frequently accompanied, more especially during the reurbanization of Europe from the twelfth century forwards, by weakening ability to reach those horizons. Where the workers concerned were simultaneously deprived of immediate support from family and communal custom there occurred a radical disorientation. In such conditions the eschatological movements provided a new sense of direction. Cohn himself notes the polarities characterizing these movements, pointing out that they 'varied in tone from pacifism to violent aggressiveness, from ethereal spirituality to gross materialism'.

The major outbreaks are those connected with the Taborites and the Anabaptists but Cohn also underlines the way in which a continuous underground movement was provided by the heresy known as the 'Free Spirit'. The widening of the gap between rich and poor led to the formation of groups which either practised extreme voluntary poverty or emulated the 'luxuria' of their social superiors. This kind of ambivalence was nicely combined with an ambivalence between sexual absti-

[16] Boas, ibid., describes this anti-intellectualism as surprisingly weak.

[17] N. Cohn: *The Pursuit of the Millennium* (London, 1957).

nence and licence. Because those who were corrupted by avarice were infallibly damned it followed that the poor were *ipso facto* in a state of grace and might indulge themselves carnally without danger. So doing the poor re-entered into Adam's sinless sexuality prior to the Fall. Not merely was paradise regained but the distinction between Creator and creature pantheistically obliterated. All was absorbed in 'nature' and God in man, so that all things might be 'used' freely, whether goods or women.

When this movement went underground it seems to have appealed to classes other than the poor, such as women of the merchant class and the less privileged strata of the intelligentsia. Being essentially anarchic it might be expected to recruit alienated segments of the middle classes rather than the very poor. These were perhaps more attracted to the idea of setting up the Kingdom of the Saints. The appeal of the movement lay in the fact that while aristocratic unmarried women were able to become nuns, and unmarried women in the peasant and artisan classes might become absorbed in industry and agriculture, there was no obvious avenue of work or interest to women in the upper merchant class. These women therefore combined with former monks, priests and clerks in minor orders, in an orgy of anarchic amoralism and in the exploration of mystical experience. They were hardly organized at all in the sectarian sense, but formed a number of like-minded loosely interconnected groups.

At the same time other members of the middle classes, men like Peter Waldo and St. Francis, renounced their backgrounds of commercial luxury and entered into an apostolic ministry for others. However, when they did so it is interesting to observe once again the appearance together of the pacifist and the eschatological themes. The pacifism of St. Francis was complemented by the *Dies Irae* of Thomas of Celano, and the later history of the Spiritual Franciscans is interwoven with eschatological expectation.

The two most striking movements of revolutionary idealism occurred in Bohemia during the development of the Hussite revolt and again all over Europe as a radical accompaniment to the Reformation. The Taborites in Bohemia and the Anabaptist wing of the Reformation were equally concerned to establish a community where equality was not only recognized in principle but realized in actuality.

The Taborites constituted a radical wing to the Hussite revolt and included an eschatological emphasis which was revolutionary and acutely aggressive. Some of the revolutionaries adopted communism of goods and sexual communism, together with tendencies to self-deification. However, when the Taborites were eventually defeated a pacifist movement was already in process of formation which based its teaching on the writings of Peter Chelcicky.[18] This writer had originally been in the army but left it because he came to believe that fighting was contrary to the perfect law of Christ. In the course of working out his ideas Peter Chelcicky attacked the union of Church and State, the condition of the priesthood, the claims of birth and the viciousness of urban and commercial life.

The group which adopted his ideas became known as the 'Unity of the Brethren' or the 'Bohemian Brethren'. They settled in Kunstadt with their leader Gregory the Patriarch, and drew at least some of their members from the licentious Adamites, now clothed and in their right mind. The Brethren were divided into three classes, beginners, proficient and perfect, the last of which possessed no private property. Military service, magistracy, oath-taking, trade, and divorce were forbidden. Although the group appeared to retain certain features of Catholic organization, such as the priesthood, this possessed no distinctive sacerdotal powers, and initially they were even half inclined to do without priests at all. The original distrust which the Brethren showed towards arts and learning did not prevent them becoming literate or from contributing to a progressive theory of education. Eventually they divided into two sections, one consisting of rural rigorists who were intolerant of members who acquired property and social responsibilities, and the other consisting of burghers who sought to mitigate the pacifistic anarchism of the original body.[19]

The second great revolutionary movement has been described

[18] *See* J. Hutton: *A History of the Moravian Church* (Moravian Publications Office, 1909) for an account of Peter Chelcicky.

[19] This division is described in G. H. Williams: *The Radical Reformation* (London, 1962).

in detail by G. H. Williams in *The Radical Reformation*. In the earlier stages two leaders are of particular interest: Thomas Münzer and Conrad Grebel.[20] Münzer's development began with a phase of millenarian pacifism. The contemporary situation was one in which peasants who had been prosperous and relatively free found themselves losing ground to civil and ecclesiastical lords who were attempting to extend and formalize their jurisdictions. Events came to a crisis in the great Peasants War of 1524–5 in which the eschatological expectations of the peasants met with a crushing military defeat. After this failure some of the spokesmen for the peasants led their followers 'into the emergent Anabaptist movement, which, except for one effort, ever thereafter was to eschew military and political action and convert its constitutional energies into the formation of self-disciplined conventicles separated from the State'.[21]

Meanwhile, in Zurich, Conrad Grebel had been gravitating from the humanism natural to one of his patrician background towards the radical evangelical position. This stand brought him into conflict with Zwingli over the question of the subordination of the Word to the magistracy. Grebel envisaged a new community which should be ruled by a regenerate and therefore non-coercive magistracy. His pacifism is of special interest because it was based neither on Erasmian humanism nor specifically on the Sermon on the Mount but on his 'still more fundamental conviction as to the captaincy of Christ over the true milites Christi, recruited for service as a suffering church, making an ideal of absolute non-violence and suffering in Christ's name a confirmation of one's salvation'.[22] The groups who held views similar to Grebel formed themselves into the Swiss Brethren, most of whom were legalistic and perfectionist, although some broke out into a frenzied autinomianism and even burned the New Testament because it was merely the letter of the law.

Another important figure in the Anabaptist movement was Johannes Hut who proclaimed the imminence of the second

[20] Short accounts of Grebel are given in Williams, op. cit., and G. Nuttall: *Christian Pacifism* (Oxford, 1958), Chapter 3. H. Bender has written a biography: *Conrad Grebel, c. 1498–1526* (Goschen, Indiana, 1950).
[21] Williams, op. cit., p. 83.
[22] Ibid., p. 99.

advent. The movement with which he was connected underwent many vicissitudes and also disagreements which turned on the place of the sword and the role of Christians with regard to the magistracy. Eventually this group of Anabaptists was welded together by Jacob Hutter, who regarded a system of communal production as the discipline appropriate for spiritual warriors persevering until their vindication at Christ's coming. Williams compares the Hutterites to the Essenes. They saw their community as a true Church driven into the wilderness, which was to serve as a provisional paradise. Within this Church they must share in brotherly love, be resigned to suffering and give absolute obedience to God and the eldership.

The outbreak of violent and aggressive eschatological expectation at Münster has been frequently described. It began in passive preparations for the advent and then threatened the 'imminent destruction of all tyrants'. During its militant phase libertinism was rife. Some walked naked to proclaim 'the naked truth of the gospel'. In this they paralleled the early Quakers. After the fall of Münster a few remained 'sword-minded', notably the Batenburgers, a polygamous and communistic group who declared death on all who did not join them. However, most of the rest gathered under the wing of Menno Simons, who formed them into a pacifist community, which rejected participation in the State and insisted on the maintenance of equality. This community still survives, notably in Holland, Canada and the United States.

The course of the radical reformation in Poland differed slightly from its course elsewhere. Nowhere else did so large a section of the gentry espouse the cause of the pacifist sectarians, which is the more surprising in view of their traditional military ethos. Moreover, there were Judaising and rationalizing tendencies at work which were less evident or absent in German, Swiss and Dutch Anabaptism. Indeed, once the rationalizing trend made headway, not only in Poland but in Lithuania and Transylvania, the spirit of genuine Anabaptism began to fade. The original Polish sectarians were pacifist and held at least some of the traditional views concerning Christ, but it seems that on the whole the development towards Unitarianism led to a justification of defensive war.

The object of the survey just completed is to provide pre-

liminary documentation of a basic ambivalence between pacifist withdrawal and revolutionary assault. The same counter-
point can be observed in the Essenes, the Early Church, the
Taborites, the Anabaptists, and even among the dualists where
it was not entirely inhibited by the strict logic of doctrine. Not
only has there been an attempt to illustrate the polar and
related extremes of pacifism and revolution, but certain other
polarities have been frequently in evidence. Most notable of all
has been the connection between extreme asceticism and total
licence, the latter being more often associated with the militant
phase in sectarian development. Communism and anarchism
are also very frequent components in the complex of sectarian
phenomena. These polarities, in particular the crucial ones
which are central to this study, will find further illustration in
the sections of the following chapter which deal with the
English Civil War.

CHAPTER FOUR

A PILOT STUDY

THE object of this chapter is to sketch an outline of the myth of the apocalypse and to conduct a pilot study into its influence in the period of the English Civil War. This may then provide more detailed evidence concerning its relationship to pacifism.

As used here the word 'myth' denotes a dynamic image or symbolic system which embodies a promise and may act as a spur to heroic action. This kind of image focuses the hopes of the disinherited and by creating a tension between things as they are desired and things as they are, sometimes brings these hopes to some measure of fruition. The myth is both true and untrue. It is 'true' in that the vitalities it releases have impressive consequences. It is untrue because the intractabilities embedded in social organization deflect and distort the mythical vision. The incubus of the past is never finally sloughed off and the tragic disharmonies of social life cannot, in principle, be overcome.

I

The myth of the apocalypse may or may not be confined without exception to Judaeo-Christian cultures but it is nevertheless very closely associated with them. The gospels themselves include the apocalyptic vision, in so far as they proclaim an entirely different scheme of human relationships. At the same time this dynamic element is balanced and grounded in reality by a profound acceptance of life's tragic dimension. In this way the dichotomy in Christian history between vision and tragedy is directly derived from its foundation documents.

Throughout Christian history one finds a socially inclusive Church, standing in a positive relation to history which is in close touch with problems of community and organization and which is sharply aware of the limits of the possible. It therefore comprehends the tragic dimension in individual and political choice and places the concept of tragedy at the centre of its historical understanding. Unhappily times of social inertia and the almost inevitable relationship of the Church to ruling groups may conspire to replace understanding by complacency. The Church sanctifies and deepens the constant and basic elements in living and this sanctity is transferred to the whole social order of which these elements are only a part.

However, the sect is also a constant element in the history of Christianity. Because the sect is separated from political pressures and necessities as well as delivered from the temptations of élite membership it is able to canalize the hopes of the alienated into a vision from which all tragic disharmonies are to be eliminated. Thus while the Church bases its understanding on a unity of past, present and future, the sect transfigures a mythical past and a mythical future.

The apocalyptic myth looks both forward and backward in each case seeking harmonies which elude men in the present. To the extent, therefore, that men acquire a stake in the present it tends to lose its potency, becoming a mild nostalgia for the past, a proximate and more or less realizable secular hope, or an aspiration towards a heaven beyond death which will remedy those things which afflict the estate of men in general rather than particular social afflictions. Should oppression end all 'normal' secular hopes or should the landmarks of 'ordinary' society be obliterated, more particularly by war or rapid social change, the mind turns towards a 'final solution'. The oppressed, excluded or alienated groups, whether nations or groups within nations, look for a reversal of their present position either by divine fiat or by the immanent and irresistible forces of history, with either of which they may or may not be required to co-operate. Some groups wait passively for the current to carry them to their desired haven, while others believe there is a time for waiting and a time when the tide of affairs is to be taken at the flood. The passivity of the former is more formal than real, since the underlying psychological attitude is often one of acute aggression. It is merely that God is seen as the Sole Executor of their will to triumph.

The prospective form of the myth envisages the Millennium in which the New Jerusalem comes down from Heaven or is captured by the strong arms of the soldiers of Christ. The Kingdom of Heaven is at hand, the Cargo is due to arrive, the Third Age is about to dawn. The keynote is expectation, releasing a spiritual vigour which overflows the dykes and boundaries of law and convention. In such an atmosphere the type of religious philosophy of history based on successive eras or ages provides a potent source of images: the four world-empires of the Book of Daniel have passed while the Fifth Monarchy now waits to be established. In a secular context the same basic psychology provides the concept of the Third Reich, *Nouveau Christianisme*[1] and Engels's idea of the Kingdom of Freedom into which mankind leaps out of the Kingdom of Necessity. The Revolution, the Day, or the General Strike[2] is seen as imminent, coming as the Day of the Lord, when the children of light or the 'New Man' of Communist society shall put to flight the armies of the children of darkness, of antichrist and of reaction.

The secularization of the apocalyptic myth not only involves a loss of poetry but renders relatively infrequent the tendency to wait passively for the dawning of the Day. Overtones of quietistic mysticism are replaced by an aggressive mystique, except in so far as eventual disillusionment with the secular apocalypse produces a desire to find an ultimate resting-point within the Self. It is a paradox that the secularization of the religious concept of history as understood in the Judaeo-Christian tradition can develop alongside a form of ahistorical world-denial very much more radically 'religious' than that of Christianity. The process of secularization also involves merging the sense of God immanent in society into the materialistic philosophy of history, and of a mystical pantheism into a militant and triumphant atheism. Shelley and Bakunin provide interesting examples of this relation between pantheism and atheism.[3]

The retrospective form of the myth has less revolutionary

---

[1] The concept of Nouveau Christianisme belongs, of course, to the Saint-Simonian Movement. Most of the usual sectarian phenomena can be illustrated from Saint-Simonianism. *See* J. F. Talmon: *Political Messianism: the Romantic Phase* (London, 1960), Chapter 1.

[2] The mythology of the General Strike derives from G. Sorel: *Reflections on Violence* (London, 1925).

[3] There is interesting material in I. Pyziur: *The Doctrine of Anarchism of Michael A. Bakunin* (Milwaukee, 1955).

potential than the prospective form. Man strives to recapture the primal felicity of Adam in the Garden of Eden before 'disproportioned sin jarred against nature's chime'. In Stoic terms it is hoped that 'time will run back and fetch the Age of Gold'. The seventeenth century, as Milton illustrates, combined the two concepts. Of course, the Fall is not always seen as unfortunate: *O felix culpa*! But there has been a persistent tendency to lament at least some of the consequences. Culture, sophistication, regulation and legalism have all been regarded as destroying an innocence and a directness to which we must return. Naturally, such a view appeals to those deprived of culture or groaning under artificial, unnatural conditions and unjust laws.

Sometimes the state of innocence and social harmony is located prior to a particular historical event: for instance the Norman conquest. In popular notions of church history the primitive Christian community is accredited with normative virtues. For Wordsworth and for Blake, in their widely differing ways, the Fall was, in fact, ascribed to industrialism. It was reserved to the twentieth century, however, to blame loss of Eden on to the previous generation, who were supposed to have ruined the natural right of the young to happiness and innocent freedom by a unique combination of sexual prurience and political turpitude.

The retrospective formulation of the myth is also to be observed in countries recently disturbed by contact with the West. The reaction to such disturbance often includes a form of primitivism which exalts the 'old ways'. The agrarian simplicity espoused by Gandhi is an example. This is perhaps not quite the same as the idea of a pre-lapsarian condition, but there are common psychological elements. Sometimes primitivism is combined with a policy of 'turning the other cheek' to the representatives of Westernization. Thus among American Indians some tribes have adopted a primitivist or pacifist policy, while others have adopted an apocalyptic which is regarded as a 'final solution' of their problems. Or an aggressive policy having failed it may be succeeded by a pacifist policy. The apocalyptic alternative is observable today in the 'Cargo Cults' of Melanesia.[4]

In ages and cultures where the imagination has been deeply

[4] The subject of many studies, but in particular P. M. Worsley: *The Trumpet Shall Sound* (London, 1957).

coloured by the story of the Fall the attempt to recapture man's first estate can result in efforts to restore primitive communism in the sphere of property relations and sometimes also in the sphere of sexual relations. Such a movement draws inspiration from the fact the Church fathers always saw communism as an absolute good pertaining to man's innocence and private property as a relative good erected as a bulwark against sinfulness. The Adamitism of the late Middle Ages and the English seventeenth century symbolized its freedom from the corruption of sexual feeling involved in 'modesty' and 'mine' and 'thine' by a form of nudism. Even modern nudism, in so far as it rises to an ideological formulation, retains drifting fragments from this current of ideas. In William Blake one finds an interesting version of the return to innocence, which constitutes an English echo of the revolutionary ferment in France. The old Adam has been subverted by the Satanic mills of Church and industry and of official culture (as represented for example in Reynolds) : but the new Adam, the Christ of the Imagination, destroys all legalism and restores the innocent play of the passions. It is interesting to note how Blake belongs to those groups in England at the end of the eighteenth century, some of which were revolutionary and some of which have been described as 'Natural Quakers', which illustrate quite clearly the linkages between revolutionary Utopianism and pacifism.[5]

An important mutation, which must be noted here, but developed later, arises from the fusion of Stoic and Christian ideas of 'Nature' which was so characteristic of the seventeenth century, but which extends in various forms up to the present day.[6] This mutation relates specifically to the evolution of liberal pacificism and optimism. The state of nature begins as a theological and philosophical 'myth', but eventually comes to

[5] See H. N. Brailsford: *Shelley, Godwin and their Circle* (London, 1936), especially pp. 36–7. There is some material on sectarianism during this period in W. H. G. Armytage, *Heavens Below* (London 1961), pp. 69–73, which illustrates pacifist tendencies in the circle of Richard Brothers and various eschatological beliefs associated with them. Brothers himself had Messianic pretensions and elaborated ideas similar to those of the British Israel Movement. The *D N B* has an entry on him and on his disciple John Finlayson.

[6] The ancient syncretism between the Christian concept of the moral order and the law of nature finds illustrations in the Quaker Robert Barclay, concerning whom there is material in R. L. Armsby: *The Early Quaker View of the State* (B A dissertation, Birmingham, 1932).

be regarded as a 'simple possibility' within history, progressively realizable in the present and the near future.

From this viewpoint the Fall of Man is ignored (along with those political realities which imply it and are implied by it) and mankind represented as naturally decent and reasonable. The emphasis now falls almost exclusively on the dignity of man, while his misery, which a Christian like Pascal sees as equally consequent on his freedom, is disregarded. The concepts of tragedy and redemption now appear irrelevant, while the element of 'vision' is transmuted into the *bourgeois* Utopia, wherein men are not so much heroically virtuous as in the ancient apocalyptic, as rational and basically well-intentioned. Thus both the dimension of man's dignity, as a being made in the image of God, and the dimension of man's misery, undergo a process of scaling-down in which the latter in particular is reduced to the status of a little local difficulty. Evolutionary thought, although in fact having diverse implications, also enabled such difficulties to be seen as roughly analogous to the residual tail in the human anatomy: a reminder but not a serious drawback.

The myth of the apocalypse has a clearly defined shape. Generally there is a preparatory figure, or even a whole series of preparatory figures, who fulfil certain expectations and proceed to witness to the apocalyptic character of the age. This character is evidenced in the 'Signs of the Times': it is a time of 'troubles', of 'lawlessness', or, in Marxist phraseology, of 'contradictions'. The world itself may be seen as about to founder and so the sect becomes an Ark of Salvation specially prepared for that catastrophic event. Or else the world awaits a transfiguration, either because the Lord will Himself lay bare His holy arm or because His servants are prepared to do so. The world is divided up into those who side with evil and those who side with good: the children of light and the children of darkness. The latter may be collectively represented in the symbol of antichrist, or that symbol is dramatically focused in one immense and diabolic figure, as for instance, the Emperor Nero or the Tsar Peter III.

The children of light frequently regard themselves as the Elect out of every nation, or in Jewish symbolism as 'the Remnant'. In a secularized situation the *bourgeoisie* may constitute a collective antichrist while the Elect become the party cadre or syndicat. Eventually the concentrated forces of evil are defeated in Armageddon or in the 'Final Clash' of Marxist mythology.

It is important to note that the more profound lines of thought in Judaism recognized the possibility of the secular triumph of 'the godless', and so tried to give a redemptive meaning to the suffering of the 'Chosen' at alien hands. The true Israel, God's elect, became a Suffering Servant whose tragic destiny brings in a universal kingdom. Thus Jesus both proclaimed this kingdom and identified Himself with the figure of the Suffering Servant, taking the evil upon Himself in order to transform its meaning.

This acceptance of sacrifice has been interpreted by liberal theology as implying a pacifist position. Much modern Christian pacifism has stemmed from a theology of the Atonement, particularly of the kind that interprets the action of the Passion as exemplary. Such theology sees the Christian era as a period in which the forces of evil are to be 'mopped up'. These forces are regarded as defeated in fact as well as in principle, and so the Atonement becomes a repeatable method of completing the operation which guarantees eventual if not immediate success. In this way liberal theology can become a form of long-range optimism neglecting the endemic character of evil.

A time of 'troubles' easily acquires a Messianic character in those cultures where a Messiah is expected. The role of Messiah, or in Islam of the Mahdi, may be taken up either by a person or by a group. The Messianic consciousness arises through the convergence of a number of factors, not all of them necessarily present in every Messianic situation. There is, first of all, the presence of an expectation which arises out of the fundamental religious postulates underlying a culture. Then there are the conditions which give that expectation intensity. If, for instance, norms have been acutely disturbed then a genuinely charismatic personality who provides a moral orientation may gather some of the aura normally attaching to the moral law itself to his own person.

Moreover, a shaking of the social foundations often produces a need for a more direct apprehension of spiritual truths and a wrestling with what is essential and what accidental in the religious tradition, which often issues, after prolonged struggles, in the experience of conversion. It also issues in what Reinhold Niebuhr calls 'crisis heroism'. With the conversion experience goes a sense of immediacy, of mission and of direct communion with God. When all the external points of reference have begun to crumble, God is either discovered within the self, or He is thought to have removed Himself to an immeasurable distance. Thus the Messianic consciousness of the individual charismatic leader, and the needs of various groups for a new point of reference and a source of salvation, together result in a Messianic movement.

Sometimes the Messianic movement takes a military form and in such cases the shock troops of the Elect can easily regard themselves as collectively executing and even constituting the immanent judgements of God, or alternatively as marching forward with the inevitable forces of history or destiny. The transcendent God of more stable times, comes down into the phenomenal world, to execute His will through human kind. This sense of destiny, vitality and power combines with the sense of immediacy and a dramatic fore-shortening of the temporal process to produce either the kind of Messianic inflation associated with egocentric irresponsibility[7] or a deep sense of identity with God and absolute dependence upon His will. The line dividing the two is thin but for the believer it must be crucial.

An awareness of divine immanence and the sense of immediacy give rise to a new moral approach. We have already observed the transition from legalistic formulae to experience and experiment. In the socially inclusive Churches associated with stable periods, emphasis is always laid on the performance of certain works of the law, this law itself being explicitly or implicitly divided into works of rogation and superogation. Any appearance of moral enthusiasm is shunted off into the quiet sidings of monasticism. But as times of change and disturbance reveal the conventional elements both in the content and the performance of these works the emphasis passes from outward performance to inner intention.[8] How this develops depends

[7] G. Huehns discusses and illustrates such tendencies in the Puritan army in her: *Antinomianism in English History* (London, 1951).

[8] The Saint-Simonians coined the notion of the *Loi Vivante* centred in a charismatic leader.

partly on whether the impact of immediacy and collective excitement strains the personality structure to breaking-point.

At this juncture the individual psychology of the leader may well have considerable importance. A disintegration of the personality in association with a sense of destiny and mission may issue in a complete amoralism regarding itself as beyond good and evil. Alternatively the awareness of intimate communion may be so canalized and controlled as to integrate the individual around the idea of dedicated service, in which the distinction between works of rogation and superogation is dissolved.

The moral direction taken also depends in part on the stage of the revolutionary movement. At a certain stage the sense of a task to be accomplished often produces a disciplinary asceticism, while at another stage consciousness of success may result in complete amoralism, perhaps reinforced by a vitalistic philosophy of the inherent rightness of the deed which serves to justify the horrors of war. Should the assault have failed in some degree then those elements inclined or forced to withdraw will need to find a new source of direction, which combines with a reaction against amoralism, to produce radical asceticism. This perfectionist asceticism in the stage of revolutionary withdrawal frequently results in a pacifism which is all the more rigid for being an element in a new orientation based on a reaction to acute disorganization and anomie. Both amoralism and perfectionism are sectarian phenomena, but only the latter is likely to produce a lasting, vertebrate organization. Thus it is that the revolution swings between the extreme which sees love or the deed as destroying the law and the extreme which sees love as fulfilling the law entirely and perfectly.

The apocalyptic myth stands in a complex relation to optimism and to pessimism about human nature. In impossible situations it can envisage a destruction of the world by a completely transcendent God, and will thus tend to be extremely pessimistic about humanity, so that even the Elect are saved by an inscrutable choice rather than by superior worth. If on the other hand, the world is regarded as on the point of transfiguration and human beings seen as co-operating towards that end then a higher degree of optimism is involved, perhaps increasing if there are any secular successes. No clear correlations are possible with social situations because so much depends on the way in which available theological elements in the pre-existing cultural tradition are selected in order to structure the situation for the alienated group.

On the other hand it is true that the sense of immanence accompanying success tends to lead to an emphasis on human potentialities which may, paradoxically, still sustain the group in its period of withdrawal. Of course secularized versions of apocalypticism must necessarily be optimistic since they have no other point of reference: all evils are referred to environment. By contrast conservative philosophies and associated inclusive Churches often espouse a mild pessimism, perhaps seeing most men as capable of recognizing their interest in maintaining the social fabric given suitable sanctions and incentives, but hardly cast in the godlike mould which can renew the whole social order.

II

Some circumstantial evidence for the interconnections so far described is provided by the apocalyptic myth as formulated in the seventeenth century during the English Civil War. During the period 1642–60 apocalypticism was able to develop in a manner unusually free from factors which might distort and intrude.

One of the most striking aspects of the Puritan Revolution is the way in which ideas were taken for a ride on the backs of events until they arrived at unexpected and sometimes entirely foreign destinations.[9] A simple example of a not unexpected destination is the way in which Lilburne's attack on prelacy developed into an attack on its political correlative, the monarchy. Similarly, and less predictably, we find the spiritual egalitarianism of St. Paul leading to levelling notions in a secular context. Those who put on the armour of God to adventure the spiritual pilgrimage came to display similar discipline with a pike, while those elect few who knew heaven for their inheritance became the many who received assurance of more mundane legacies. An emphasis on the 'perspicuitas' of the gospel became the right of private interpretation, then the superiority of untutored exegesis, and finally a form of populism.

[9] As described in W. Haller's *The Rise of Puritanism* (New York, 1938), especially Chapter 3.

The irresistibility of divine grace developed into an immanent grace which destroyed the difference between good and evil or which curved back on itself in the doctrine of works still characteristic of the debased Calvinism residually lodged in the English character. The assertion of Christ's supremacy within the Church was expressed in denominational structures which implied democracy.

The transmutation of the predestination of the Elect into the destiny of the people meant that when the Puritan 'Spiritual Brotherhood' reached their godly Utopia the sectarians were already forging ahead towards New Jerusalem. Especially relevant in this connection is the fact that many of those who were redeemed from the consequences of the Fall in principle supposed that they were also redeemed from those consequences in fact, and therefore attempted to return to the communism, equality and peaceableness pertaining to Adam's first estate. The more religiously minded emphasized their rights as possessors of Paradise Regained, while the more politically orientated also emphasized their rights under the law of nature.[10] Thus the apocalyptic myth was formulated both prospectively and retrospectively.

The consequent ideological spectrum was related in a confused and complicated way to the various interest groups, and Christopher Hill has warned against a tendency to regard these as rigid classifications. In any case this is an issue where it would be more than foolish for a sociologist to rush in where so many historians have rushed in already. All that one dare do is to indicate certain types of groupings.

First of all, there were the groups making up the rival Churches with their competing forms of inclusiveness: Roman Catholics, Anglicans and Presbyterians. Secondly there were the Independents and the Baptists who in some degree represented the right and left centre of the revolution politically, but who can be distinguished in religious terms both from the rival 'churches' and from the sectarians. The Baptists, and the politically minded Levellers with whom they were partly

[10] *See* J. Frank: *The Levellers* (Cambridge, Mass., 1955). William Walwyn is particularly interesting amongst Leveller leaders as combining optimistic rationalism with romantic primitivism.

[11] Together with strains of Renaissance humanism.

associated, were concentrated in the trades and the less prosperous sections of the middle class. The same is partly true of the sectarians, although these were characteristically the 'decent poor', while the Quakers were originally distinctively rural and northern in distribution. The lowest levels of society, more capable of a *jacquerie* than a revolution, were in any case more inclined to the royalist cause, or simply indifferent.

Perhaps the two most interesting aspects of this situation are, firstly, the tendency of some individuals to run through the whole political and ecclesiastical gamut from right to left[12] and secondly the defection of distinguished Puritan clerics and intellectuals to the radical wing particularly those from the University of Cambridge.

The spectrum of opinion and interest groups may for analytic purposes be separated out into three broad bands, Churches, denominations and sects, with logical political correlatives. The dichotomy of Church history which we have noted undergoes a mutation in the seventeenth century to produce in embryo a fresh type of ecclesiastical organization: the denomination. The category of denomination has already been referred to in Chapter One but some further formulation, comparing it with Church and sect, is relevant here.

The Church is a socially inclusive institution with the function of conservation and unification. Its social theory is organicist and its organization hierarchical. By contrast the sect is the voluntary association of the disinherited, expressing social cleavage and marked by differing kinds of extremism: thus it is either anarchist or quasi-military, pacifist or aggressive, perfectionist or antinomian. In outlook it tends to millenarianism and adventism. The denomination (notably the Independents, the General Baptists and later also the Methodists) is the organization of the lower middle classes and of the artisan: individualistic in character, democratic and pragmatic in organization, liberal in politics. Its relative indifference to adventism indicates its stake in society and so completes its differentiation from the sect.

These three formulations are very important for the analysis of pacificism and pacifism in the centuries following, but they

---

[12] Illustrated in G. Nuttall: *The Holy Spirit in Puritan Faith and Experience* (Oxford, 1946).

can be illustrated in principle from the seventeenth-century material. We find the unified, 'conservative' organicism of Romans, Anglicans and Presbyterians; the relative tolerance, liberalism and democracy of the denominations, and the sectarian extremism of the aggressive theocratic Fifth Monarchy Men on the one hand and the anarchic quietism of Seekers and Quakers, together with the communitarian pacifism of the Diggers, on the other.

It is to these sectarians that attention should be turned, since an apolitical doctrine, like pacifism, is necessarily a phenomenon of sectarian extremism, just as pacificism is related to the denomination. As we have seen, the sects may be divided into acutely aggressive and acutely quietist. The psychological affinity between these apparently opposed positions is illustrated by two facts. In the first place both Fifth Monarchy Men and Quakers drew a large proportion of their adherents from a common source, the radical wing of the Baptists. There was also a notable tendency for the Fifth Monarchists (and the aggressive Ranters) of the earlier stages in the revolution to become Quakers in the latter stages,[13] when the 'good old cause' was clearly on the wane. In the second place both Fifth Monarchy Men and Quakers contained quietist and aggressive minorities respectively, in the latter case known as 'Proud Quakers'. The quietist wing of Fifth Monarchism expected the revolution to be completed by divine fiat, whereas the quietist majority in Quakerism progressively spiritualized the concepts of the revolution into a doctrine of immanence.[14]

The other polarities characteristic of sectarianism lie partly along and partly athwart this fundamental polarity between aggression and pacifism. Thus antinomianism is more symptomatic of the aggressive than the passive attitude but the correlation is not complete. Conversely, perfectionism is generally associated with pacifism but many perfectionists also anticipated the temporal rule of the 'Saints'. Fifth Monarchism was theocratic whereas Quakerism was anarchic in

---

[13] Confirmed from several sources, including L. Fargo Brown's *The Political Activities of Baptists and Fifth Monarchy Men* (Washington, 1912) Chapter 3; N. Cohn op. cit., Appendix, and H. S. Barbour: *The Early Quaker Outlook on 'the World' and 'Society'* (Ph.D. Thesis, Yale, 1952), p. 41.

[14] The Quakers, unlike Winstanley and the Diggers, just succeeded in avoiding a doctrine of complete immanence.

tendency, but anarchism was also characteristic of the Ranters. Similarly doctrines of immanence belong both to the aggressive, amoral Ranters and the pacific perfectionist Diggers. What is significant here is the close relation of opposites, which have this in common, that they are both related to a political philosophy which rejects politics. Politics are based on consensus within disunity, but since the sect is based on acute cleavage it can envisage only rule by fiat or withdrawal,[15] neither of which are political in the liberal sense of the word.

Something needs to be said about mysticism and rationalism since both are present in the ideological amalgam of the seventeenth century and both are significant for the complex of ideas associated with pacifism in the twentieth century.[16] In itself mysticism is a psychological rather than a sociological phenomenon. In so far as it achieves social expression *per se* it does so merely as a 'parallelism of spontaneities' and so erects no lasting organization. Being psychological and therefore sociologically evanescent it possesses little historical impact: its importance in history is as a psychological overtone to sociological forms with a more particularized content. Mysticism has no content, just as a colour has no content except in relation to a shape. It may provide psychological overtones both in Church, sect and denomination, but whatever specific ideological content it possesses in history will be derived from the type of organization with which it is associated. Certainly it has its own language, but this is a form of descriptive psychology in relation to an ahistorical impulse: an impulse, that is, to rise above content though not necessarily to reject it. Mysticism rises above ideological and organizational particularities, but this aspiration can as well be achieved through as apart from these particularities.

Since this type of aspiration, taken in itself, devalues the contingent and the particular, it may issue in a form of passivity which expresses mystical indifference. The alone pursues its flight to the alone and cuts the social roots of religion. But this is of no concern to the sociologist, whose focus is on the social interactions of religious awareness: those giving rise to it and

[15] Its 'political' view implies absolute power or no power at all.

[16] *See* R. Jones' *Mysticism and Democracy in the English Commonwealth* (Cambridge, Mass., 1932).

those arising from it. He can only note this mystical passivity of the individual as an interesting irrelevance and pass on to mysticism as a psychological overtone to social organization. As such it is distributed along the whole ideological spectrum of the seventeenth century from Henry Vaughan and Thomas Traherne to George Fox and Gerrard Winstanley. This being the case one can only suggest that the relation between immediacy and mysticism, whether of the integrative or disintegrative kind, leads to a relatively greater tendency to mysticism among both the pacifist and aggressive sects in their initial stages, and in this way is related at one remove to the social disorganization from which these sects are derived and the psychological turmoil concomitant with it.

Rationalism in the seventeenth century is normally still within the Christian tradition. One finds it embedded in quite unexpected material: in Ludovic Muggleton's[17] rejection of miracles and in Winstanley's psychologization of the central symbols of Christian dogma. This type of rationalism merely corrodes certain sorts of traditional belief, but it is not yet the dogmatic rationalism to be found in the eighteenth century.

However, it is worth indicating here just how this later doctrine partly took over from the older apocalypse. Dogmatic rationalism is not only concerned with reason as an instrument but with reason as a means of determining ends. It is also a form of optimism, ignoring both the intractabilities written into society and the primary importance of passions and interests in political choice. This is perhaps the central delusion of liberal *bourgeois* intellectualism: one tap with the golden hammer of reason will open all doors. A thing has only to be explained and understood to issue in action. Evil is ignorance: good is enlightenment.

The way is therefore open for the construction of any number of abstractly conceived Utopias divorced from history and empirical politics. It is the intellectualism of such Utopias which, in part, differentiates them from the imaginative and passionate creations of the older apocalyptic. In the seventeenth century the transition from apocalypse to Utopia begins by an emphasis on the divine 'seed' or image in man characteristic of the pacific

[17] There is a useful article on Muggleton in the *D N B* (Vol. xxxiv, London, 1894).

left-wing of the revolution, which is then reinterpreted as the divine reason in man. Eventually this becomes a faith in reason itself. Both in its theological and its philosophical form it is equally optimistic and may issue in a form of pacificism peculiarly attractive to the enlightened intelligentsia. The rationalistic Utopianism of a Bertrand Russell is the final term in this development.

III

Having sketched in the general background of seventeenth-century apocalypticism one can now turn to the more particular history of the Quakers and of their peace testimony.

The Battle of Naseby in 1645 brought about the victory of the alliance between Parliament and Puritanism and simultaneously destroyed Presbyterian hopes for the establishment of a godly Utopia. The decisive part played by Cromwell, himself an Independent, and his New Model Army composed of Independents, Baptists and sectarians, was crucial for the development of religious diversity in England and for the future of democratic voluntarism. But the progress of the fighting and the disorganization following in its wake produced forms of sectarianism which had begun to make progress in 1642 and which by 1645 were in full spate.

The army itself conscious of being a vanguard of things to come, was deeply affected by antinomianism, but the anarchic sectarianism with which it was associated was necessarily incapable of producing a coherent programme. However, the denominational core of the army, particularly the Baptists, standing as they did to the left of the Cromwellian centre, did succeed in producing a political programme consonant with their democratic liberalism in the sphere of Church organization. This political programme was the platform of the party known as the Levellers, which flourished from 1647 until 1649, when it was suppressed by Cromwell.

The year 1645 brought long-standing material and spiritual uncertainties to a head. The collapse of the Catholic Church a century previous, had been followed by the undermining of the Elizabethan settlement and the failure of the Presbyterian alternative. These successive collapses could hardly fail to have profound psychological repercussions. Then the year 1649 saw both the execution of the King, an event which had traumatic effects on many minds, and the suppression of the radical political wing of the denominational centre, the Levellers. This latter event meant that the insurgent populism inspired by pamphleteering and Bible-reading was deprived of its last point of political reference and its source of political expression. Unsettlement, disorientation and frustration were thus complete.

Into this situation came a fresh kind of sect offering a new kind of hope and fresh norms whose very rigidity was a relief from constant moral and social flux. Groups like the Seekers[18] and the 'shattered' Baptists began to appear, some of them succumbing to secularization and some of them waiting helplessly for the new revelation. They were, in Penn's phrase, 'as sheep without a shepherd'.

The shepherd, both literally and figuratively, was George Fox. In him the shattered radicalism of the period reset into a definite form, even though that form was a kind of formlessness. In the movement which he started the egalitarianism of the Levellers received a second extension of life, albeit in a religious rather than a political frame. The religion of Fox showed clear evidence of the struggles of the time. The acrid character of theological disputation produced in him a strong antipathy for all 'notional' religion. The amoral vitalism of the Ranters reinforced a reaction to perfectionism.[19] The failure of all external authorities led him to find an authority within the soul, while the anarchism of the sects led him to control individualistic tendencies by a doctrine of unanimity within the religious community. Doubtless the individualism was itself partly derived from the Baptist background of so many early Quaker recruits.

Broadly Quakerism represents the progressive spiritualization of the apocalyptic myth in the stage of revolutionary withdrawal. Ranters, Fifth Monarchy Men and Levellers, conscious of failure, more and more tended to canalize their remaining

[18] The Seekers and their relation to Quakerism is described in Rufus Jones, op. cit., Chapter 3.

[19] Something of the dialectic relation between Quakerism and antinomianism appears in G. Nuttall's discussion of 'The Grindletonian Movement', op. cit., Appendix 1.

hopes into Quakerism.[20] In this way the Society of Friends became the residual legatee of the Puritan Revolution. Levelling principles became the Quaker refusal of hat-honour. The spiritualization of the apocalypse is illustrated by the way in which the 'Day of the Lord' sounded by Fox lost its temporal reference. The Fifth Monarchy was realized in the soul and in the Quaker 'Israel' delivered out of the nation. The Messianism which they associated with Cromwell became subjectivized into an immanent 'God' within the believer, the point of change being symbolized in Naylor's 'triumphal entry' into Bristol, in which the political Messianism of the earlier stage and the religious Messianism of the later, were mixed in an unstable compound. Certainly Messianic language as applied to Fox referred to an immanent divinity rather than to any political mission. Finally, and only after some uncertainties, the carnal war against principalities and powers became 'the Lamb's war' against sin and 'the World'.[21]

With regard to the 'peace testimony' of early Quakerism, Friends have themselves questioned its consistency. It was not until 1660 that the 'good old cause' finally crystallized into 'the Lamb's war'. The expulsion of Friends from the army (against which Fox protested) was not due to their pacifism but to their egalitarian refusal of 'hat-honour'. The appearance of an uncompromising attitude against war in the very year in which the Restoration marked the final defeat of their political hopes, indicates the conclusion of a gradual process, which from the failure of the Nominated Parliament of 1653 is noticeable also among the Baptists, whereby the rule of the saints by the sword gave way to the sword of the spirit. The tendency of some Friends in the temporary revival of 1659 to arm themselves shows that the earlier attitude was still a live option for some members.[22]

Fox's own doctrine of the divine seed in every man might

[20] John Lilburne, the leader of the Levellers became a Quaker. The suggestion that Winstanley also became a Quaker is apparently incorrect, according to Sabine in *The Works of Gerrard Winstanley* (Cornell, 1941), p. 11.

[21] G. Nuttall, op. cit., p. 111 describes a progression from the earthquake and the fire to the 'still small voice'. He also points out that in Mid-Wales the chief sources of Quaker recruitment were the millenarian congregations of Vavasor Powell.

[22] This is convincingly detailed in W.A. Cole: 'The Quakers and the English Revolution' (*Past and Present*, November 1956).

indeed have pacifist implications. One could make a moral appeal to that immanent spark of good, and its presence made every individual an object of reverence. At the same time there is something approaching a double standard in Fox's approach since he based his rejection of war on his own personal deliverance from those 'lusts' of the flesh which the New Testament declares to be the root of all war. Nevertheless against evil-doers the sword is a 'praise'. One finds a parallel instance of this double standard, one for the redeemed and one for the unredeemed, in Isaac Penington.[23]

The declaration of 1661 signalizes the final stage of withdrawal and spiritualization. It affirms 'that the Spirit of Christ which leads us into all Truth, will never move us to fight against any man with outward weapons, neither for the Kingdom of Christ nor for the kingdoms of this world'.

IV

Having indicated the general conditions giving rise to revolutionary assault and withdrawal we may turn to certain specific conditions relating to the areas and the social strata from which Quakers were recruited. Recent researches by H. S. Barbour[24] and W. A. Cole[25] have shown that Quakers were recruited from areas and classes where the social distresses and disorganization of the time were especially acute. These were not the lowest elements in the social hierarchy, which had not at that time attained self-consciousness, but those elements in the lower middle class and decent poor sufficiently conscious to share in the general expectations of the revolution and therefore correspondingly disappointed when the revolution stopped short of their expressed demands, particularly as articulated by John Lilburne and the Levellers.

Ephraim Pagit in his *Heresiographie* (1645) delineates the

[23] Ruth Armsby, op. cit. pp. 104 ff., describes two dispensations, one for the 'Remnant' and one for those 'yet in the mixture'. The same idea is to be found in Barclay.

[24] H. S. Barbour, op. cit. It is worth noting that Barbour discusses the process of the 'spiritualization' of the apocalypse among the Baptists, Fifth Monarchy Men and Muggletonians (pp. 38–41).

[25] W. A. Cole: *The Quakers and Politics 1652–1660* (Ph.D. Peterhouse, Cambridge, 1955).

general social character of the radical left, saying that 'since the suspension of our church government everyone that listeth turneth Preacher, as shoemakers, cobblers, buttonmakers, ostlers and such like . . .'[26] Cole in Appendix A of his thesis gives this broad hint some precision by presenting the results of a careful analysis of Quaker records. He gives these results as a 'cumulative impression', subject to certain minor caveats which need not concern us here.

He found, firstly, that although a substantial proportion of Friends in rural areas came from the land, they were heavily outnumbered by those in trades and handicrafts. 'In this respect the main body of Friends differed from their leaders, at least half of whom were directly connected with the land' (p. 320). Amongst both leaders and rank and file the husbandmen were generally more numerous than the yeomen, while the numbers of clearly identifiable labourers was insignificant. Secondly, he found that substantial groups were engaged in commercial activities in several areas, but that in most districts these were clearly outnumbered by those engaged in industrial occupations. Thirdly, Friends were particularly strong in the textile trades. Cole argues there must be some significance in the fact that the leading centres of cloth manufacture were generally also regions of strong Quaker influence, although the more prosperous areas, as for instance Manchester and East Anglia, retained a less radical form of Puritanism. Many Quakers were weavers, a traditionally heretical occupation. Tailors and shoemakers, workers in wood and leather, workers in the building trade and sailors were all occupations which contained strong Quaker groups.

'Finally, and most important,' says Cole, 'the general consensus of evidence suggests that the early Quaker movement drew its main support from the more depressed sections of the *petite bourgeoisie*' (p. 321). The preponderance of Quaker husbandmen, weavers, tailors and shoemakers favours the view that it was among the more hard pressed sections of the middle strata that Quakerism was most influential. Cole goes on to say that the movement derived its main support from precisely those sections of the population which found their economic position threatened and their political demands frustrated by

[26] Quoted in W. Braithwaite's *History of Quakerism* Vol. I, p. 13.

the political and social changes of the seventeenth century (pp. 324–5). In other words, the revolution aroused radical hopes among such parts of the lower strata as were self-conscious and their disappointment aroused equally radical alienation.

Initially Quakerism was a northern movement which spread south to the cities of London and Bristol. H. S. Barbour makes some interesting comments about the religious geography of the time which throw further light on sources of alienation. He points out that the movement arose among the Dales and Fells of North-West England, where Church life and organization, whether Presbyterian, Roman, Anglican or Baptist, had been neglected. In these areas a tradition of social discontent had persisted among the tenant farmers, who felt themselves disinherited both with regard to their social superiors and with regard to the Church.

Of the sixty-six first active preachers some fifty-nine were from the north-west. This was partly related to isolation and provincialism but Barbour underlines the interesting fact that in the north-west the Pilgrimage of Grace in the previous century was a revolt solely of the commons, without benefit of clergy or gentry. Attitudes engendered at this period between commons and gentry became important for the genesis of Quakerism; moreover, in areas where gentry and commons had risen together, Quakerism made little headway. Thus the social antagonism in these areas allied to the disorganized and deteriorating condition of Church life provided the initial social base from which Quakerism might move forward. Where this social antagonism was absent and where Church life was vital (as for instance in Presbyterian Scotland and Catholic Ireland) Quakers achieved small success. It is also interesting to note that in the wildest regions of all, Northumberland, Durham and North-east Cumberland, where the border earls maintained more personal and direct feudal relations, neither Quakerism nor the Pilgrimage of Grace won much support (p. 95).

Quakerism was thus initially a northern movement with a considerable component of husbandmen, which spread south among artisans and those in trades. The initial impulse derived from radical Puritanism, probably through Quakers in the New Model Army who came into contact with its radical chaplains. Barbour agrees with Cole that in general Quakers were not the lowest stratum of society and that they were nevertheless disappointed groups. 'We gather the general impression,' he says, 'that the Quakers were drawn from classes and areas which had once felt themselves thoroughly disinherited, but which had risen above the bottom' (p. 110). He also says, what is specially relevant to our theme, that:

> in the south of England there were active radical Puritans, such as Penington and Lieut-Col. Jubbes who became disillusioned with war and violence. Nevertheless, the combination of social radicalism with aloofness from war and government which is found in Quakerism, though it appealed to these men, did not originate from them. Its first soil was the outlook of the commoners of the north-west (p. 105).[27]

V

It remains now to bring together certain broad considerations as regards the aetiology of the apocalyptic myth and to raise more precisely the question of the way in which pacifism is related to it.[28]

The material so far cited shows that apocalypticism can appear at any social level, though it is very much more likely at some social levels than others. It is the conditions which affect any given social level, in particular rapid changes, which are crucial. It would be particularly interesting to study the few cases where groups with high status have adopted an apocalyptic or for that matter a pacifist attitude. One would want to uncover the predisposing factors and to see in what way subsequent development differed in pattern from that obtaining at lower social levels. The Minor Church in Poland for example would provide such a field for research, and a later section of the present study is to be concerned with the problem caused by

[27] It is interesting that H. R. Trevor Roper in *The Gentry 1540–1640* (Economic History Supplement, No. 1) interprets the non-resistance policy of the squirearchy as a form of withdrawal following the failure of the 'declining gentry' to maintain the Cromwellian revolution. This might be regarded as analogous to the Quaker withdrawal discussed here.

[28] There is a discussion of millenarianism by Yonina Talmon in 'The Pursuit of the Millennium (*European Journal of Sociology*, Vol. III, No. 1, 1962). My characterization of the apocalyptic myth is an independent construct but her comments regarding aetiology have been utilized in this section.

apocalypticism and pacifism in a comfortable segment of the middle class during the present century.

However, on the whole the apocalyptic myth is a symbolic system to be anticipated amongst the deprived sections of a society, especially where the deprived are in some way marginal, either in having been recent migrants or in constituting ethnic minorities. Deprivation in itself is perhaps less important than a sudden worsening of conditions, such as might be occasioned by natural disasters or by social changes, for example those initiated by the impact of capitalist on peasant economies. Such changes are apt to arouse fantastic expectations either as a reaction to absolute despair or because mild improvements in material conditions are accompanied by social dislocations. An example of the latter situation is provided by recent increases in the Communist vote as a response to the dislocations associated with the Italian economic miracle.

It follows from the whole analysis so far that the aetiology of pacifism is substantially identical with the aetiology of apocalypticism. This established it becomes necessary to investigate under what conditions the response of a sect will be either pacifist or activist. Of course this problem is so complex that one can do little more than indicate some directions in which answers may be sought. The tasks confronting future research are enormous and it will be some time before a comprehensive framework emerges which can be incorporated in sociological theory. When it does one may anticipate a partial fusion of conclusions in the sociology of religion with conclusions in political sociology and in criminology. What one would hope for is a general theory of deviance.

Pacifism accompanies apocalypticism in three basic ways and some discussion of these is a relevant approach to the problem of the differentiating factors. Firstly, pacifism may be proto-revolutionary, in which case the response will be withdrawal but the symbolic system will indicate acute revolutionary potential. In some cases, however, this potential is realized, in others not, and one needs to ask what conditions act as a catalyst from the potential to the actual. The question is complicated by the fact that one cannot easily assess types of relation between theological doctrines and various social situations. But it is possible that the stage of quiescence is dominated by a traditionalistic 'reification' of the social order, in which situation it may appear that salvation could come only from God alone. Then, some initial social changes, perhaps assisted by a symbolic defeat of the existing forces of order, touch off an awareness that revolution may be assisted by human agency.

There would seem to be an association between a stress on human agency and secularization. Nevertheless withdrawal is still possible in a secularized situation, but it is very much more likely to be viewed as a temporary tactic. In other words it is likely to be a form of 'revolutionary defeatism'.

Secondly, pacifism may be post-revolutionary. In such a case pacifism is a radical deposit left behind by revolutionary failure.[29] Such constituents of the revolutionary programme as can be retained within the self-selecting community are organized into the pacifist sect. The apocalyptic myth is internalized and spiritualized and the light from the clouds becomes a light within. The revolutionary spirit bound up in apocalyptic symbolism has been worked out and the emphasis is on introversion. In this type of development it would be of interest to study what differentiates a group which withdraws into a sphere of inner light from a group whose revolutionary ardour outlasted political and military failure. Conceivably individual leaders play an important role in structuring the situation: whether for example the leader is a Fox or a Major-General Harrison.

Finally apocalyptic and pacifist movements may parallel each other as alternative responses to a similar situation. As has been shown in the eschatological ferment in the early sixteenth century Conrad Grebel and Thomas Münzer adopted diametrically opposed responses. In a loose social grouping such as the twentieth century intelligentsia individuals in almost identical situations may react in a revolutionary or in a pacifist manner. In this type of situation the analysis of differentiating factors becomes extremely complicated, since it includes not only minor variations in the social situation and different stages

---

[29] E. Hobsbawm emphasizes this aspect. In his *Primitive Rebels* (Manchester, 1959) he says that some millenarians accept the *status quo* 'Or, what is more likely, they may withdraw into the passionate inner life of "the movement" or "the sect" leaving the rest of the world to its own devices except for some token assertions of millennial hopes, and perhaps of the millennial programme: for instance pacifism and the refusal to take oaths' (p. 63).

in the development of the situation, but the previous social experience and particularly the education of individuals, especially where these individuals act as leaders of opinion. No attempt has been made in this study to unravel such factors: the substantial point is to indicate the existence of certain organic connections between revolution and withdrawal.

PART II

Pacifism in Britain

The categories and relationships so far analysed are now discussed with reference to Britain, particularly in the period of the two world wars. In this context the category of 'the denomination' acquires greater importance and the discussion therefore begins with a chapter on 'The Dissenting Mind'.

PART II

Pacifism in Britain

CHAPTER FIVE

OLD AND NEW DISSENT:
A PROLOGUE

THE object of this chapter is to provide a background to the dissenting and sectarian tendencies which are later to be described in relation to the inter-war period. It is, in particular, an introduction, first to the dissenting mind in general, and then to the contributions made to that mind by economic Liberalism and liberal Socialism. Economic Liberalism is focused for the sake of expository convenience in the person of Lord Courtney and liberal Socialism in the writings of Angell, Hobson and Brailsford. So far as war and peace are concerned the one develops out of the other without the major discontinuities one might expect. The Marxist analysis had little influence on Britain prior to the First World War, so it is not given any consideration at this point. In any case the position of Marx and Engels with regard to war is sufficiently well known and excellently expounded to require no further illustration. The same applies to the actual theory of economic Liberalism: the sources are plentiful and adequate.[1]

The dissenting opposition to war discussed here is *pacificist*[2] not pacifist. The dissenters did not hold that war was always wrong but that it should be avoided wherever humanly possible. The immediate ideological source of this pacificism is the enlightenment, with its universalist message of the likeness of all

[1] Among important sources are E. Silberner: *The Problem of War in Nineteenth Century Economic Thought* (Princeton, 1946); K. Waltz: *Man, the State and War* (New York, 1959); F. Hinsley: *Power and the Pursuit of Peace* (Cambridge, 1963); and A. Bullock and M. Short: *The Liberal Tradition* (London, 1956). There is also a PhD thesis by P. S. Wandycz on: *Liberal Internationalism: the contribution of British and French thought to the theory of international relations* (London 1950).

[2] The usage of 'pacificist' is identical with that of A. J. P. Taylor in *The Trouble Makers* (London, 1957). However, it will be clear that the usage of 'dissenter' is not entirely coextensive with Taylor's.

human beings, but a succession can be traced back to the tradition of international law, in particular Grotius, and to the pacific Christian humanism of Erasmus. Basically it was held that just as individual men were essentially good and rational so also nations were capable of behaving morally and rationally. Again, just as individual men were equal so also nations were equal. The concepts of *raison d'État* and of the normality of war belonged to the era of absolute monarchs and aristocracies not to the liberal society of nations in which policy was openly determined by the pressure of public opinion. Democratic nations as such had no conflicting claims: the interests of each, small or great, were the interests of all.

This natural harmony was to be realized through the rule of law and the agent of its realization was commerce and free trade. Free trade was believed to encourage moral and intellectual progress. It also favoured international prosperity by promoting an international division of labour which was beneficial to all.

These concepts served the interests of economically advanced countries like Britain and France, and were correspondingly deleterious to the retarded economy of a country like Germany. So far as Britain is concerned a great tradition may be traced lasting some hundred and fifty years. It runs from the opposition of Charles James Fox to the wars against the French to John Bright's noble denunciation of the Crimean War. Later exemplars in the same succession are Sir Henry Campbell-Bannerman, protesting against the concentration camps in South Africa and Arthur Henderson devoting his energies to the cause of disarmament.

An honourable niche in the tradition is held by the peace societies.[3] Though these were originally Quaker-inspired, both here and in America,[4] and therefore strictly pacifist, they tended more and more to the broadly pacific position. None of the great names in the British peace movement, W. R. Cremer, Henry Richard, W. T. Stead and John Bright him-

[3] The standard history of the peace societies is A. C. F. Beales's *The History of Peace* (London, 1931).

[4] It is impossible to include the voluminous American data in the present study but some titles are given in the bibliography. There is a comprehensive history by M. Curti: *Peace or War. The American Struggle 1636–1936* (New York, 1936).

74

self, were pacifist: they were rather concerned with the organization of peace by federation, arbitration and international
law. These men saw peace as in some sense natural, but both
within the State and between States peace needed to be
ensured by laws based on reason. The world could be integrated
on a basis of a common interest expressed through voluntary
co-operation rather than through force and diplomatic intervention.

However, within the mind of the pacificist there has always
been an unresolved contradiction between preaching the good
tidings of peace and setting the captives at liberty. Lloyd
George remarked that it was not easy to launch crusades and
to reduce the navy at the same time. The generous Liberal
wished to avoid the entanglements of power politics, and to
save the Persians from the Russians, the Armenians and the
Bulgarians from the Turks, and Liberal nations everywhere
from their oppressors. Unfortunately political isolation necessitated arms for defence while crusading required arms for
attack.

The term 'dissenter' as used by A. J. P. Taylor and applied
to this whole tradition is clearly appropriate.[5] With a few
exceptions the pacific doctrine has received the support of
religious nonconformity. Moreover, this religious dissent has
mingled with and, in the eighteenth and nineteenth centuries
part produced, other forms of dissidence, some of it even
specifically anti-religious. The 'nonconformist conscience' has
increasingly undergone a mutation into 'nonconformity' and
'conscience'. Pious nonconformists and nonconforming sceptics
have together confronted the political and religious establishment. Religious humanitarians have allied themselves with
humane rationalists for whom reason was a principle of development, not merely an organ of adaptation to environment.
Within the body of dissenting opinion has coexisted the rationalistic Unitarianism of Richard Price, the philosophical radicalism of Herbert Spencer,[6] the 'old-fashioned' rationalism of
Charles Bradlaugh, the 'old Whig' utilitarian rationalism of

[5] A. J. P. Taylor, op. cit.

[6] Spencer is particularly important for having given the commonplace nineteenth-century distinction between military and industrial societies a careful conceptual formulation. This is available in C. Wright Mills: *Images of Society* (New
York, 1960).

Bertrand Russell, and the working-class nonconformist radicalism of Thomas Burt and Arthur Henderson.

Taylor traces dissent up to 1939. Yet in some ways its
demise can be located some years before while in another
sense its ghost is clearly still with us. The dissenters were
sharply divided during the First World War, and Arthur
Henderson, by his support for the war and for the League
succeeded in merging many of them with a much wider body
of opinion. Both political and religious dissent went underground in 1931, by which time there were few so poor as felt
constrained to say a good word either for Liberal democracy
or Protestant nonconformity. There have been those who
wished to place the prophetic mantle on the shoulders of
Anthony Eden, by reason of his devotion to principle and
support for the League. But Eden was really a Broad Churchman who does not masquerade convincingly in the severe
vestments of a dissenter. A mere two years in the political
wilderness is just not good enough.

The attitude which united all the different elements which
have been mentioned was the personal, Protestant conscience:
noble, fallible and selective. All adhered to the moral principle
in politics, whether validated by reason or by scripture or by
both. Thus John Morley criticized Machiavelli on the grounds
that he was oblivious to the 'potent arms of moral force'. In
Morley's view to declare war was to suspend 'not merely
habeas corpus but the Ten Commandments as well'.[7] Similarly
Bertrand Russell early took to heart the text: 'Thou shalt not
follow a multitude to do evil.' When John Bright explained his
resignation over the bombardment of Alexandria he 'said
something about the moral law'. Morley tells us this drew a
'sharp retort' from Gladstone, who, as a good dissenter in his
periods out of office, regarded the moral law as his own personal
political property.[8]

The dissenters undoubtedly exaggerated the extent to which
politics could be moralized. Yet what they proposed was at
least some form of politics, whereas the sectarians who succeeded

[7] From Morley's *Miscellanies*, fourth series (London, 1948) quoted in F. R.
Flournoy: 'British Liberal Theories of International Relations' (*Journal of the
History of Ideas*, Vol. VII, No. 2, April 1946).

[8] J. Morley: *Life of Gladstone* (London, 1908), Vol. 2, p. 244.

them believed in an end to politics. Their policy was an alternative policy, not a negation of policy. They differed from the foreign policy of the Establishment in this, that while the latter saw all morality as subservient to the safety of the realm, the dissenters regarded morality and safety as coequal, and even, in the long run, as coincident. Whatever might be lost materially on momentary swings would be gained on eventual roundabouts. Conservatives were clear that foreign policy provided many instances where morality and interest parted company but their opponents regarded such instances as arising solely in connection with the interests of Conservatives. The result was that when the Liberals eventually found themselves willy-nilly involved in a world war in which existence appeared to be at stake they refused to see it in such terms but elevated it into a final war for freedom and democracy. Liberal idealism either crusades for peace or treats war as a crusade.

Such attachment to principle means that dissenters rarely achieve power. When they do it is either because they have something else to offer besides righteousness, like big loaves instead of little ones, or because the Conservatives have failed to deliver the goods. Attachment to principle is also a fruitful source of fission and inflexibility. Every dissenter knows he is right, and as Cromwell found out, it is very little use beseeching them, even 'in the bowels of Christ', to consider the possibility that they may be wrong. Should they for a moment doubt the righteousness of their cause or be confronted by a tragic and unavoidable dilemma they may well descend to power politics with startling rapidity.

Exclusion from power enables dissenters to enlarge on the dire consequences of the past policies of their opponents on the present. And they are nearly always right. The only flaw in their analysis is to assume that politics is simply a matter of evil decisions and intellectual errors rather than of pressures. Alternatively they illogically combine a moralistic critique with an analysis based on economic determinism. Occasionally dissenters regard the responsibility of their opponents for the past as divesting them of any responsibility towards the present.

When dissenters do acquire power, however, their attitude undergoes a change of key. It would appear that they are held prisoner by wicked and persuasive sirens in the Foreign Office who somehow succeed in corrupting their morals. The voice with which they speak is no longer their true voice. Alternatively one can only suppose that their previous attachment to principle was of doubtful sincerity and they are now appearing in their true colours. A good man in the Foreign Office executing evil policies is an enigma to the dissenting mind : they conclude he is acting on false information and hasten to acquaint him with the facts.

International affairs is thus a field in which the good are mysteriously led astray. The Lloyd George of pro-Boer fame makes a jingoistic speech at the Mansion House, the Wilson of the fourteen points is found consenting to Versailles, and the Ramsay MacDonald of the Union of Democratic Control becomes the secretive premier who signs the White Paper on Rearmament. Faced with such daunting facts, both when in and out of office, dissenters easily fall back on a conspiratorial theory of politics. In the twentieth century their favourite conspiracy was that of the armament manufacturers.[9]

Finally the dissenters believe that the freedom of action occasionally belonging to Britain at the height of her power belongs to political decisions in general. This leads them to indulge a curiously inverted patriotism in the belief that Britain has no right to be wrong. An ideal role is cast for her and the effect of Britain's imperial position is to lead dissenters to see this role as potentially decisive. If only Britain sets an example then other nations can hardly fail to follow. In the event of her failing to do so they fall back on a fretful, consciously righteous, criticism.

Such virtue is, in a sense, parasitic on the vice of the Establishment. One cannot dramatically throw away one's arms unless the Establishment is first misguided enough to manufacture them. The redemptive gesture in order to have any moral meaning requires to be made freely and political freedom depends on power which in turn depends on armaments. So there is a sense in which the moral gesture is not repeatable. Should it fail then the political situation reverts

[9] A classic of this approach is P. Noel Baker's *The Private Manufacture of Armaments* (2 Vols. London, 1936) For another example see W. Holtby's Apology for Armourers', Chapter 6 of a symposium *Challenge to Death* (London, 1934).

to its normal unregenerate state. Nevertheless some dissenters have talked as if policy could be composed of a series of such gestures.

I. PORTRAIT OF AN OLD DISSENTER

An admirable focus of the pacific doctrine in the nineteenth and early twentieth centuries is provided by the career of Leonard Courtney. In almost every respect he sums up the varied strains in the older Liberalism. His concept of democracy depended on the fullest possible extension of political rights, even to proportional representation. In his desire for retrenchment he was a Gladstonian economist of the old school; in his opposition to war a philosophic radical.

L. S. Amery summed him up as follows: 'Lord Courtney represented, in its most clear cut and uncompromising form, the Liberal Individualism of the Victorian age, with its unquestioning faith in the Free Trade, its dislike of all forms of State action, its dislike in the British Empire, its whole-hearted pacifism.'[10] It is also historically proper that such a man, imbued with Victorian piety and a communicant of the English Church though he was, should have held to a rationalistic Socinianism linking him to old Whig dissent. It is doubly proper that he should come from the Celtic fringes of Cornwall and have been educated at the University of Cambridge.

The chief mark of Courtney's political creed was its consistency. His beliefs remained almost unchanged from the time when he first entered Parliament as member for Liskeard in 1874 to his death in 1918 as a member of the House of Lords. Moreover, these beliefs were logically consistent one with another. His adherence to political democracy did not baulk at any of its implications: he not only introduced a bill for women's suffrage in 1878 but actively campaigned for proportional representation. Nor did he ever waver in devotion to peace and conciliation. When he rose to speak in the debate immediately preceding the South African War he was able to say quite truly that he was taking the same stand 'that I took in 1877 when, as a new Member, I pleaded against an unwise

[10] Quoted in G. P. Gooch: *Life of Lord Courtney* (London, 1920), p. 441. The material for this section derives almost entirely from Gooch.

annexation of the Transvaal. Then, as now I pleaded for for-
bearance and conciliation.'[11]

This consistency (or inflexibility) was based on a vigorous
sense of 'the majesty of the moral law' and the authority of
conscience. In his Presidential Address to the Universal Peace
Congress in 1908, Courtney claimed that 'the force which really
governs the world . . . is the force of morality'.[12] It was therefore
not surprising that he and his brother-in-law Lord Parmoor
(Alfred Cripps) should become the chief protagonists of the
rights of conscientious objectors during the First World War.
Indeed so clearly did he sense the moral imperative that he
was ready to prophesy in season and out for reason and common
sense, whether the occasion was the world war or the war in
South Africa. For him the foreign policy of Britain needed above
all a moral basis and it was policies based on alliances which
deprived her of freedom to espouse the cause of justice wherever
that cause might be found.

Personal integrity allied to intellectual consistency made him
relatively indifferent to the claims of party. He was a genuine
independent for whom the caucus politics of a Joseph Chamberlain or a Randolph Churchill were anathema, although,
ironically enough, the very democracy he advocated was undermining the basis of his political independence. His integrity
also aggravated what his sister-in-law Beatrice Webb called his
one fault: 'his inveterate habit of thinking everyone who dis-
agrees with him immoral and unenlightened'.[13]

The result was his partial disablement as a politician. Although gifted with outstanding abilities he held only two brief
under-secretaryships. A period as Secretary to the Treasury
from 1882 to 1884 ended with his resignation over the issue of
proportional representation. He left the Liberals for the Liberal
Unionists because he believed a thorough programme of reform
in Ireland was preferable to a policy of Home Rule. Then,
in the aftermath of the South African War his pro-Boer sym-
pathies cost him his seat and cast him out into the political
wilderness.

Perhaps his portrait is most clearly drawn by his attitude to

[11] Ibid., p. 366.

[12] Ibid., p. 551.

[13] B. Webb: *Our Partnership* (London, 1948).

the Agadir incident, one of the major crises preceding the First World War. The crisis occurred in 1911 and rudely interrupted the discussions which had been going on between Britain and Germany about disarmament. The choice before Britain lay between the Anglo-French Entente, operative since 1904 and the Treaty of Algeciras which safeguarded the integrity of Morocco and to which Britain, Germany and France were signatories. When the French sent troops to Fez, Germany interpreted this as being a breach of the Treaty and sent a gunboat to Agadir. However, Grey, the British Foreign Secretary approved the French action and felt indignant about German interference. On July 21st Lloyd George, now no longer the pacific pro-Boer of a decade previous, made his famous speech at the Mansion House threatening Germany with war if she treated Britain 'as of no account in the Cabinet of Nations'. In the event a treaty was signed between France and Germany on November 4th by which Germany renounced her claims in Morocco in return for a part of French Congo.

In the ensuing debate in the House of Lords Courtney argued that the Foreign Office gave greater weight to the Anglo-French Entente than to the Treaty of Algeciras. Since our treaty obligations were to maintain the integrity of Morocco we ought rather to have partnered Germany in protesting against any unilateral action by France. Lloyd George's speech he described as a shrill outcry of slighted self-importance. All in all the policy of Grey had made our friendship with France exclusive.

Courtney then went on to a statement of political faith. 'His [Grey's] conception is a divided Europe. He seems to regard as impossible the notion of a unity of Christendom, a family of nations, a concert of Europe.' The concept of balance of power had been:

> . . . the bane of successive generations. We want a new conception of international duty, a foreign policy based on a federation of powers in one body, not in two camps. The main principle of Lord Salisbury's foreign policy was the maintenance of a concert. We sometimes regretted that it moved slowly. It always will move slowly. But the Concert of Europe is a guarantee of peace compared with which your calculations of the relative strength of this or that combination are idle and frivolous. It is to a European

concert and to that alone, that we look for a restoration of right feeling in European politics.[14]

II. THE NEW DISSENTER

Courtney represented the old dissent, but in the last quarter of the nineteenth century and the beginning of the twentieth a new dissent had appeared. Men like T. H. Green, L. T. Hobhouse and J. M. Keynes represented a liberalism which maintained its pacific attitude but came closer to an economic analysis of the causes of war in terms of the incoherence of the capitalist system. At the same time the new dissent had to face the split in the liberal mind between those who retained the pacific doctrine but who also retained a suspicion of State activity and those who wished to extend State welfare but whose attitude to foreign affairs was imperialist, even protectionist. As the Liberal Party moved nearer to Socialism it loosened its grasp in free trade and pacificism.

By a parallel paradox the Labour Party maintained its pacific faith to the extent that it imbibed the spirit of liberalism. It was helped in so doing by those Liberals who seceded to the Labour Party at the close of the First World War. These Liberals, whose primary concern with foreign affairs earned them the title of the 'foreign legion', maintained the continuity of the pacific witness between the Liberal and Labour Parties. Roden Buxton and Noel Buxton had been Liberals engaged in the support of many good dissenting causes, such as the Boers, the Congolese, the Welsh, the Irish, the Macedonians, the Bulgarians and the Armenians. After the war they became Labour M.P.s and sat on the Labour Party's highly distinguished and influential 'Advisory Committee on International Questions'.[15]

Three other distinguished members of that committee, J. A. Hobson, Norman Angell and H. N. Brailsford are important as having written classics which became received texts in the dissenting exegesis of foreign politics. It is these which we must now examine. The first was Hobson's *Imperialism* (1902), followed by Angell's *The Great Illusion* (1910), and Brailsford's

[14] G. P. Gooch, op. cit., p. 570.
[15] Some useful comment on this committee is available in W. P. Maddox: *Foreign Relationships in British Labour Politics* (Cambridge, Mass., 1924).

The War of Steel and Gold (1914). Before considering their contributions to the dissenting mind it is interesting to note that
whereas in the case of the Buxtons the old evangelical tradition
was transmuted into the social concerns characteristic of the
'Christian Social Union', in the case of these three writers one
finds a continuation of the rationalist tradition. Hobson for
example was a rationalist of the type associated with the South
Place Ethical Society.

Hobson's *Imperialism*, which contained the basis of a later
book by V. I. Lenin on the same theme, saw imperialism
primarily in economic terms. It was a question of a demand for
raw materials, for markets and for profitable investment, made
more urgent by the tendency of industrial productivity to out-
run the rate of home consumption. In thoroughly Keynesian
manner he diagnosed this as due to underspending and over-
saving rooted in the maldistribution of wealth as between the
classes. The consequence of expansion in several countries at
once was colonialism, protectionism, the armaments race and
hence clashes of interest which led to wars, of which the war in
South Africa provided a prime example.

Norman Angell[16] regarded war as an intellectual error and
in so doing typified the rationalist element in dissent. Those
who agreed with him, who included a number of industrialists,
some of them Quakers, sponsored The Garton Foundation to
propagate his ideas among those possessed of power and influence. According to Angell war was a mistake and conquest
an illusion. Modern communications and the interdependence
of modern financial arrangements carried two implications.
Firstly, force was futile as a means of imposing either ideas or
institutions. Secondly, a conquering nation could not expro-
priate land or lay its hands on potential or realized wealth.
The cosmopolitan structure of credit would be so shaken by
war as to almost ensure that the victors emerged weakened and
impoverished. War was not indeed impossible, but neither was
it inevitable. The crucial factor was information, not human
nature.

Brailsford criticized Angell in that while it was quite true

[16] Angell has sometimes been cited as a pacifist who believed war was impossible.
In fact he was not a pacifist and eventually became a firm supporter of League
sanctions.

to say that war was irrational from the national viewpoint, it was not necessarily irrational from the viewpoint of a narrow governing class. There might be no great gain for Germany in conquering a Britain already saturated in capital, but there was gain in her conquering India. Although it is true that conquest may not benefit a nation, the purpose of arms was not so much war and conquest as the exercise of diplomatic pressure, particularly in new spheres of influence. Those who had a new view of international affairs must consider three main courses: to make democracy bear on diplomacy, to regulate the export of capital to underdeveloped countries and to conceive a European organization which might supersede the balance of power.

He further pointed out that the idea of a fundamental opposition to war had usually taken root amongst men whose outlook was ethical and individualistic and who were, therefore, primarily concerned with personal righteousness. On the other hand those whose prime concern was to prevent suffering might be more inclined to resist evil by war. Men united in non-resistance but otherwise divided and individualistic could never create a formidable opposition to a Government: it therefore remained for Socialists to create a united party of peace.

CHAPTER SIX

THE LABOUR PARTY AND
THE I.L.P.

I. INTRODUCTION

THE Labour Party, in common with the Liberal Party, may be regarded as a political denomination. Some of the implications of this terminology will be drawn out in the conclusions to the present chapter but it will probably be useful to make some preliminary remarks at the outset of our discussion.

Clearly an analogy is being sought between the religious denomination and political organizations which display certain similar characteristics. At the most formal level this analogy depends on the simple fact of dissent, meaning by dissent disagreement which occurs within the context of shared presuppositions. These shared presuppositions distinguish a dissenting situation from a sectarian situation, since in the latter disagreement is absolute.

The denomination, then, is involved in limited conflict and there is consequently no need either for the violence of repression or the violence of revolution. The existence of broad and mutually acceptable criteria allows change to occur without any major lesions in the body politic. Political life proceeds in a steady and peaceful evolution which permits a continuity of dissent to subsist alongside a continuity of established power.

Thus to label the Labour Party a political denomination is simply to indicate the familiar fact that its ideological dissidence has been expressed within an overall framework of broad national agreement, as set, in this particular instance, by the conventions of Liberal parliamentary democracy.[1] It also in-

[1] See R. Miliband: *Parliamentary Socialism* (London, 1961), especially p. 13.

G   85

dicates that the change from Liberal dissent to the dissidence of Labour was more apparent than real. Indeed a striking evolution of attitudes is observable as between the Liberal Party and the Labour Party and this is particularly remarkable with regard to the whole question of violence.[2]

These preliminary remarks concerning the meaning of the term political denomination are highly formal as well as obvious, but they are capable of expansion and of acquiring a more particular content once the historical material has been discussed. For the moment, however, they serve the purpose of indicating two questions which merit some examination. The first is the historical relation between religious dissent and political dissidence, and the second is the relation between the Liberal Party and the Labour Party. Each of these questions is crucial if the attitudes of the Labour Party to war and peace are to be understood.

The parallelism between religious dissent and political dissidence has been frequently noted but it has also been subject to exaggeration and misunderstanding. The two have certainly not been coextensive. To give but one example the official policy of the Wesleyan branch of Methodism during the first half of the nineteenth century was more inclined to favour the political establishment than otherwise.[3] The most prominent leader of the Wesleyans, the Reverend Jabez Bunting even went so far as to declare that Methodism was as opposed to democracy as it was to sin.

Nevertheless it is certainly true that during the second half of the nineteenth century and first quarter or so of the twentieth, English and Welsh nonconformity made significant contributions to the Liberal Party and to the Labour Party. It is probably correct to say that the majority of nonconformists remained Liberal throughout the period. Perhaps in the earlier years they were relatively more prominent in local associa-

---

[2] 'The history of the Labour Party has been particularly marked by the development of what is best described as radical liberal internationalism.' G. W. Shepherd: *Theory and Practice of Internationalism in the British Labour Party* (Ph.D. Thesis, London, 1952), p. 8.

[3] See E. R. Taylor: *Methodism and Politics, 1791–1851* (Cambridge 1935), and K. S. Inglis: *Churches and the Working Classes in Victorian England* (London, 1963).

tions[4] than in the highest circles of Liberal leadership[5] or of the intellectual defenders of Liberalism, but by 1906 they had broken through to very considerable political power within the Liberal Party.

At the same time the leadership of the Labour Party also contained a surprisingly large number of nonconformists, probably drawn more particularly from the ranks of skilled workers and artisans. Such men sometimes found the path to political expression through the Liberal Party blocked and therefore turned to the nascent Labour Party. The high tide of this particular influence lasted up to 1931 with residual effects remaining till 1951 and even to the present day.[6]

Something of the extent of the nonconformist contribution to Labour's leadership may be gauged from the briefest consideration of key figures in the Labour Party of this period. Any list of outstanding leaders would certainly include nonconformists such as Keir Hardie, Philip Snowden, Arthur Henderson, and Ernest Bevin: men who learnt their political craft and rhetoric through the chapel as well as through the branch and local party.[7] Perhaps the principal figures are Henderson and Bevin, both with lay preaching backgrounds. Some idea of the influence of nonconformity at a slightly lower political level may be gained from the fact that of 192 Labour M.P.s questioned in 1925 by J. M. Gaus, forty-five were lay preachers, mainly in dissenting bodies.[8]

Few of these dissenters at the forefront of the Labour leadership were sectarian in their attitudes, either in adopting a

[4] E. Halevy points out the relatively poor showing of nonconformists at parliamentary level prior to 1906 on p. 209 of his *Imperialism and the Rise of Labour* (London, 1929), which is Book V of a *History of the English People in the Nineteenth Century*. He also documents the nonconformist triumph in 1906 on pp. 64–5 of Book VI in the same series.

[5] Some documentation regarding nonconformity and the Liberal Party in Parliament is provided by W. L. Guttsman: *The British Political Élite* (London, 1963), p. 170 and pp. 180–2.

[6] See an article by K. J. W. Alexander and A. Hobbs entitled: 'What Influences Labour M.P.s' (*New Society*, No. 11, November 13th, 1962).

[7] It is interesting that Cripps and Attlee were religious men in the Anglican middle-class tradition of social service. Lansbury moved uncertainly between Anglicanism and the Ethical Society. All three Anglicans were decidedly left of centre in the inter-war period.

[8] J. M. Gaus' *Great Britain: a Study in Civic Loyalty* (Chicago, 1929), p. 108. Gaus also cites twenty-eight Labour M.P.s as active in pacifist organizations and seven as having spent a term of imprisonment as objectors.

pacifist or an aggressively apocalyptic political ideology. Like Bevin and Henderson, they were not ideologues at all, but brought to their politics certain characteristic denominational attitudes: a temperate idealism, pragmatic as well as pacific, democratic and parliamentary in the fundamental sense of the word. Moreover, they helped to carry forward their own version of individualism from the Liberal to the Labour Party.

It is here, in the denominational attitude and sentiment, considerably wider than the formal frontiers of nonconformity, that the Labour Party owes more to what Morgan Phillips loosely called 'Methodism' than it does to Marx. The theoretical basis of the Labour Party owes little to nonconformity or any form of Christianity.[9] The 'theory' of Labour politics goes back to Robert Owen and is rooted in predominantly anti-ecclesi-astical, even irreligious, sources. It is rather the comparative unimportance of theory which is owed: on the one hand a dominance of humanitarian feeling over dogma and on the other a doctrinaire attachment to the forms of political demo-cracy. Whereas some segments of the middle class might respond to rationalistic egalitarianism or Marxism, or some uneasy juxtaposition of the two, there were earnest members of the working class who imbibed the Protestant social conscience. Certainly many of them read the works of the rationalists and (later) of the secular visionaries, but they also paid impressive tribute to the fact that a major impulse of their political faith, particularly in the formative years of the 1890's, was the attempt to translate the Sermon on the Mount into political terms.

We turn now to a consideration of the relationship between the Liberal and the Labour Parties. According to the constitu-tion of 1918 the Labour Party became a Socialist party but reference has already been made to the striking continuity of attitudes which it shares with nineteenth-century liberalism, and, in particular, even with liberal individualism. This in-dividualism has two sources: the denominational tradition already discussed, and *bourgeois* rationalism. With reference to

[9] Except in so far as Henry George provided some theoretical basis in his *Progress and Poverty*. The 'social gospel' in America had a very strong influence on the Labour Party in its formative period, mainly through the writings of George and Bellamy.

the former it is an individualism expressed within a religious structure which vigorously inhibits it. As such it is necessarily grounded in the accommodations which are inherent in subordination to collective purposes. Moreover, nonconformist bodies have shouldered various social responsibilities which have involved empirical experience of political possibilities, even though exclusion from real power has encouraged tendencies to ignore the necessities and paradoxes of politics and to develop the logic of the pacific position in the abstract.

But *bourgeois* rationalism, being largely irreligious, includes the possibility of the type of individualism which develops without restraint both practically and ideologically. Not necessarily so, of course: the early work of the Webbs shows a pragmatic rationalism at work within the possibilities of power as understood in groups close to Government. Moreover, within the practical world of commerce rationalism may well mean an egoistic individualism for which reason is purely instrumental. But within the world of thought the way is open for a rationalistic Utopianism progressively divorced from empirical realities and historical contingencies. The value of this development lies in its critical attitude, but the devotion given to the abstract idea of Reason makes it extremely difficult to derive either positive loyalties or immediately practicable policies from it.

The continuity of the Labour Party with liberalism and with the Liberal Party can as clearly be seen in relation to this type of individualism as it can be seen in relation to denominational Christianity. Moreover, the growth of the middle-class intelligentsia in the twentieth century has given rationalistic Utopianism increasing weight within the Labour Party.

Paradoxically it is the so-called left, with its apparently Socialist slogans, which provides clearest evidence of this inheritance from the anarchic tendencies of nineteenth-century liberalism.[10] Thus the left has been able to recruit middle-class liberals directly to its ranks. To the extent that it is concerned with domestic issues the emphasis rests on the rationalistic (*'bourgeois'*) egalitarianism of the French Revolution rather than the Marxist economics of the Russian. But the broad emphasis

[10] S. Davis: *The Labour Party and Foreign Policy 1933–1939* (Ph.D. Thesis, London, 1952), describes left-wingers as 'strongly individualistic in their thinking' (p. xxvii). See J. Jupp: *The Left in Britain* (M.Sc. Econ, London, 1956), p. 248.

of these anarchic Socialists of the left hardly rests on domestic issues, but on those issues which are most germane to our thesis: foreign affairs and the whole question of violence.

In relation to foreign affairs and the practice of violence the non-Communist left holds to attitudes and postures directly reminiscent of that *laissez-faire* section of the Liberal Party which preoccupied itself with such questions. It is around the issue of war and all the related issues concerned with main force that the emotional vehemence of the left characteristically gathers. As A. J. P. Taylor has observed, 'The great emotional question for the middle-class left was foreign policy . . .'. While the trade unions expected an enlightened foreign policy to produce economic benefits, the politicians preached welfare in order to have a free hand for their foreign policy. 'Left foreign policy had a simple prescription. Germany and Russia were justly aggrieved; the redress of their grievances would secure the peace and prosperity of the world.'[11]

But if liberal causes have peculiarly agitated the mind of the middle-class left this is not to suggest that the Labour Party as a whole has not evidenced the liberal aversion to violence, both internally as between classes and externally as between nations. Of course to the extent that that left has imbibed Marxism it tends to recognize conflict between classes, whereas the right has been more inclined to recognize conflict between nations.

It is also worth stressing that aversion to violence, both internal and external, connects with an essentially liberal objection to military or industrial conscription through the agency of the State. The question of the total organization of the citizen is closely tied in with the issue of violence and it sharply demarcates all shades of opinion within the Labour Party from the Communist Party. Historically this is the fulcrum on which Labour's rejection of Communism has turned. In this respect the denominational character of the Labour Party is particularly clear. Marxism has no primary aversion to violence and in principle approves of both military and industrial conscription.

A final example of the liberalism of the middle-class left may be found in its attitude to alliances. Middle-class progressives have never ceased to believe that somehow Britain can both

[11] A. J. P. Taylor, a chapter on: *Confusion on the Left* in. *The Baldwin Age* (London, 1960), edited by John Raymond, pp. 68–9.

avoid conscription or military preparations and also play a decisive role in international politics entirely outside the framework of alliances.

II. TYPES OF OPINION

Some five broad bands of opinion with respect to peace and war may be discerned within the Labour Party. There is, first of all, a thin line of nationalistic fervour, particularly evident in the period prior to the First World War and up to the summer of 1917. After the war it maintains itself, but generally in an attenuated form, as a simple dislike of Germany. This attitude was probably more widespread in the broad, inactive mass of working-class unionism than at the level of trade union representatives and administrators. It is evident enough in the writings of a working-class Socialist like Robert Blatchford, both during the Boer War and in the period of arms rivalry with Germany. Similarly so in the unions related to armaments, in the Seamen's Union during the actual course of the war, and amongst some M.P.s sitting for dockyard constituencies.

It also found expression in a middle-class spokesman of the extreme left like H. M. Hyndman and in the nationalistic minority of the Social Democratic Federation which he led during the course of the war. A representative of a similarly intense nationalism can be found on the extreme right of the Labour Party during the thirties in the person of A. L. Rowse. It is interesting that Rowse himself contrasts the heroic ethic and realism of the working class and the aristocracy with the prudential and pacific ethic of the *bourgeoisie*. This alliance of aristocrat and proletarian is obviously only marginally distinct from the Socialism of Oswald Mosley in the earlier stages of his career. However, in so far as it was no more than a fear and suspicion of Germany, such as was shared by Hugh Dalton, it enabled those who were imbued with it to recognize the menace of Hitler more clearly and quickly than those whose prejudgements were less firm.

Secondly, there is the realist school of thought which believed in the League as an organization for the elimination of the international anarchy only for so long as this seemed genuinely possible, and which recognized both that the League could **do** little but reflect existing alignments and that such alignments might be necessary. Prior to the First World War realists saw the British Empire as the only existing instalment on world government and the attitude of the Webbs and of Shaw was coloured by this point of view. After the war by far the most important exponents of realism were to be found amongst trade union leaders, although it is important to recognize that in the period immediately following the war many trade union leaders shared in the widespread feelings of revulsion, in spite of their formal engagements to the League. Whereas before the war the unions had been relatively little concerned with foreign affairs, apart from some liberal and pacific gestures in the nineteenth century, the world-wide economic dislocations of the twenties forced foreign politics on their attention, while the instructive fate of the German and Austrian movements in the thirties completed their education in political realities. Moreover, trade union leaders wielded concrete responsibilities which made them realize that such doctrines as the general strike against war represented little more than a momentary genuflection towards an illusion.

There is, thirdly, what may be called the League view, both in a 'weak' and in a 'strong' version. Each version may be brought under the heading of collective security, though the term might well be restricted solely to the 'strong' version of League doctrine. Broadly the 'weak' interpretation of the League doctrine was based on a suspicion of the use of sanctions, partly because the League itself was so imperfect a structure, partly because sanctions would tend to petrify the injustices of the *status quo*, particularly those brought about by Versailles. A correct approach lay rather in gradually building up machinery for disarmament and arbitration through which norms of justice might become customary and peaceful change enabled to take place. Disarmament and arbitration once established the need for sanctions might never arise.

The 'strong' version of belief in the League, which gained very wide acceptance in Labour's ranks after 1934, tended to see the sanctions at the League's disposal either as the crux of the international order or, at least, as an essential element in it. Law might depend mainly on custom but custom partly depended on power. National forces should be conceived in terms of the League's requirements, however, not in terms of competitive alignments between sovereign States. The essence of foreign policy was the defence of the League concept and the enforcement of its decisions against recalcitrant powers.

A fourth view, located among the non-Communist left, stressed the unity of the international working class and the consequent efficacy of a general strike against war. War was the creation of capitalist Governments, and to many the League was an association of such Governments. Capitalist and imperialist régimes were incorrigibly immoral and it was therefore impossible to concede them armaments. Once the proletariat gained power, international relations would recover a state of innocence. In so far as the non-Communist left was solicitous for the national security of Russia it tended to become a halting reflection of the Communist Party, proposing or rejecting alliances accordingly, but to the extent that a purist attitude was maintained it required various stages in the development of the international crisis to dislodge various groups into accepting the necessity of compromise. Cripps, leading the Socialist League, did not abandon his belief in the independent action of the international working class until 1938. The I.L.P. maintained its faith to the end. Apart from the I.L.P., which had influence in the Scots–Irish working class of West Scotland, and apart from some left-wing areas in South Wales and East London, this view was particularly strong amongst the middle-class supporters of Labour.

Finally, there is the pacifist view, which rejects war as such, sometimes on religious grounds, in which case it remains constant, sometimes on utilitarian or rationalist grounds, in which case it may easily embrace a diametrically opposed doctrine should circumstances alter cases. Both religious and utilitarian pacifism can appear to merge with the League view, either because they have confidence in the purely moral force wielded by an international body, or because they rely on various sanctions short of war. Everything depends here on which sanctions are thought likely to provoke war. The problem also arises of the near-pacifist, who does not rule out resort to force *a priori*, but who in any particular war is so conscious of the defects pertaining to his own side, or to the international body, or both, that he will almost certainly reject it as unjust. Many

Liberal recruits to Labour, like H. M. Swanwick and Noel Buxton, held such views.

The pacifist and near-pacifist attitudes were primarily found amongst the Socialist and extreme liberal segments of the middle class, except in Wales where pacifism was tinged with nationalistic and religious influences, and Scotland, where nationalism combined with a pacifism which was more frequently political.

At this point one must pause to note the extraordinarily complex way in which all these views were related to each other. A proponent of international working-class unity might on suitable occasions emerge as a supporter of the 'strong' policies by the League; a supporter of League sanctions might momentarily fall back on working-class unity. Believers in the 'weak' version of the League could easily take a pacifist stand in particular circumstances; alternatively they might, after experience of power, gradually revert to a foreign policy of the purely national variety. Religious pacifists were capable of seeming to align themselves with 'weak' supporters of the League; utilitarian pacifists were capable of seeming to take the same course, and then of switching to the starkest realism. Realists, for their part, habitually presented their case in terms of a strong League policy, rather than of national exigency. Those who accepted the necessity of ultimate sanctions nevertheless often pursued the 'weak' principle of League action so long as it appeared remotely viable.

What is interesting about these combinations is the number of them which were capable of assimilation under the rubric of collective security so long as it was chiefly identified with the possibility of disarmament. Only the realistic attitude was not capable of such assimilation given appropriate circumstances. Moreover, as will be shown below, underlying most of these attitudes was the conviction that the current difficulties were the making of capitalist and Conservative miscreants. Doubtless in part they were. But Labour felt falsely free to suppose that it need not face things as they now existed, since its own advent to power would automatically be for the healing of the nations. The brighter possibilities were indeed genuinely present at times: the difficulty arose from automatically assuming their existence.

We now turn to illustrate how these various strands of opinion reacted to events from the period of the First World War to the end of the Second.[12]

III. THE SEQUENCE OF EVENTS

(a) *1914–1919*

In the period before the First World War many Labour leaders reposed their trust in the doctrine of a general strike against war.[13] Keir Hardie himself pleaded for 'war resistance', not indeed on grounds of the class war but on the basis of the international brotherhood of man. Even MacDonald envisaged the general strike as a possible tactic in the event of an unpopular war. However, it seems unlikely that the movement as a whole was converted. The brunt of the opposition came from the unions, led by Henderson, and when the issue was debated at the Leicester Conference in 1911, Keir Hardie found himself in the minority. At the conference in the following year Tom Shaw, another union leader, expressed a scepticism similar to that of Henderson. In his view the general strike policy was merely a pious aspiration and would be revealed as such as soon as a situation of war arose.

In any case, Labour spokesmen were simultaneously giving vent to patriotic sentiments which seemed likely to clash with attempts at war resistance in the event of a full-scale crisis. Philip Snowden, speaking in 1910, insisted that he would vote 'for any sum, however large, if it were absolutely necessary for the defence of our shores'. J. R. Clynes declared that his party would agree to fight in any circumstance where 'life and honour' were involved. It was safe to predict that the majority of the party would see life and honour involved once the moment of truth was on them.

The war crisis developed in two stages. The first stage, prior to the invasion of Belgium, revealed a substantial opposition to war, coming from the radical and pacific rump of the Liberal Party and from the I.L.P. The former group, including men as diverse as Lord Courtney and Norman Angell,

[12] Only material directly relevant to pacifism has been discussed. The major conclusions rest on the very detailed work of G. W. Shepherd and S. Davis, op. cit.

[13] See R. Miliband: *Parliamentary Socialism* (London, 1961), p. 40.

immediately organized a newspaper campaign to back up political pressure in favour of neutrality. At this time Angell was engaged in working for the Garton Foundation, an organization supported by some industrialists concerned to demonstrate the irrationality of war, and the tone used by the proponents of neutrality was strongly tinged with the prudential rationality of British capitalism. The I.L.P., however, combined such *bourgeois* objections to war with Socialist analyses of its economic basis and with religious objections. Labour's belief in peace found its most impressive expression in a historic mass rally in Trafalgar Square.

It was all of no avail. The 'rape of little Belgium' swept aside this substantial body of opinion, leaving only a few isolated pockets of resistance among middle-class radical intellectuals and the hard core of the I.L.P. Only these groups gave support to MacDonald when he made the first parliamentary protest against the war. The trade unions were almost unanimously in favour of fighting and the majority of Fabians were moderately inclined towards participation. Indeed, one Fabian, H. G. Wells, sometime apostle of peace and world government, rapidly came to regard the dissentients as 'the scum' of the Labour movement. So violent a conversion may indicate that many men of liberal mind, faced by an intolerable dilemma, necessarily underwent a process of reversal. Pacific and idealistic in approach, they could only reconcile themselves to the *fait accompli* of war by misrepresenting it as a crusade for international righteousness.[14]

Henderson now became leader of the party while MacDonald and Snowden went into political exile. Yet neither of them were pacifist,[15] and the majority of those for whom they spoke were more inclined to radical pacificism than to pacifism or to revolutionary defeatism on the Marxist model. They had little

[14] This reversal is described in I. C. Willis *How we went into the war* (Manchester, 1918), *How we got on with the war* (Manchester, 1920) and *How we came out of the war* (London, 1921).

[15] MacDonald's position appears to swing uncertainly between radicalism, socialism and pacifism. In his *National Defence* (London, 1917) he makes pacifist statements not congruent with his more usual attitude as set out in Lord Elton's *The Life of James Ramsay MacDonald 1866–1919* (London, 1939), p. 255 ff. A most interesting study could be made of MacDonald in terms of the special moral difficulties and peculiar pressures attendant on leadership, whether in or out of power.

wish for a split within the nation: Keir Hardie himself spoke of a need for national unity. MacDonald, employing the language of radicalism, saw the war as manufactured by 'about half a dozen men' engaged in secret diplomacy. It was the shortsightedness of Grey which had 'brought all this upon us'. In like vein Snowden regarded the war as the creation of politicians for which the ordinary people were being made to suffer. A more Socialist attitude might be found in the *Labour Leader*, which issued a declaration calling for international solidarity, but the solidarity was as much that of the human race as of the international working class. Similar sentiments animated George Lansbury, who as editor of the *Daily Herald*, made it an organ for propaganda against the war.

Although the I.L.P. was separated from the great mass of Labour support in its stand for peace it could nevertheless co-operate with the unions and many of the Liberals in rejecting the idea of conscription. Influential Liberals like Sir John Simon and sections of nonconformity shared Labour's intense dislike of conscription. In September 1915 the Trades Union Congress was as unanimous in its denunciation of conscription as it was united on support for the war.

The opposition to the war itself, whether Independent Labour or Liberal, included two partly conflicting approaches to internationalism as well as an undercurrent of Socialist solidarity. On the one hand the major concern of the Union of Democratic Control founded in November 1914 (and not in itself a stop-the-war movement) was with the democratic control of foreign policy exercised through Parliament and with open agreements openly arrived at. It aimed at the repudiation of exclusive alliances and the democratization of diplomatic personnel. Many of its members followed MacDonald and Mrs. Swanwick in suspecting attempts to camouflage sectional aims behind supposedly unbiased supra-national decisions enforced by a pseudo-international police force. As A. J. P. Taylor has pointed out, this attitude regarded the League somewhat as an afterthought or as 'quackery'.[16]

For other internationalists the League was central and sanctions an important part of its organization. A group centred around Lowes Dickinson, which came to be known as the

[16] A. J. P. Taylor: *The Trouble Makers* (London, 1957), pp. 142–4.

Bryce Group, discussed international organization as early as 1914 and formed one of the nuclei of the League of Nations Society established in 1915. Eventually this amalgamated with the League of Free Nations Association to form the League of Nations Union. The first definite plans for shaping the League came from a research group under Leonard Woolf which published its conclusions in the *New Statesman* during July 1915. All these various groups were, of course, overwhelmingly middle class in composition, with special centres of activity in Blooms-bury and Cambridge.[17]

However, a working-class opposition to the war was develop-ing concurrently, which differed from that typical of middle-class internationalists or of the stand so far characteristic of the I.L.P. The Shop Stewards Movement, with particular influence on the Clyde, had originally emerged just before the war and it now developed in an anti-war direction on a basis of class conflict. One of its first leaders was Gallacher, the future Communist M.P. who became chairman of the Clyde Strike Committee in February 1915. Another leader was David Kirk-wood, who had been a member of the Marxist (De Leonite) Socialist Labour Party and later became an independent Labour M.P. His friend, James Maxton, the future leader of the I.L.P. in its extremist phase, was also a Clyde agitator and political objector to the war. An analogous working-class op-position also existed in South Wales, perhaps more particularly in syndicalist areas, but modified and penetrated by Christian Socialism and nationalism to produce a blend of political and religious pacifism. Its major figure was A. J. Cook, who had begun his career as a Baptist preacher and was later to become leader of the Miners' Federation.

The broad alignment of forces sketched above remained in being until 1917 when the trade unions began to rethink their position and the peace party at Westminster began to recover its confidence. As regards the unions the change of attitude was, of course, partly due to the appalling losses of the war. However, various other influences were operative; the new Kerensky Government in Russia had provided the Slogan 'No annexations

[17] See E. M. Forster *Goldsworthy Lowes Dickinson* (Cambridge, 1934), especially Chapter 12, and G. D. Crosby *Disarmament and Peace in British Politics, 1914-1916* (Harvard, 1957), Chapter 2.

and no indemnities', while President Wilson had spoken of 'Peace without victory'. The new approach crystallized not around the question of peace so much as around the supposed aims of the Allied Powers. Suspicions about these aims were later felt to be confirmed when the Bolshevik Government in Russia published the secret treaties.

The beginnings of a change became evident when the Labour Party Conference held from January 23rd to 25th, 1917 voted approval of the League concept. Thenceforward the Labour Party was officially committed. Parallel stirrings at Westminster became evident in February 1917, when a debate was held on war policies in the House of Commons. In April 1917 a resolution put down by Snowden, which called for a declaration similar to that of the Kerensky Government, received the vote of thirty-two members. These and similar efforts culminated in the letter from Lord Lansdowne, published in the *Daily Telegraph* on the 29th of November. However, the idea of a peace of accommodation which it promoted received support only from the *Manchester Guardian* and the *Nation* among the more important journals.

The crucial shift of opinion within the trade unions became clear at a special conference held on August 10th, 1917. At this gathering a large majority of delegates voted for participation in the International Conference of Labour Parties to be held at Stockholm, provided such participation should be on a consultative rather than on a mandatory basis. Henderson supported this move, in spite of being Labour's representative in a War Cabinet which strongly disapproved of the whole idea. In so doing he precipitated his own resignation and became free to co-operate with MacDonald and Webb on a memorandum regarding war aims which was presented to and passed by a special conference held on December 23rd, 1917. Speaking to this conference Henderson combined the arguments of the U.D.C. and of the League protagonists. He attacked conscription, the arms manufacturers and secret diplomacy, and also looked forward to a League of democratic nations. Once again, it was not over pacifism that the Labour Party reunited, but through common opposition to imperialism and a corrupt foreign policy.[18]

[18] See P. Kellogg and A. Gleason: *British Labor and the War* (New York, 1919), Chapter 7.

The efforts of the peace party in the Commons continued to give evidence of recovered confidence. Between May 1917 and February 1918 there were five divisions on resolutions concerned with the problem of peace terms. It is interesting that moderate peace resolutions received strong support from a group of members attached to the pacific wing of the Liberals. Altogether thirty-seven Liberals and nine Labour members voted on one or more of these resolutions opposing the Government. Amongst them were a significantly high proportion of industrialists, merchants and bankers, indicating that the spirit of commercial pacificism was not dead in the Liberal Party.[19]

However, the temporary German successes in the spring of 1918, followed by the immediate onset of the Coupon election after the Armistice, set back the protagonists of a moderate peace at crucial points. The Coupon election is notorious, perhaps too notorious, for the atmosphere of nationalistic phobia in which it was conducted. The results much reduced the number of peace advocates in the Commons and completely eliminated the representation of the U.D.C. This in itself contributed to the paucity of Parliamentary opposition to the Treaty of Versailles when Lloyd George eventually presented it to the House. Moreover, those Liberal and Labour members who doubted the wisdom of the Treaty could still envisage the League as a means whereby its provisions could be progressively ameliorated. Thus the major voice in opposition to the Treaty came from outside Parliament: from the *Labour Leader*, and the I.L.P., from the *New Statesman* and the National Executive of the Labour Party—and from John Maynard Keynes.

(b) 1919–1931

Keynes's *The Economic Consequences of the Peace* provided radicals with an Authorized Version of the peace to set alongside the received texts of Brailsford, Angell and Hobson. Of course, the Treaty of Versailles was indeed unwise, unjust and predatory, but as R. B. McCallum has pointed out, the critics failed to concede the fairly narrow limits within which those who framed the Treaty had necessarily to work.[20] Moreover, the character

[19] Names are listed in G. D. Crosby, op. cit., Appendix A.

[20] R. B. McCallum: *Public Opinion and the Last Peace* (London, 1944). See especially pp. 90–100, 171–189.

of the Treaty, which was perhaps not noticeably below the usual level of international morality, should not have led critics to conclude that all its constituent elements deserved indiscriminate and total reprobation.

Yet this was almost precisely the conclusion which substantial segments of opinion came to draw. The Treaty was the outcome of the war and the war had partly originated in the doctrine of the balance of power. Therefore all wars left behind problems more recalcitrant than those they solved; and the balance of power was totally discredited. The Treaty had been the work of the older generation: in future only the young could know how to shape a world from which such happenings were absent. The Treaty had been framed by Governments and professional diplomats: it followed that one must look to the peoples themselves to ensure that such devious and disastrous policies were never pursued again. Since the Governments concerned were British and French one could only conclude that these Governments were by nature even more infallibly vicious than others of their kind. And especially so the French Government, whose anxieties and animosities had been so central to some of the Treaty's more offensive provisions, and who would therefore the more justly reap the whirlwind which the radicals predicted. Only when the moral balance had been restored, and when the sometime victims were in a position to more than restore it, would it once again be possible to sympathize with a French Government.

Finally, and for the left most important, the British and French Governments were capitalist governments, mere executive committees of the ruling class. Like tools in the hands of high financial gods they had carved the letters of their own doom and nobody need feel the slightest obligation to ameliorate their justly deserved difficulties. Versailles was the corrupt fruit of capitalism: thenceforward the tree was fit for nothing but to cut down and cast into the oven.

So it was that most radicals came to hold that only one good thing came out of Versailles: the League. Plainly only the League could provide even a remotely commensurate justification for the war. But devotion to the League was not an immediate reaction in every quarter. Large segments of the Labour Party, including some important voices in the T.U.C., shared in a revulsion from Versailles so bitter that even the League itself came under grave suspicion. The left suspected the League of being a thin disguise for an alliance of the Allies (and in particular a disguise for France), while liberal doctrinaires like Morel strongly disliked the provision for sanctions. In the eyes of large numbers of Labour supporters Geneva could be little more than the sepulchre of capitalism, however assiduously it might be whited by its proponents. It required all the dedicated propaganda of Henderson, Clynes and their allies to rehabilitate the League idea, aided by the fact that the Conservatives themselves were less than enthusiastic for the machinery of the League. The concept of the League remained part of Labour's official policy throughout, but it was some time before the idealists recovered from the shock of 1919 and came to see the League as a potential instrument of progressive purposes.[21]

A more immediate effect of the Treaty was to justify all the opponents of the war and to reunite the party in a common sense of betrayal. Those who had gone into the political wilderness, the prophets of the U.D.C. and the I.L.P. felt their position minutely vindicated by events. The exponents of working-class internationalism and those who believed in liberal internationalism could for the moment work together fairly comfortably until the coming of a Labour Government should reveal the extent of differences between them. Meanwhile unity prevailed in a mood of common denunciation. This reached its climax in the resolution condemning all war which was carried at the party conference in 1922. Taken at its face value this was a direct declaration of pacifist policy by the one body supposed to be the official repository of Labour doctrine. Nevertheless the resolution was not introduced by the National Executive and it was tacitly rescinded at future conferences when the I.L.P. demand for 'disarmament by example' met with an unambiguous rejection. When in power the party ignored it and Shepherd, in his study of the period, dismisses it as an 'emotional upsurge'.[22]

Many pacifists undoubtedly shared the root and branch

[21] See H. R. Winkler: 'The Emergence of a Labor Foreign Policy in Great Britain 1918–1929' (*Journal of Modern History*, September 1956).

[22] G. W. Shepherd, op. cit., p. 478.

view held by a majority on the left: they believed that wickedness had finally been located in the particular institutions of capitalism. For some, therefore, it was merely a matter of waiting until the deified forces of history encompassed the system's inevitable ruin. But others were gradually tempted to see whether the League might not after all provide a narrow path through the political impasse. Rhys Davies was an example of a pacifist both tempted and disillusioned by the League. It was just possible that it might assume the role of arbiter in international affairs, and by gradually absorbing national armaments to its own purposes, limit the need for sanctions to moral suasion, or at most, to economic pressure. It was conceived possible that such arms as Britain retained, even during periods of Labour government, were eventually to be placed at the disposal of the League. In fact, by an appropriate stress on the aspect of disarmament, the League was capable of seeming to be a pacifist idea.

Tempted in this way many pacifists were able to participate in Governments which maintained armed forces and to support the League; substantial numbers were converted outright.[23] Pacifists were even to be found in the Service Ministries, although William Leach, Under-Secretary of State for Air in MacDonald's first Government, took the opportunity to include the Sermon on the Mount in his speech bringing in the air estimates. Philip Noel-Baker, a Quaker who had been instrumental in organizing the Friends' Ambulance Unit, became one of the converts, not only to the League, but also to its role as policeman in international affairs.

According to Shepherd, the Labour Party was still basically committed to liberal internationalism, and, as in previous situations, the constant norm of its position was Henderson. It was liberal internationalism, with its repudiation of secret diplomacy and alliances, which became the basis of foreign policy in Labour's first Government. Thus, the system of mutual assistance pacts involved in the Draft Treaty was rejected, because revision of Versailles was regarded as more important than a scheme for military security against Germany. The Draft Treaty was seen as likely to increase British armaments and to encourage alliances. The preferred alternative

[23] S. Davis, op. cit., p. 3.

was a system for the arbitration of international disputes. The core of the problem was seen in arbitration, disarmament and the rule of law, not in collective military arrangements.

At the same time questions of enforcement had to be faced. In the discussions concerning the Geneva Protocol, which aimed at a procedure for dealing with disputes, both 'strong' and 'weak' versions of the League concept were argued within the Labour Government and the Labour movement. In the Government's view the essence of the Protocol lay in proposals for a Disarmament Conference, whereas the French Government was principally concerned with incorporating sanctions against aggressors. MacDonald, now Foreign Secretary as well as Prime Minister, still suspected the activity of self-appointed international police forces, but he gave way to French pressure, although with substantial reservations. His position had wide support from those who, like Norman Angell, were disinclined to give guarantees which might fossilize the injustices of the *status quo*. Others, amongst them Noel-Baker, accepted the proposed sanctions as an integral part of League provisions, though it may be doubted where the full implications of this acceptance were genuinely faced.

The conclusion of Labour's brief period of minority rule brought to power a Conservative Government which replaced the idea of the Protocol by the Pact of Locarno. This provided for mutual assistance in Western Europe while rejecting extensive and unpredictable commitments elsewhere. Though partly mollified by the actual terms of Locarno the Labour Party not only regarded this move as a retreat from the League idea but also suspected the Government of lack of devotion to disarmament. If the Conservatives were indeed reluctant about the League it was possible for Labour to move from formal acceptance of the idea to positive enthusiasm. The Labour Party now redoubled its propaganda in favour of disarmament through the League and felt free to attribute recent increases in international friction to Conservative policies. The Labour case was put by Ponsonby, himself gravitating towards a pure utilitarian pacifism, in the House of Commons on July 11th, 1927. 'There has not been the change that we expected. The voice is still the voice of war; the language is still the language of nationalism; the manner is still the manner of the old diplomacy; and the method is still the method of alliances and pacts.'[24] This indictment gathered wider acceptance as the leaders of the League of Nations Union now began to move towards the Labour position. At the same time, however, a unilateralist minority remained active in the party (only partly pacifist and largely located in the I.L.P.), which urged disarmament by example.

The Labour Government of 1929–31 was notable for the great efforts of Henderson to make liberal internationalism the basis of a viable foreign policy. True to his creed, Henderson, while accepting the ultimate possibility of sanctions, saw first priorities in a system of arbitration and a disarmament conference. He was assisted in his efforts by Noel-Baker and Hugh Dalton, the latter being then a strong believer in multilateral disarmament as central to any policy of peace. These years were the apogee of liberal internationalism, and, at the same time, the beginning of the end. Differences soon arose, not simply over the usual questions relating to sanctions and the petrifaction of the *status quo*, but also over the position of the Commonwealth. Yet some progress was made. Preparations for the Disarmament Conference were successfully completed and Henderson eventually became its President. By this time, however, Labour was once more out of office and the international scene had been clouded over by Japanese aggression in Manchuria and by the beginnings of Hitler's rise to power in Germany. In any case, the ending of the free-trade era destroyed the economic base on which liberalism rested.

The consequence of these events within the Labour Party was first of all an emotional swing towards war resistance, followed by an espousal of collective security in which sanctions were to play a more central role. However, only slowly and belatedly was this acceptance of sanctions seen to imply a system of alliances and military power only formally within the framework of the League.

(c) 1931–1933

The depression and the circumstances of the 1931 election brought Labour closer to the Marxist view than ever before or since. Whatever the Government might do it was bound to be

[24] *Parliamentary Debates* (Vol. 208, Col. 1773, July 11th, 1927.)

wrong. Even the French Government had to yield its place as the chief source of international difficulties to the British Government, which Labour now regarded as principally to blame for the failure of the Disarmament Conference to make any headway. The ruling class in Britain cared neither for the League nor for disarmament: it was more concerned with preserving 'the use of the bombing plane' on the frontiers of the Empire and the safeguarding of capitalist property. Since the National Government cared neither for disarmament nor the League, Labour might care for both with uninhibited passion, and might link them together under the common rubric of 'peace' without inquiring too closely whether events would eventually render them incompatible.

The electoral débâcle had several effects which assisted the position of pacifists. In the first place it pushed Labour representation in Parliament back towards the Celtic fringes in which both pacifism and war-resistance had greater influence. Secondly, it removed a whole generation of leaders, many of whom were major proponents of the League view. Leadership now fell on the shoulders of George Lansbury; soon to be assisted by Stafford Cripps. Lansbury had been First Commissioner of Works in the MacDonald Government and was recognized as the chief advocate of pacifism within the party. Besides being a devout Christian and a marginal member of the Church of England, he was also well to the left of the party. He believed that the cohesive forces of international Christendom might be an influence in stabilizing the world order. This last belief had also been a favourite idea of Stafford Cripps. Cripps himself reacted to the events of 1931 with a personal version of Marxism which led to an increasing devotion to the concept of war resistance by the international working class. He was not a pacifist, but he and many who veered in a similar direction could appear to agree with the pacifists through their mutual opposition to arms in the hands of a capitalist government.

This potent conjunction is important, because the *political* impact of pacifism in this period, as distinct from its impact on sections of the middle class, depended partly on the events just described and partly on the capacity of pacifism to combine with viewpoints based quite differently. Immediately after 1931 pacifism was frequently able to combine with both war-resistance and with those proponents of the League who continued to lay emphasis on the prior necessity of disarmament. Thus while the climax of pacifism in terms of numerical support may well have come round about 1935–6, its period of maximum political influence came in the years before 1936 when combinations with incompatible viewpoints were still plausible. By 1936 the League view plainly implied sanctions, while most war-resisters had become intensely militant over Spain. It was even possible for pacifism to coalesce on occasion with the realist viewpoint, as for instance in relation to Italy, but when this occurred the difference of attitude was so plain as to prevent any plausible confusions. Nobody could suppose that those who wished to overlook the issue of Abyssinia so as to be better placed in the coming struggle with Germany had anything in common with those who rejected force in principle.

The Far Eastern Crisis: Manchuria and the Shanghai Incident
The crisis over Japanese aggression in Manchuria illustrated precisely this combination between pacifism and trade unionist realism. As regards the Manchurian incident the unions were largely passive, reflecting a widespread feeling amongst the general public against crusades in the Far East. Not only the unions but partisans of the League were affected by the public mood. It was widely recognized that unilateral action by Britain was impossible, and that the support of the United States, now in an isolationist phase, was not likely to materialize to any appreciable extent. Moreover, League supporters were unwilling to criticize the League during a period of initial uncertainty in case the League idea should itself be discredited.

In these circumstances Lansbury was able to count on broad support for the view that Britain should do all she could to promote arbitration and that the League should try to curb aggression by moral authority without resort to economic sanctions. Only the left championed strong League action against Japan, partly because this was directly contrary to the policy of Simon, the Foreign Secretary, and partly because Japan was suspected of designs against Russia. But when the Far Eastern crisis was over the left mostly ceased to support the League.

The Shanghai incident came closer home since British property and interests were involved. Labour's League adherents stood firmly for sanctions, backed actively by the left and passively by the unions. The position of the pacifists was contradictory. Initially, early in 1932, they too seemed to be pressing for strong League action. Lansbury not only wanted the League to exercise its moral authority but, in an interview on February 1st, argued that sanctions could be employed without war ensuing. Ponsonby, now Labour leader in the Lords, even rebuked the Government for failing to protect British life and property in Shanghai, and for failing to uphold British prestige. Wellock, also a pacifist, was continuing to criticize the Government, outside of Parliament, for its previous failure to halt Japan.

Then Lansbury suggested that an appeal should be made to Japan to stop aggression in return for a just consideration of her economic difficulties. Britain was to tell Japan that she was not solely to blame and that this country recognized such behaviour had been learnt from other imperialist powers. Britain would have 'no part or lot' in boycotting her. In the House of Commons on February 22nd Lansbury brought the pacifist position into focus by demonstrating how it ultimately depended solely on the issue of averting war. Pacifists could not agree to economic sanctions enforced by Governments since these might lead to war. However, some pacifists thought a private boycott might be harmless, while a few, like Rhys Davies, thought it might even be possible to get away with economic sanctions.

Lansbury could neither make any recommendation to the Government which was not an equivocation, nor could he consistently speak for his own party. Meanwhile the League group called for sanctions and when Japan was in due course condemned as an aggressor the party policy changed from an arms embargo on both sides to an embargo on Japan alone. In the House of Commons on February 27th, Lansbury found himself having to put forward this viewpoint on behalf of his party while adding that he personally wished to refuse arms to either side. It was Lansbury's personal view that Simon adopted. Seymour Cocks, a belligerent Leaguer, wanted aid to China. From the left, Wallhead asked for an economic boycott of Japan. No group, of course, asked for unilateral action by

Britain and in any case as the crisis simmered down Labour's demands became less vocal.

In fact, according to Davis, it is possible to exaggerate the extent of Labour's effort to secure League action: '. . . only for a few days, early in 1932, and then with much confusion, had Labour itself called for sanctions. And that demand faded out when the Shanghai crisis eased off'.[25] As for the pacifists, trusting essentially to moral force, the Far Eastern crisis brought disillusion with the possibilities of League action. The crisis defined the limits of pacifist policy, bringing out the logic of the position. Lansbury had to speak with two voices, one for himself and one for his party, knowing that whenever he spoke he might weaken his party's policy, since the Government could always challenge him personally on the issue of sanctions.

Moreover, it became clear that in terms of practical politics a pacifist was forced to refuse to make any meaningful distinction between an aggressor and a victim. Pacifists might co-operate in government at various levels to avoid the fruitless alternative of complete withdrawal, but the dilemma of Lansbury as leader illustrated that their central tenet was in fact entirely apolitical. Once moral authority had failed it was only possible to stand and wait.

(d) 1933–1945

After the Far Eastern crisis the character of the combination between pacifism and other viewpoints changed. In that crisis there had been some partial coalescence between pacifists and those who recognized the difficulty of making any substantial impact on such distant events. There now appeared a combination more characteristic of the middle thirties in which pacifism and war-resistance and disarmament through the League united under the common rubric of the word 'peace'. Yet this development is paradoxical because it was precisely at this period that Labour adopted a fully-fledged policy of 'collective security' in the strong rather than in the weak sense of the phrase. One must inquire how it was that the theoretical adoption of collective security collapsed in political practice.

As has been said, the years 1933–5 mark both the adoption of collective security and the climax of pacifist influence in the

[25] S. Davis, op. cit., p. 58.

Labour Party. One may, like A. J. P. Taylor see Labour's adherence to collective security as little more than a gesture of respect to Henderson. But this is perhaps to over-simplify. The bulk of the Labour Party probably meant what it said about collective security but could not envisage a situation in which this would mean supporting a British Government which cared so little for the League. So far as the foreign policy of the Government was concerned the party was both pacifist and war-resisting: hence the extraordinary situation at the Conference of 1933 where resolutions equally supporting collective security and war-resistance were passed. And in any case the bulk of the Labour Party still believed that if only Labour were in power they could reverse the drift towards war and return to the policy of all-round disarmament. It was in this way that collective security became confused with pacifism and with war-resistance, and it was on this account that the collective-security policy collapsed fairly soon after its inception.

The temporary disposition within the Labour Party to favour vigorous action through the League was supported by the realists, like Hugh Dalton, who had early recognized the menace of Hitler, and by union leaders, activated by the peril of the German unions. Thus by the late spring of 1933 Labour was coming to favour economic coercion of Germany through the League if such were necessary to prevent her throwing off her treaty obligations.

Yet the left, while very hostile to Fascism, allowed itself to be blinded by the doctrine of the class war and refused to entrust arms to the Government even through the medium of the League. In such circumstances war would be capital-ist–imperialist in character and they could not participate. Meanwhile the pacifists and near-pacifists concentrated their attention on Treaty revision, because they analysed the ab-normal psychology of Germany in terms of a reaction to injustice. In similar vein, many League supporters accepted the justice of Hitler's case against Versailles, even though they were against yielding to threats. The British people as a whole were reluctant to recognize the drift of the continental situation, and so provided the Labour Party with an almost irresistible temptation to reverse the freak verdicts of the 1931 general election.

It was against this confused and ambiguous situation that war-resistance motions were introduced at the Trades Union and at the Labour Party Conferences in 1933. At the Trades Union Conference the General Council asked for the matter to be remitted for further consideration, though Bevin was afterwards characteristically irritated that peace proponents should try to unload the brunt of war-resistance on to the unions. At the Labour Party Conference, the National Executive did not subscribe to the semi-Marxist arguments employed, but, wishing to conciliate widespread feeling among delegates, it promised to consult the T.U.C., knowing full well that the T.U.C. was opposed to the whole idea. Henderson and Noel-Baker posed the League view of collective security against that of the international working class and the conference saw no contradiction in applauding the League view as enthusiastically as it applauded war-resistance. 'Thus, the Labour Executive had made no more than a pretence of accepting the general strike principle. Nevertheless, far from urging the conference to stand strongly in favour of firm measures to halt Hitler's lawlessness, it had weakly given way before the popular feeling that all war should be resisted.'[26]

We have located this equivocation in a revived pacifism and a growing Marxism allied to an unrealistic view of the possibilities of League action. Its plausibility lay in the capacity of Labour to see their own Government as the root of all international evil. Thus when in due course Germany left the Disarmament Conference, Lansbury found himself able to announce that the Labour Party was against sanctions without provoking any major controversy. In addition many people believed that Hitler would collapse provided the German people were left alone.

However, the trade unions not only recognized the weakness of international working-class action against Hitler or against war, but also suspected that these hopes of Hitler's collapse were illusory. The first object was, therefore, to make quite clear that the Labour Party was really in earnest about collective security rather than in favour of the aberration towards war-resistance. Hence both the Trades Union and the Labour Party Conferences in 1934 were persuaded to adopt a clear

[26] Ibid., p. 83.

exposition of collective security principles. Conceivably the union leaders were not entirely representative of the movement in this: at their own conference collective security was overwhelmingly adopted but at the Party Conference their block vote was responsible for a majority only of 1,519,000 as against 673,000. Naturally the left-wingers in the Socialist League protested against dropping the general strike principle. Moreover, the reaffirmation of collective security did not mean an end to ambivalence and equivocation. Large numbers of Labour Party supporters still saw collective security as being primarily concerned with the priority of disarmament rather than as involving stronger guarantees.

So the political atmosphere was prepared for the East Fulham by-election and for a whole series of subsequent by-elections in which Labour utilized the appeal of 'peace', until such time as the dangers were more apparent and the appeal yielded diminishing electoral returns.

The Labour candidate at East Fulham, John Wilmot, was not a pacifist. Indeed, local Liberals supported him as a League man, and one of the prominent speakers in his campaign was Dalton. Nevertheless when Germany left Geneva on October 14th, 1934 he turned to attack the Government's peace policy. 'Wilmot dwelt on Labour's devotion to peace and disarmament, made much of the machinations of private munitions manufacturers and declared that the Government's intentions would lead to war.'[27] Whereas Wilmot had originally emphasized the menace of Germany and the importance of collective action this element in his policy was now discreetly dropped. Lansbury gave him support from a pure pacifist point of view. Moreover, some of the other speakers on his behalf even voiced the isolationist attitude that Britain should withdraw from her commitments under the Locarno Pact, which was after all, an important bulwark of the collective system. The result of the election turned a Conservative majority of 14,521 into a Labour majority of 4,840.

In varying degrees Labour used similar tactics in subsequent by-elections. The five elections occurring in the six weeks following Germany's departure from the Disarmament Conference provided Labour with a sudden increase in support.

[27] Ibid., p. 116.

It is interesting to note the religious connections of many of the Labour candidates. At Kilmarnock the candidate was a pacifist, the Reverend Barr, while at Skipton the candidate was a Quaker. At Rusholme the candidate was the Reverend Wood, who attacked his opponent on a straight issue of peace or war. Much the same approach was employed at the Rutland and Stamford elections.

The elections in the new year showed a similar pattern. The Labour candidate at Cambridge was the pacifist Dr. Alex Wood. The candidate at Upton, Ben Gardner, and the candidate at Monmouth, the Reverend Hughes, both did their best to appeal to the peace sentiment. However, the candidate at Lowestoft, the Reverend Sorensen, although personally a pacifist, did not employ the East Fulham tactics. Of course, the questions of peace and the responsibility of the Government for the failure of the Disarmament Conference were not the only or always the dominant issues at all these elections. But it is difficult to see the increase in Labour support simply or mainly as a recovery of nerve after the scares of the previous general election.[28] It is also difficult to lay the onus on the zeal of local candidates : political leaders also contributed, although the more irresponsible speeches against Locarno were eventually prohibited since these directly embarrassed the party in Parliament.

The equivocations and ambivalence lying at the root of Labour propaganda also evidenced itself in connection with the attitude which Labour took up towards the arms estimates. The policy of voting against estimates was not, of course, based on pacifist grounds, but was adopted in order to protest against a foreign policy which preferred national security to collective security in terms of the League. The increase in the estimates in 1934 was in fact not large and mainly centred in the air : Labour voted against the increase not so much on its own account as because the Government did not envisage the Air Force as part of the collective sanctions of the League. Here again, the pacifist viewpoint and the League viewpoint were joined together in a basically incompatible manner.

The same logically incompatible coalescence between collective security notions and pacifism lay behind the Peace

---

[28] This view is argued in pamphlet No 1 issued by the University Group on Defence Policy entitled : *The Role of the Peace Movements in the 1930's* (London, 1959).

Ballot. It is this coalescence which probably accounts for the very small number who actually took the strict Christian option.[29] The ballot itself was concerned both with the rejection of armaments and with sanctions, but the centre of controversy turned on the former rather than the latter issue. At the Putney by-election in particular, and generally outside Parliament, Labour tended to pose the question around the simple issue of peace or war. Taken strictly, the vote in favour of the ballot was a vote in favour of sanctions, a large majority being for economic and a smaller majority for military sanctions, but since so many of the voters saw the question of disarmament as primary, the political meaning of the ballot is less clear. In general, whatever the formal implications of the ballot, one may say that neither the public nor the Labour Party showed themselves fully alive to the menace of Hitler. Only when Hitler introduced conscription did Labour begin to argue that once Germany had eliminated the injustices of Versailles it would become imperative to fortify the Covenant of the League.

The crisis over Abyssinia in 1936 marks Labour's specific repudiation of pacifism and of war-resistance. Whatever the confusions hitherto, collective security and pacifism became clearly demarcated from each other under the impact of Italian aggression. Contradictions in official policy remained but these were now largely between those who saw foreign policy in starkly realist terms and those who talked, like Attlee, in terms of the international control of arms.

The central bastions of Labour regarded the Abyssinian crisis as crucial for the League's authority. The League must thwart Mussolini otherwise Hitler would see the green light. Perhaps the high-minded were more specifically against Italy while the realists wished to restrain Italy as a warning to Germany. Some ultra-realists, like A. L. Rowse, would have been willing to overlook the Italian aggression in order to retain her as an ally against Germany. The Communist Party, obedient to the necessities of Russian foreign policy, had likewise come to favour sanctions. Only the I.L.P. and the Socialist League, after some doubts and internal dissidence maintained the line of pure war-resistance and adherence to sanctions

[29] 17,000. For an account of the Ballot see A. Livingstone: *The Peace Ballot*: The *Official History* (London, 1935).

114

operated solely by the international working class. The pacifists naturally remained against any action likely to end in war.

The opposition of the pacifists, particularly Lansbury and Ponsonby, and of the Socialist League angered the unions. Ponsonby had already resigned, however: the stage was now set for the final show-down with Lansbury to take place at the Brighton Party Conference from September 30th to October 4th. This conference decisively rejected both pacifism and war-resistance. Bevin took the opportunity to make his notorious assault on Lansbury and in the upshot the leadership passed to Attlee. This conference may be regarded as a climax in Labour's devotion to the League and many war-resisters and some pacifists (like Rhys Davies) were tempted to support the collective security concept.

This did not mean that Labour was inhibited from attacking the Government for its rearmament policy. Moreover, however much Labour supporters might call for sanctions against Italy, the memory of Versailles still preserved sympathy for Germany, so much so that there was little substantial protest when Hitler marched into the Rhineland in March 1936. Indeed Labour's immediate reaction to that event was not to attack Germany but to blame Britain for the frictions generated by an arms policy conceived outside the League, and France for her betrayal of collective security over Abyssinia.

Yet, if Hitler's advent in the Rhineland provoked little immediate reaction it did mark the commencement of the series of crises which were to point up the contradiction between the idealistic interpretation of collective security exercised through the League, which formed the current orthodoxy, and the realist interpretation of collective security which progressively focused attention on Germany. Walter Citrine, General Secretary of the Trades Union Congress and Bevin's principal ally, now took up a position close to that of Norman Angell and Winston Churchill, virtually recommending that the League become an armed alliance. The development of this split, with its obvious implications for the illusory character of the League hopes, pushed some who had been attracted by the idealism of collective security back in a pacifist direction. Others, like H. N. Brailsford, who were not specifically pacifist, began to adopt a policy of isolationism which found support from Lord Beaverbrook: not, of course, the last of such incongruous alliances.

The Leaguers and the high-minded had cared about Italy but the view began to gain ground that the crux of the matter was Germany. If that were so, the alienation of Italy might be dangerous and unwise: a close approximation to the French view and an explicit return to the politics of power and the calculations of alliances. It was becoming clearer that the League only papered over a situation of structural anarchy. Nevertheless in the early months of 1936 the combined influence of the idealistic Leaguers, of the pacifists and of the Socialist League overruled pressure from Dalton and his union allies.

At the same time the implications of the Brighton Conference were gradually drawn out. Opposition to the main provisions of the arms estimates was abandoned and the adverse vote on the estimates was now understood largely as a token of dissent over a nationalistic interpretation of foreign policy. The slogan 'arms mean war' was dropped and patience with pacifism lessened. So much so that in May 1936 the National Executive declined to approve the selection of a pacifist by the Lewes Divisional Labour Party.

Thus the situation at this juncture may be summarized as follows. At the official level pacifism had been explicitly repudiated and the struggle now lay clearly between the idealistic and the realistic conceptions of collective security. The former was concerned with asserting the authority of the League, while the latter was concerned with progressively focusing attention on Germany. Meanwhile the Socialist League and the left generally maintained an attitude of war-resistance: for them the Italian fiasco could only underline the unity of all imperialist powers in the condonation of mutual crimes.

Then came the Spanish crisis and provided the war-resisters with their opportunity. Conflict with Germany or Italy might have been plausibly interpreted as imperialist war, but in Spain the children of light faced the children of darkness with no intermediaries of doubtful purity. War-resistance now took on an acutely militant character and those who most vehemently opposed arms in the hands of the democratically elected Government of Britain became intensely enthusiastic for arms in the hands of the democratically elected Government of Spain.

The militancy of war-resisters over Spain ended their alliance
with the pacifists, apart from a few purists of war-resistance like
Emrys Hughes, and the *Forward* group in Scotland. The pacifists were now deprived of a second group of allies in that war-
resistance clearly had nothing to do with the rejection of war
as such. Moreover, the other erstwhile allies of the pacifists
amongst the proponents of the League demarcated themselves
from the pacifist cause even more clearly by holding that Spain
represented (another) last chance to save the League.

Having lost two groups of allies with whom there was some
possibility of plausible confusion the pacifists now regained
allies amongst the realists with whom there was no possibility
of confusion at all. In this respect the alignment resembled that
obtaining during the Manchurian crisis. Dalton and the union
leaders, in particular Bevin and Citrine, by now saw the League
as a broken instrument and could only regard involvement in
Spain as a 'hopelessly indirect approach to the main problem
of curbing German ambitions'. They were also necessarily concerned to take note of the difficulties of the French Government,
which was pressing a policy of non-intervention. However, the
arguments of the realists in favour of non-intervention began
to fall on increasingly deaf ears as it became clear that both
Germany and Italy were giving the rebels material assistance.

A turning point in Labour's evolution away from an official
policy of non-intervention occurred at the Edinburgh Conference. The delegates were particularly impressed by impassioned
appeals made by Spanish representatives. The international
situation and the arms question were debated on the second
day of the conference and the debate was interesting in the
way it revealed the outstanding differences between the League
and the realist view. Dalton rose to move a resolution the key
paragraphs of which were . . . 'this conference declares that the
armed strength of the countries loyal to the League of Nations
must be conditioned by the armed strengh of the potential
aggressors' . . . 'realizing the relationship between foreign
policy and armaments, and having regard to the deplorable
record of the Government, the Labour Party declines to accept
responsibility for a purely competitive armament policy'. Dalton
and his realist allies stressed the first half of the statement,
attacking the policy of unilateral non-rearmament, while Attlee

and Morrison stressed the second half of the statement. By so doing they provided continuing justification for Labour's parliamentary vote against the arms estimates. Clearly Labour's attitude still remained contradictory.

This internal contradiction now centred on divergent views with regard to the arms estimates. The issue duly came up for discussion within the Parliamentary Party. Dalton himself has left an interesting account of the evolution of opinion within the party.[30] There had now been twelve months in which Labour supporters had clamoured for arms for Spain and in Dalton's view it was becoming increasingly difficult to justify a vote against arms for Britain. It was all very well to interpret the vote as a gesture against an unpalatable foreign policy but to the plain man it could not appear otherwise than as a vote against armaments as such.

When Dalton raised the question on the Executive he was defeated but he then proceeded to raise it again at the party meeting. The meeting was persuaded to upset the majority recommendation of the Executive and voted in favour of abstention as regards the estimates. In this division of opinion Dalton's view was supported by all the co-operative M.P.s (except Woods), by the railwaymen, the Lancashire miners and some of the Durham miners. Against him in support of Morrison were the Yorkshire and the South Wales miners. However, once the majority had declared itself the party was unusually united in its loyalty to the decision. When the service votes came up they were officially challenged only by the I.L.P. and, apart from the four I.L.P. members, support for the challenge was restricted to one Communist and six members of the Parliamentary Labour Party. These lonely six now represented what remained of pure pacifism plus the remnant of strict war-resistance. The realist view was clearly in the ascendant.

So, by the end of 1937 the attitude of Labour relating to arms was comparatively settled and the policy of appeasement became thenceforward largely associated with the Conservatives. From this time onwards Labour's criticism tended to fasten on the inefficiency of the arms programme rather than its scope. This does not mean that the Labour Party now rejected negotia-

[30] H. Dalton: *The Fateful Years* (London, 1957), pp. 133 ff.

tions and reasonable concessions to Germany. Versailles was not thus forgotten. But alongside reasonable concessions the Party wanted strong security commitments both as regards Spain and Czechoslovakia. When the crisis over Czechoslovakia eventually came to a head the Labour Party stood firmly against capitulation.[31] Yet it is probably true to say that this firmness attracted little positive mass support. The British people were not pacifist but the Munich settlement brought them relief if not satisfaction.

Of course pacifism and war-resistance remained within the Labour Party throughout this period, but much weakened and internally divided. For example, the Parliamentary Pacifist Group, formed in 1936, had always been divided over Spain, and then in 1938 some of its members actually resigned from the Labour Party altogether. Whereas the pacifists could not avoid accepting appeasement their occasional allies in the I.L.P., the Socialist League and the Communist Party were now combined in an attack on arms which concentrated on the fact that these were in the hands of a capitalist Government. Moreover, first the Communist Party and then the Socialist League dropped this negative approach in favour of a coalition between all democratic elements, of whatever political hue, against the Fascist threat. Sir Stafford Cripps, who had at one one time declared that the outcome of a war between Germany and Britain was a matter of indifference now came out in favour of an armed alliance between Britain, France and Russia. Only the I.L.P. maintained a form of war-resistance capable of allying itself with pacifism. For the I.L.P. the collective security of alliances could only be a disguise for the 'collective insecurities of Versailles injustice'.

The leadership of the pacifists rested with George Lansbury and Salter. Lansbury had become President of the Peace Pledge Union on the death of Dick Sheppard and in company with Salter he engaged in various peace embassies on behalf of the International Fellowship of Reconciliation. The basis of their policy, apart from its religious objection to war as such, rested on a vigorous anti-imperialism. It was argued that righteous indignation could not be justified unless the imperialist powers,

[31] S. Davis, op. cit., gives an account of the attitudes taken up by the *New Statesman* towards the Czechoslovakian crisis. See Chapter 7 of the present study.

and Britain in particular, agreed to a redistribution of the world's resources. Here again was the argument that Lansbury had used in relation to Japan at the very beginning of the successive crises. From such an analysis it was possible, in 1938 as in 1932, to regard the warlike preparations of others as solely due to the moral failures of Britain and France.

Just prior to Munich the pacifist groups within the Labour Party expressed their opposition to the stand which the party had taken in a manifesto. The manifesto is interesting because it brought together all the various strands of opinion which have run through the narrative of Labour history up to this point. These strands were pure pacifism, the remnant of strict war-resistance and a much diminished radical liberal rump surviving from the First World War. Of these last, Mrs. Swanwick, a founder of the U.D.C., still remembered Versailles and maintained a pro-German attitude. So also did Clifford Allen, once of the I.L.P., and now a supporter of National Labour. But it is from Noel Buxton that one has an illustration of the degree of formalism underlying the radical liberal position. In his view the existence of the Sudeten Germans meant that any allied stand in favour of Czechoslovakia could only be regarded as denial of self-determination.

Such views could not, of course, influence the Labour Party on its fundamental position. It is true that the Parliamentary Party voted against conscription even in the spring of 1939, but this decision was based solely on technical advice and not on ideological grounds. Labour continued to favour an alliance with France, and if possible with Russia and the United States as well. When the final crisis arose over Poland the Labour Party stood behind the British guarantee without ambiguity or reservation. Thereafter the political history of pacifism is largely associated with the I.L.P., and it is that party to which we now must turn.

IV. THE INDEPENDENT LABOUR PARTY: FROM DENOMINATION TO SECT[32]

The history of the Independent Labour Party may be sub-divided into various periods and these may be loosely related

[32] The material in this section leans heavily on A. J. B. Marwick: *The Independent Labour Party 1918–1932* (B. Litt-Thesis, Oxford, 1960).

to changes in social composition and changes in ideological attitude. We begin by delineating these phases and the social and ideological changes associated with them before considering the actual sequence of events.

The history of the I.L.P. falls into the following phases: From its foundation in 1893 until the Labour Party acquired a new constitution in 1918 the I.L.P. provided the core of Labour support and propaganda. When Labour representation in Parliament began in 1900 it depended on a coalition between unions and Socialist societies, and the I.L.P. was the political nerve centre of this coalition. The local manifestations of Labour politics were generally branches of the I.L.P. But when Henderson prepared the new constitution of 1918 the relationship entered a new phase. The Labour Party now had an alternative local organization and the I.L.P. therefore needed to find a new role. For a while it seemed to have done so through acting as a ginger group which provided policy and leadership for the larger body. However, this role proved to be increasingly incompatible with loyalty to the wider whole. Tensions grew. Moderate members began to leave and the domination of extremists grew more complete. The coming of the second Labour Government and the timidity of the policies which it pursued provided the occasion for a series of crises, the eventual outcome of which was disaffiliation in 1932.

After 1932 the I.L.P. entered a third phase as an elect remnant, retaining some of its traditional influence in West Scotland, particularly through the journal *Forward* but ideologically rigid and politically futile. The party gradually grew weaker and weaker, partly because successors had taken its place in terms of role and attitude. First the Socialist League, and then the Bevanite schism, the Victory for Socialism Group and the Campaign for Nuclear Disarmament, filled the role vacated by the I.L.P.

The various phases just outlined may be related to changes in social composition and ideological content. Prior to 1918 the I.L.P. was coextensive with the Labour Party. It was therefore mainly upper working class in composition and deeply infused with idealistic religious fervour, much of it nonconformist in character. A. J. B. Marwick shows that the contribution made by lay preachers and ministers of religion in this period was a notable one. The result was a stress on an attitude of moderate idealism allied to a relatively loose grasp of Socialist theories and of techniques for gaining and manipulating power.

However, the advent of the war and the stand which the I.L.P. made against it, brought two new groups into the party who were successively to dominate it. The first of these groups consisted of upper middle-class liberals (mainly high Anglicans, Quakers and rationalists) who had some association with the U.D.C. The adhesions of these influential and sophisticated people altered the class composition of the I.L.P. at the level of leadership. It also turned broad religious attitudes into specific political programmes. The liberals were specially concerned with the study of international issues but they also set about providing the party with a viable domestic policy which eventually came to brilliant fruition in 1926 with the publication of the *Living Wage*. The leader of this group was Clifford Allen. Allen, scholar and rationalist, succeeded Snowden, the self-taught product of Wesleyan Methodism, as party treasurer, and then became chairman of the party from 1922 to 1925. During the period of his leadership the object of the party programme was to provide specific radical policies which might maintain a fruitful and friendly dialectic with the more dilatory gradualism of the Labour Party itself.

The second of the new groups to enter the ranks of Independent Labour was more explicitly revolutionary. The most notable component in this group was provided by the Clydesiders who made their Parliamentary début in 1922. As regards social composition this group consisted of working-class people or lower middle-class people of recent working-class origin. Much of its voting strength was derived from a Catholic working class, and the religious motivations of the earlier period became markedly less evident. The militant Socialism of Maxton and his followers soon clashed with the radicalism of the upper-class liberals, and the triumph of the former was signalized when Allen resigned his chairmanship in 1925 to be succeeded by Maxton in the following year.

These various groupings were fairly predictably associated with appropriate attitudes towards foreign affairs. Before the war the central doctrine was the Brotherhood of Man. The solidarity of peoples was the rock on which the machinations of diplomats would be broken. As indicated above the leaders of the I.L.P. were not pacifists but advocates of the pacific doctrine, complete with a liberal critique of war in terms of professional diplomacy and secret treaties. Although there were many doubts about the League, particularly with reference to sanctions, these doubts were partly based on liberal premises. Eventually the League idea gained their support. In similar vein the converts in the U.D.C. approved the League but only on condition that the Covenant was heavily revised and sanctions rejected. Ponsonby, for example, accepted the League, trusting that sanctions would be thrust progressively farther into the background. But for Maxton and for politicians like Fenner Brockway[33] the League was simply a capitalist alliance. The revolutionaries therefore repudiated the pacific doctrine and espoused war-resistance.

It is now possible to turn to the actual sequence of events within the period under review. When the First World War was declared the vast majority within the I.L.P. rejected it. Only a minority of about one in five supported it, including two M.P.s, Clynes and Parker. Yet in spite of the strains which this division caused within the Labour movement as a whole there was no overt organizational split and a move for disaffiliation within the I.L.P. was defeated.

At its Annual Conference in 1915 the I.L.P. produced the first real formulation of peace terms, framed along lines characteristic of the U.D.C. But the conference also debated a motion, supported in particular by Salter and the Bermondsey branch which declared the party opposed to all war. This explicitly pacifist resolution was eventually passed with only three dissentients at the Conference in 1916 and again passed against more organized opposition at the Conference in 1917. On the latter occasion it is significant that the opposition was led by Ramsay MacDonald and W. C. Anderson.

Meanwhile a sentiment was rapidly establishing itself in favour of war-resistance. While the older generation of leaders, like MacDonald, partly assimilated their views to those of the

---

[33] Brockway was the son of a Congregationalist missionary in India. It is interesting to note that he was influenced in early years by the *New Theology* of R. J. Campbell, which combined a stress on immanence with Christian Socialism.

U.D.C., the younger generation were engaged in a new type of propaganda against war. This took two forms. One of these was the No Conscription Fellowship, in which the moving spirit was Brockway. Rather typically he regarded it as a movement of youthful protest against 'war-making elders'. The Fellowship was not exclusively pacifist but existed to unite individualists, anarchists, Socialists, Quakers and members of other sects in an opposition to war based on 'the sacredness of human life'. After the war its supporters tended to merge in the No More War Movement and the War-Resisters International both of which developed away from '*bourgeois* pacifism' and towards Socialism. The other movement was that led by Maxton, Kirkwood and others in the West of Scotland, which aimed at industrial democracy and from the first formed a specifically Socialist objection to war. It was contact with this militantly Socialist agitation which turned Brockway from the pacifism of the U.D.C. towards a revolutionary outlook.

Yet it was the *bourgeois* ex-Liberals who made the major contribution to domestic as well as to foreign policy in the immediate post-war years. As regards foreign policy they provided the party with a philosophical strategy to supplement the broad basis of religious and idealist sentiment. In particular they concentrated attention on the effects of reparations on the home market and so tied in unemployment in Britain with mistakes abroad. In this way the fact that they were not fully Socialist in outlook was obscured.[34] Naturally the I.L.P. as a whole rejected reparations not only on economic but on moral grounds, although it accepted the justice of an indemnity. It is interesting to note that the *bourgeois* concentration on foreign policy as the key to domestic difficulties was a further source of contention between ex-Liberals and Socialists of the Maxton type. But there remains an element of paradox in the fact that Maxton and his followers utilized Hobson's analysis of unemployment in terms of over-saving and under-consumption at home to re-direct attention to the primary importance of the internal economic structure.

It is worth noting that during this period the *Labour Leader*

[34] I should acknowledge the usefulness at this point of R. E. Dowse: 'The Independent Labour Party and Foreign Policy 1918–1923' (*International Review of Social History* Vol. VII, Part I, 1962).

was converted into an organ of the radical intellectual criticism of foreign policy. Under Clifford Allen's aegis the paper acquired an editor of high distinction in H. N. Brailsford and was renamed the *New Leader*. The new paper evolved a type of journalism and an ideological stance which resembled that characterizing the *New Statesman*. It combined Liberal and semi-Marxist arguments with a brilliance hardly likely to appeal to the uncomplicated idealism of the earlier generation. Amongst the first causes it espoused were opposition to Lloyd George over the possibility of war with Turkey in 1922, and opposition to the French over the occupation of the Ruhr in 1923. As regards this last Francophobia was a common denominator of every position within the I.L.P.

Indeed, it was possible for the intellectual Liberals and the revolutionaries to find a common cause during the immediate post-war years in the denunciation of Versailles. In any case some of the intellectuals like Brailsford himself, were already on the far left. But whereas the Labour Party, under the devoted tutelage of Henderson, gradually recovered an emotional identification with the decision made in 1917 to support the League, the I.L.P. retained an attitude of negation. It rejected both the Treaty and the current form of the League as integral parts of the capitalist conspiracy, simultaneously utilizing the Liberal notion that the peoples would be peaceable providing open treaties were openly arrived at with the Socialist belief that war lay located exclusively in the institutions of capitalism. If the League were inclusive and made representative of the peoples it might yet be serviceable. But sanctions were universally suspected, either on strict pacifist grounds, or on the ground that once the peoples and/or the international working class controlled the League, sanctions would automatically recede into the background. There was anyway no immediate problem since all instructed persons knew that sanctions were no more than a cover thrown over the warlike designs of France.

In 1924 the I.L.P. found itself faced by a real test of principles. Over half the M.P.s in the first Labour Government were members of the I.L.P., so the party found itself faced by the problem of power for the first (and as it happened the last) time. The question therefore arose as to the implementation of pacifist and unilateralist motions passed at conferences in the war and even so recently as 1922. A move was made to ensure that all votes of supplies were rejected. However, this was frustrated in favour of a pragmatic decision to allow M.P.s individual freedom of action.

Although votes of supplies were not rejected, many I.L.P. members were inevitably worried by the Government's acceptance of the Dawes Plan for scaling down reparations and by the Geneva Protocol. They were worried by the first because it accepted reparations as right in principle, and by the second because an imperfect League was to be provided with sanctions. Further than that the absence of Germany and Russia from the League meant that these countries could not be signatories to the Protocol.

Yet these questions apart there was a fair degree of satisfaction with MacDonald's handling of foreign policy. The divisions now threatening between the followers of Allen and the followers of Maxton really turned on domestic issues. Allen was engaged on a comprehensive programme of research and in order to retain some chance of implementing his new proposals politically he was anxious to maintain friendly links with MacDonald. The revolutionaries had no patience with gradualism or with the concrete difficulties faced by Allen and MacDonald.

In the struggle which followed the chairmanship passed from Allen to Maxton, and Maxton followed up his victory by an independent campaign waged in conjunction with the miners' leader, A. J. Cook, which again sharpened dissension within the party. Further signs of an increasingly leftward swing showed itself in a preoccupation with imperialism, particularly on the part of Brockway, and in the recruitment of a small group of intellectual Marxists to the party.

A point of maximum strain was reached during the term of the second Labour Government. The executive of the Parliamentary Group of the I.L.P. wished to launch an attack against the Government's insurance policy but found the majority of M.P.s in the group determined to construe such an attack as disloyalty to the movement. The result was a purge of the Parliamentary Group which reduced its membership from 140 to 19, a number soon to be further reduced by the loss of some members to Oswald Mosley's *New Party*. So it was that what had been an internal struggle within the I.L.P. now became an external confrontation between the I.L.P. and the Labour Party over the right to vote against the Government. Soon after the Government fell the I.L.P. became disaffiliated.

The foreign policy which the I.L.P. advocated thereafter had all the purity, predictability and consistency possible to a small minority. However, two issues are worth some brief discussion: the relation of the I.L.P. to the Communist Party and the difficulty which the party encountered in deciding whether any particular crisis had resulted in 'capitalist peace' or 'capitalist war'.

As regards the Communist Party the actions of Russia following Hitler's advent to power left the I.L.P. shocked and disillusioned. For just at the moment when the party wanted a boycott of Germany by the international working class the Russians proceeded to extend their previous trade agreements with Germany. Harry Pollitt then stigmatized the boycott as not a weapon appropriate to the working class and the *Daily Worker* described the unfortunate Brockway as a 'hound of war'. Moreover, the Russians joined the reactionary League (no longer a 'thieves kitchen') and started negotiations for an alliance with the reactionary Government of France. From the I.L.P. viewpoint such actions gravely compromised the class struggle in France and undermined the work of the 'League against Imperialism' with which the party was much identified.

A similar type of situation occurred in 1937 and 1938 when the I.L.P. was involved with the Communist Party and the Socialist League in the agitation for a United Front. The I.L.P. rejected the current idea of a Popular Front which should include all progressive forces, and the proposal to link Russia, Britain and France in a common defensive alliance. For the I.L.P. the only correct course was to intensify the internal class struggle in the West and engage only in alliances between working-class forces.

Of the successive crises which raised the issue of 'capitalist peace' or 'capitalist war' two are particularly interesting: Abyssinia and Munich.

As regards Abyssinia the problem was how to obstruct Italian imperialism without simultaneously endorsing the imperialist aims of Britain and France. Fenner Brockway, writing in the *New Leader* again recommended a boycott operated by the international working class. However, the Inner Executive, swayed by Maxton, urged the impossibility of distinguishing these working-class sanctions from those of the League. In his capacity as party secretary Brockway accepted Maxton's line until the annual conference should allow the matter to come out into the open.

Meanwhile controversy continued. In the course of it the leader of the Marxist Group,[35] Jack Gaster, resigned from the I.L.P. to join the Communist Party, even though he was critical of Communist support for League sanctions. When the conference was held a resolution was debated dissociating the party from the Inner Executive. In reply the supporters of Maxton now argued that Abyssinia was a nationalist cause, and that, in any case, Haile Selassie was himself a dictator who did not represent the international working class. They also urged that the only effective sanctions would be those of the League. Nevertheless the resolution was carried and at a special meeting of the I.L.P. National Council, Maxton resigned as chairman on the ground that the Parliamentary Group would be unable to carry out what was now party policy. The impasse was resolved, however, by holding a plebiscite of members which gave a three to two majority in favour of the Parliamentary Group.

The most acute crisis arose at Munich. Maxton disturbed many loyal members by wishing Chamberlain well, by congratulating him on his return and by failing to denounce the settlement as evidence of capitalism's inability to provide a just alternative to war. But for Maxton war was 'the one great over-riding evil that humanity has to face'. He declared himself revolted at the idea of going out to slaughter his German comrades of the Social Democratic Party. Brockway therefore issued a statement to the *New Leader* declaring that they were allowing themselves to acquiesce in a 'capitalist peace'. But this time, when the issue came before the annual conference (in 1939), the delegates endorsed Maxton's position.

When the war came the I.L.P. stood alone, except of course, for the period between November 1939 and the entry of Russia in 1941, during which the Communist Party diagnosed the war

[35] Known as the 'Revolutionary Policy Committee'.

as imperialist in character. The lonely group of three I.L.P. members co-operated with some half a dozen Labour members led by Lansbury in seeking ways to peace. A wider group of twenty to thirty members also met to promote peace negotiations. The existence of continued support for negotiations is shown by the fact that over seventy constituency parties and twenty to thirty trades councils declared themselves in favour of a truce. However, after the collapse of France in 1940 pacifist and war-resisting activity rapidly dwindled.[36] Thus whereas in the First World War opposition had slowly increased in volume, in the Second World War it steadily diminished.

The development of the I.L.P. has been described from the time when it was a pacific body partly sustained by religious inspiration until it became a revolutionary body which rejected the ideology of '*bourgeois* pacifism'. Gradually the departure of its more moderate members left it free to take up the fully sectarian position. However, while the party leaders in the revolutionary phase formally repudiated pacifism their position remained pacifist in practice. It is possible that the early history of religious objections to war still had some influence on the party even when it theoretically accepted violence for working-class ends. The conditions under which the I.L.P. would accept violence were so stringent that it is difficult to envisage any real political situation which would have altered the party's pacifist stand. It was, in fact, highly reluctant to use force for any ends: its negotiations with the Third International are some indication of its attachment to non-violence.

Basically the I.L.P. seems to have acted as if capitalism would disintegrate of itself. Although it regarded capitalism as the root of all evil it still believed the Satanic mills would collapse of their own accord. It thus resembled those religious sects whose adventist response to the situation is pacifist. Moreover, since Satan was about to compass his own ruin, the members of the I.L.P. need frame no practical policy in terms of distinctions between relative good and relative bad. Capitalists were bad; workers, whether British or Russian, were good. War was of the former, peace of the latter. Since the lines of

[36] An account of residual opposition to the war as well as sections concerning the attitude of minor or ancillary bodies (like the Co-operative Movement) can be found in J. Jupp, op. cit.

battle were clear and the outcome fore-ordained it was only necessary to blow the trumpet with a sufficiently certain sound and the walls of Jericho would come tumbling down.

V. GENERAL CONCLUSIONS

At the beginning of this chapter the Labour Party was characterized as a political denomination analogous in type to the religious denominations of Protestant nonconformity. It is appropriate at this juncture to draw out a few of the implications of political denominationalism, showing how they relate to the practice of war and violence.

Considering that it is a body bent on political power the Labour Party accepts the right of other political bodies to their existence. This same relative tolerance is mirrored internally in an acceptance of a wide range of opinions amongst supporters. Provided certain broad centralities are safeguarded the party is not averse to the continuous expression of minority opinions. It does not seek the unanimity of the sect or the subtle but binding formulations of the Church. Like the Methodist Church it has 'doctrinal standards' but these are neither comprehensive in the ecclesiastical manner nor rigid after the manner of the sects.

Linked with this internal and external tolerance is a rejection of the concept of a political élite. The Conservative Party implicitly recognizes the need for a group who are to the political manner born and who exercise rule by right of their caste. This is the ecclesiastical principle whereby a particular order has the sole right to perform the mysteries and to interpret the scriptures. The revolutionary parties explicitly recognize themselves as an élite since to them are given the secrets of the coming political kingdom. Like the religious sectarians they are the only possessors of truth. But the Labour Party has a faith in the ordinary man and in the judgements of its ordinary membership. The ordinary man and the ordinary member are, in principle, capable of political responsibility in a way quite different from the pattern of paternalism and deference historically characterizing Conservatism, and from the sectarian contempt for all ordinary people not vouchsafed the true faith. Hence the Labour Party has never yielded in any important way to the sectarian principle of a total, segregated environment. Like Protestant dissenters its members remain 'in the mixture'.

All these characteristics imply a qualified optimism: men will choose their political salvation without any need of first being dominated by an appropriate theocratic environment. In other words, the Labour Party is based on the liberal faith in individual conscience and individual reason: in Protestant Christianity and the liberal variant of the Enlightenment. It is in this individualism with its correlatives of a qualified optimism and relative tolerance that one must seek the roots of the Labour approach to the question of violence.

Qualified optimism envisages a steady progression towards humane political objectives accompanied by a gradual elimination of the need for violence. In this it compares with the kind of unqualified optimism which expects a total and violent change in the future and remains meanwhile unqualifiedly pessimistic about the present. Similarly the individualism of the Labour Party is allied to a pragmatic *ad hoc* approach which does not necessitate violent change in the way demanded by the holistic theory of Marxism. And again, if men as men are susceptible to the appeals of reason and conscience then the role of violence in human affairs both within and between nations is that much the more restricted.

At this point an element of unreality has clearly entered in. Reason and conscience require to be allied with the cohesive forces of both interest and sentiment. The Marxists understood the former and the Conservatives the latter. Thus the Labour Party was ideologically unprepared for situations where interest partly or completely nullified the appeal of reason and conscience. When such situations occurred it could only attribute them to the machinations of cabals rather than to the structure of politics as such. It was also unprepared for the power exercised by the non-rational and at times irrational appeals of cohesive sentiment, particularly as rooted in the nation. Thus it failed to come to terms with the roots of violence in the essentially interested character of *all* politics and in the non-rational forces of nationalism and religion.

This failure was not completely crippling as regards the internal politics of Britain. Within Britain a constellation of favourable circumstances had canalized the tensions of interested forces along non-violent institutional channels and had made steady and progressive change possible without resort to force. Moreover, the rational and moral appeals of the Labour Party sufficiently coincided with the forces of cohesive interest to give them some degree of political viability. But an approach which was partially viable within Britain was less valid in the sphere of international politics. The faith which was the strength of the Labour Party in the domestic sphere became first an amiable and then a dangerous weakness in the sphere of international relations.

In consequence the Labour Party, schooled in the non-violent pressures of Liberal politics and inexperienced in the control of foreign policy, projected a false image on to international politics. This image exaggerated the possibilities available, partly because it assumed that such possibilities were continuously present. Thus openings which may have existed in the twenties were often assumed to exist equally in the thirties. Each time the image was falsified the party tended to fall into the negative position of blaming the British and French Governments. Moreover, the exaggeration of the degree to which contemporary international politics were susceptible to moralization and rationalization led to two paradoxical attitudes. One of these suspected all attempts to give power to international organizations because these only reflected existing alignments. The other idealized the League and the sanctions it might wield, and in so doing was in danger of converting every outbreak of violence into a universal war. Thus the policy of the idealists either involved a withdrawal from such highly imperfect structures of power as might partly make for international order, or it involved war on a scale calculated to alarm even the most militant of Conservatives. Moreover, the automatic and idealistic employment of sanctions required a foreign policy dangerously calculated to increase the forces aligned against Britain when the issues of national life and death came to a final crisis.

So far the Labour Party has been discussed in terms of denominationalism and the pacific doctrine with which it is associated. But as in the religious denomination so in the political there is always the possibility of sectarian attitudes influencing the beliefs of a minority. The history of the party shows that it has never been either pacifist or aggressively eschatological but it is equally clear that pacifist and acutely aggressive movements have greatly influenced important minorities. These two interrelated forms of sectarianism affected sections of the middle-class intelligentsia, more particularly in the thirties, and found working-class roots in those areas of Scotland, East London and Wales which had suffered most acutely from bad conditions and unemployment. In Scotland the movement took the form of 'revolutionary defeatism' whereas in parts of South Wales the continuing influence of a pacific tradition rooted in nonconformist religion produced a pacifism more inclined towards Christian Socialism. In each of these areas the existence of ethnic minorities, the Scots–Irish of Glasgow, the Jews of East London and the Welsh, provided a factor reinforcing the sectarian tendency.

Yet the Labour Party as a whole has been accused of pacifism, not merely by Conservative propagandists but by serious students of the inter-war years. It therefore remains to say how this false impression has been created. Firstly, we have seen how a combination of circumstances in 1931, notably the accession of George Lansbury to the leadership, might have created a superficial impression of a pacifist policy. But this is not the major cause of confusion. The impact of pacifism from 1931 to 1935 lay in its capacity to effect temporary liaisons with viewpoints which were in fact quite different in outlook. Pacifism was capable of confusion with collective security so long as the emphasis of the latter lay primarily on the need for multilateral disarmament. It was capable of confusion with war-resistance so long as the issues involved only referred to the iniquity of arms in the hands of a capitalist Government. The confusion with collective security ought to have ceased in 1934 when the party officially accepted the principle of sanctions, but the combined influence of pacifists, war-resisters and those League advocates who still saw disarmament as the crucial issue, prevented the distinction between the two doctrines becoming clear until 1936. The confusion with war-resistance also collapsed in 1936 when the left became militant over Spain. Thereafter pacifism, though still as strong as before, had to stand on its own feet, and being thus deprived of erstwhile allies its political impotence was evident.

It is true, of course, that the Labour Party did not recognize that action against Germany would necessarily take place within the framework of national rather than of League requirements until 1937. It is also true that the left did not recognize that the effective restraint of Fascism depended on forming alliances of the old-fashioned type until 1938. But as the foregoing narrative has shown, in neither case was the delay due to a rejection of force as a sanction in the field of politics.

CHAPTER SEVEN

PACIFISM AND THE
INTELLIGENTSIA

THE sequence of discussion is as follows. Firstly there is the question of defining the term intelligentsia and of elaborating certain types of development which characterize intellectuals. Then there is the broad outline of historical development as regards pacifism during the period of what has been called the 'thirty years war'. Next there is a more detailed discussion of two key components in the complex of pacifist ideas, which have been labelled 'romantic anarchism' and 'rationalistic anarchism'. Finally some comments are made by way of interpretation, emphasizing the association between pacifism and Marxism.

For present purposes the term intelligentsia refers to a variety of social groupings, separated from production administration and power, whose principal concern is with academic study, critical investigation, or creative activity of various kinds. With regard to creative activity one would wish to exclude those artists, writers and musicians who not only produce for a market but who subordinate their activity *to* the market. Entrance to the intelligentsia, whether the writer is artistic or intellectual, depends on regarding one's activity as at least in part having value in itself irrespective of current demands or commands. Thus it is possible for people of high intelligence to be excluded from the intellectual stratum because they apply that intelligence in a purely manipulative way to commerce, administration, or applied science and technology. Where there is no freedom there can be no intelligentsia, only bureaucrats and technocrats.

Plainly there are difficult intermediate cases. It is not always easy to distinguish between those who exercise responsible power or who engage in activities geared in to basic social requirements and those who concentrate their work in thought and creation for its own sake. The Webbs, for example, are members of the intelligentsia to the extent that their work was critical, advisory and personally motivated rather than subject to the normal processes of government.

For the intellectual and the artist truth is an end in itself. This does not mean that, as in the case of Lord Acton, knowledge is sought purely for its own sake, but that it possesses status in its own right apart from whether or not it is necessary, useful or appreciated. So understood, the intellectual belongs to a contemplative order and it is his membership in an order which is both his strength and weakness. In the effort to achieve objectivity he conceives his role as that of participant observer, when in fact he is neither entirely participant nor entirely observer.

As regards observation the intellectual is always also participant. This is true even in the 'objective' natural sciences in so far as a conceptual pattern is imposed on the flux of experience. But in the sphere of the cultural sciences the intellectual produces frameworks of interpretation in which the subjective element is very much greater. In history and sociology for example the subjective is only 'limited' by the objective, thus leaving considerable play for factors derived from personal psychology, social experience and interest. In other words the shape of a given intellectual framework partly derives from personal participation. Moreover, there is no transfer of objectivity when an intellectual worker in the natural sciences enters the field of the cultural sciences. Indeed his scientific experience may prove a barrier to understanding.

As regards participation, the intellectual always remains partly observer, and it is this partial withdrawal which actually vitiates his understanding of social processes. In his approach to social processes, more especially those of politics and religion, the intellectual resembles a celibate priest on a marriage guidance bureau: more objective than the actual participants but less experienced. Social cohesion and social action involve crudities of formulation, limitations of perspective and group mechanisms of relative uniformity which are highly uncongenial to the intellectual. As a critical individual he possesses a refinement of thought, a variability of perspective and a freedom of action not open to the group. Thus his very position as a relatively objective observer is a source of misunderstanding in that he analyses social processes, particularly those of religion and politics, in terms of presuppositions which belong only to his own special position within society. Of course his activity in this respect is of paramount importance in any free society but it is none the less important to recognize that the perspectives of the intellectual in relation to politics are partly Utopian and therefore incapable of being universalized as a basis for social action.

This special position of the intellectual as the observer who is also participant and as the participant who is also observer results in a creative tension with other types of social position. Separated as he is from power, from production, and from the more restrictive requirements of social cohesion, the intellectual is at odds with those who are not so separated. Intellectual man is separated from working man, commercial man, political man, administrative man and religious man. As regards the tension between intellectual man and commercial man this is exacerbated by differential rewards as between the two strata. Politicians and priests are likewise the objects of criticism because they are integrally bound up in the system of social cohesion.

In denigrating the role of others the intellectual exalts the importance of his own role, exaggerating the degree of impact which it has on society at large. He moulds the shape of reality in terms of his own special activity, whether it be the logic of abstract reason, the manipulation of words or the shaping of dramatic and plastic materials. Reality is too easily conceived as conforming to his private vision: the word is the source of power.

The foregoing analysis in terms of distortions of viewpoint, Utopian perspectives, social tensions and allied exaggerations of role have certain implications as regards the political and religious affiliations of intellectuals once they attain self-consciousness. However, we are here concerned only with two types of implication, the pacifist and the Marxist, in connection with the particular circumstances of the British intelligentsia in the first half of the twentieth century.

The intelligentsia is a late product of the division of labour and its attainment of consciousness is therefore of recent occurrence. Once attained there arises a crisis of political identity which takes place under conditions of peculiar difficulty. On the one hand the intelligentsia is already partly alienated from capitalist society. It rejects the pecuniary values of the commercial classes and compares the viewpoints of administrator and politician unfavourably with its own Utopian perspective. On the other hand it is confronted by the commanding world-view of the proletariat which appears to demand a decision either for or against capitalist society. Faced by this demand the intellectual is weakened by guilt over his association with the *bourgeois* middle classes and over the degree of privilege associated with his special activities. Moreover, he recognizes that in a Communist society a diminution in the freedom of the intellectual will be compensated by a higher evaluation of intelligence.

There are a wide variety of possible reactions to such a crisis. But important sections of the intelligentsia take the paths of withdrawal and revolutionary activism. When the latter alternative is espoused the proletariat becomes the embodiment of the Utopian perspective, the living vehicle of reason and truth. The intellectual no longer cares for 'abstract' individual truth because he has discovered a corporate truth validated in action. Having found that the 'word' in itself is partly impotent he delights to discover in the proletariat a means whereby his 'word' may come with power. His feelings of guilt enable him to reverse all his previous attitudes with a shudder of masochistic joy. The freedom of contemplation is now an illusion and the intellectual a charlatan. His snobberies now become inverted so that the worker is ruler and the man of intelligence his exalted servant. Eventually of course he may discover that action is no guarantee of truth, but for the moment he is mesmerized by the contact between his study and 'life'. Apart from such contact nothing is real, nothing is strong and nothing is holy.

The alternative is withdrawal. The intellectual may hold that truth is truth entirely apart from action. The word is self-validating. Whereas the Marxist has found a new object of social attachment in the international working class and in

Russia, the pacifist has only Utopia. Provided one is right the world will conform to one's wishes.

I. HISTORICAL RESUMÉ

The actual history of the pacifist movement (as distinct from the peace movement) may be sketched very briefly. The major difficulty relates to the distinction between those who were nearly pacifist or who objected only to certain wars and those who rejected war as such. There is also the problem of people who simply wished to insist on the right of the individual to decide whether or not a war deserved his participation. One has the broadest impression that so far as the intellectuals were concerned the period of the First World War produced objections mainly in terms of the pacific doctrine; objections to conscription and affirmations of the right of private judgement. It was between the wars that strict pacifism became more prevalent.

The intellectual objections to the First World War were rationalistic in tone, tinged with aestheticism and occasional hedonism. It will be remembered that the groups concerned were influenced to some extent by the doctrines of Moore, which envisaged morality as concerned with the attainment of certain states of mind. Those who leaned towards rationalism remained in contact with Liberal politics both during and after the war, while aesthetes and hedonists were inclined to be apolitical. Rationalists like Russell and Clifford Allen actively associated themselves with the Independent Labour Party whereas a hedonist like David Garnett was much less directly concerned with political matters.

The centres of intellectual opposition to the war were Cambridge[1] and Bloomsbury. Around these two places gathered various groups comprising many of the most brilliant of contemporary minds. Virginia Woolf, Lowes Dickinson, the Stracheys, Keynes, Duncan Grant, the Huxleys, Clive Bell, Roger Fry, Middleton Murry, Kathleen Mansfield, the Lawrences and the Hon. Bertrand Russell: these people were linked

[1] The Oxford University Socialist Society was also pacifist in attitude but its objections were probably more specifically Socialist. See M. P. Ashley and C. T. Saunders: *Red Oxford* (Oxford, 1930).

together in literary and intellectual coteries. In particular they came into contact at the homes of Lady Ottoline Morell in Bedford Square and at Garsington. A mouthpiece for their viewpoint was provided by the *Cambridge Magazine* edited by Dorothy Buxton. The organizations in which they worked included the Council for Civil Liberties and the No Conscription Fellowship.

Broadly they believed that war was irrational and ruinous and that conscription was an affront to individual responsibility. Keynes for example, held that it was for him personally to decide the moral character of the war. The habitués of Bloomsbury felt a contempt for the politicians and the newspaper lords which they were at no pains to conceal, particularly so during their various appearances before courts and tribunals.[2] Their martyrdoms were lightened by these feelings of superiority —feelings which D. H. Lawrence noted with some distaste. None of them were objectors to the war on religious grounds. Indeed they contrasted sharply with a middle-class Christian like Stephen Hobhouse, who had been engaged in slum work in the East End prior to the war and who came before his tribunal both as a believer and as an advocate of international Socialism.[3]

Clive Bell the ('eminent') art critic spoke for some of their views in his *Peace at Once* (1915) which demanded a negotiated peace as soon as possible and pointed out that the war was ruining everybody. The war was seen as the fault of Grey, who had allowed himself to be entangled by Slavs plotting against Austria and by French ambitions for the recovery of Alsace-Lorraine. There was little sentiment in favour of Germany but a strong disinclination to sacrifice anything in order to shore up the Russian Empire. Once a stalemate occurred on the western front it was time to make peace. To continue the war could only mean the militarization of England.

The peace of 1919 not only produced Keynes's classic protest but deeply disillusioned those who had seen themselves as fighting for a better world. Herbert Read speaks of the revulsion

---

[2] Keynes appeared for some of his friends when they came before a tribunal, complete with Treasury brief-case and insisting proceedings be arranged so as not to clash with an important appointment.

[3] See S. Hobhouse: *Forty Years and an Epilogue* (London, 1951).

felt at the hypocrisy of statesmen and the indifference they showed to the hopes of returning soldiers.[4] Some of the disillusioned, for example Vera Brittain, set to work for the League of Nations Union; others turned to various avocations—art criticism and dramatic criticism, poetry, novel writing. Yet disgust with the war seems to have lain partly dormant until the history of the twenties had shown that the disarmament of Germany was not to be followed by Allied disarmament and by a better world for all.

As Victor Gollancz points out, the war and peace question was 'not very obtrusive' during this decade.[5] However, the appearance of R. C. Sherriff's *Journey's End* in 1929 seemed to act as a detonator to a whole series of plays, novels, books and films whose theme was the pity and waste of war. In slightly different vein Aldington's *Death of a Hero* (1928) and Graves's *Good-bye to all That* (1929) also expressed a feeling of utter cynicism about the English way of life. Indeed, disillusion with the possibilities of political action seems to have become very widespread. Eric Gill, for example, in his autobiography says that while the actual war had been 'no concern of his' at the time, he now felt a deep disgust with the whole political atmosphere.

The literary productions towards the close of the twenties may be seen as mainly a delayed psychological reaction amongst those who had fought and suffered during the war. Round about 1933, however, this stream of feeling joined up with a fresh current which also recognized that what had happened in 1914 was a prospect in the fairly near future. The second wave of pacifist feeling contained a considerably larger religious component than had previously been the case in the First World War. Beverley Nichols, for example, expressed his pacifism within the framework of a Christian rejection of war. It may have been that some people became Christian because they were pacifist, as compared with those of an earlier generation whose pacifism followed from their Christianity.

Not all the influences were Christian. Pacifism found a lodgement in even more radically religious adjustments than those of Christianity. Aldous Huxley was now interested in

[4] H. Read: *Poetry and Anarchism* (London, 1938), p. 43.

[5] V. Gollancz: *More for Timothy* (London, 1953), p. 350.

Eastern forms of mysticism and the doctrines of ahimsa or non-violence. Part of this interest derived from Gandhi's campaigns in India and the current prominence of the Indian question. An influential popularization of ahimsa appeared in R. B. Gregg's *The Power of Non-Violence* (1934). Another book widely influential was *The Conquest of Violence* by the Dutch anarchist, B. de Ligt.

These unco-ordinated stirrings dramatically came together in the Peace Pledge Union formed on the initiative of Canon Sheppard towards the end of 1934. The distinguished sponsors of the P.P.U. ranged from representatives of the nonconformist conscience like Dr. Donald Soper and Dr. Maude Royden to Lord Ponsonby and Bertrand Russell. Its first secretary was the Christian mystic Max Plowman.

The P.P.U. formed a kind of analogue to the Left Book Club, with which it partly overlapped, although the two organizations held very different views on the conditions necessary for peace. In the eyes of the main sponsor of the Left Book Club, Victor Gollancz, the objectives of his organization included peace just as much as the fight against Fascism, but the tendency was for local groups to become proto-Communist cells.[6] While the P.P.U. asked with Aldous Huxley, 'What are you going to do about it?' the Left Book Club answered with C. Day Lewis, 'We are not going to do nothing.' The policy of the P.P.U. included a protest against British rearmament, refusal to take part in air-raid precautions and proposals for a reconstruction of the League in which there should be a court of equity and no provisions for sanctions. At its height around 1937 the membership was close on 150,000.[7]

In common with Marxism the pacifist movement had particular influence in the universities. The famous Oxford Union debate was indicative of pacifist feeling even though the motion about refusing to fight for King and Country was not necessarily pacifist. Student pacifism came to a climax with the election of 'Dick' Sheppard as Rector of Glasgow University in 1937.

Sheppard died almost immediately afterwards and thereafter Middleton Murry became a major pillar of the Union. Murry

[6] Ibid., Chapter 8.

[7] An account of the P.P.U. is given in S. Morrison: *I Renounce War* (London, 1962).

had followed up his conversion to Marxism, signalized in *The Necessity of Communism*, by a conversion to pacifism, signalized in *The Necessity of Pacifism*. When the war came Murry remained with the Union as editor of *Peace News*. In so doing he had the difficult job of reconciling a wide variety of pacifist viewpoints. Moreover, of the original intellectual sponsors only a few, amongst them Laurence Housman, Canon Raven, Alex Wood and Max Plowman remained.

The position of the pacifist in wartime was one of peculiar difficulty. For one thing the varieties, nuances and degrees of pacifism made any unified policy beyond the common denominator of peace almost impossible. Moreover, it was not easy to find the 'moral equivalent of war' while fighting was actually going on. Some pacifists resolved the problem by taking up work on the land, by becoming medical orderlies, firemen, and fire watchers, and by submitting themselves to medical experiment. The absolutist objectors sometimes found the problem resolved for them by imprisonment. Others who saw some force in the arguments concerning national obligation were able to join the Non-Combatant Corps.

A major problem turned on securing a focus of identification. Once confronted by fellow pacifists the conscientious objectors sometimes found themselves without a vehicle of group identity. It was distressingly easy to become analogous to those Marxists who transferred their patriotism to the Soviet Union, except that the pacifists tended to transfer feelings of identity to the enemy.[8] The principal source of the war had to be found in the policies of their own country. The evils of the Hitlerite régime had to be minimized. Many pacifists refused to believe in the sufferings of the Jewish people, understandably enough in view of the usual fate of truth in wartime. One consequence of these psychological difficulties was the possibility of violent revulsion. A pacifist might suddenly renounce his status and take up combatant work involving the maximum danger.

Of course, many of the pacifist criticisms were true. The Allied Powers were not blameless and propaganda was never less than tendentious. It was also true that Britain was not a

[8] The phenomenon of transferred national identity is worthy of separate study. During the thirties many pacifists thought England should aspire to the condition of Scandinavia, in particular Denmark. After the war and until quite recently India played a similar role to that of Scandinavia.

knight in shining armour but a defender of her own interest. Moreover, at a certain level Germany and Britain were implicated together in the evils of the war and the peace. But the pacifists concluded that these considerations obliterated considerations of relative good and evil based on the choices actually available at the moment.

The absolutists often saw their position as a 'witness' against the dehumanization bound up in modern warfare. This was viable in terms of the concept of an order but not the basis of a universal ethic. Other absolutists believed in total unilateral disarmament. Many pacifists viewed this as a futile proposition in wartime and wished to elaborate a policy which was politically more relevant. The results were paradoxical. The absolutists were capable of being equally absolute in their attitude to Hitler while the relativists found themselves seeking ways to a peace of accommodation. In this respect some attempt was made to distinguish between necessary defensive measures and provocative policies like the economic blockade. There was an underlying hope that the German Government might somehow collapse of itself provided it were not attacked. Supposing, for example, German hegemony in Europe were recognized then the evils of Hitlerism might begin to evaporate.

These psychological difficulties and the variety of positions ensured that the pacifist movement emerged from the war weak, shaken and divided.

II. ANARCHS OF THE IMAGINATION

Up to the period of the great depression the characteristic ideology of alienated intellectuals was an anarchism either of the imagination or of the intellect.

Romantic anarchism in terms of a return to nature, to spontaneity and the life of the small group is a distinctively middle-class ideology. Its basis is fundamentally individualistic. When one examines the exceptions to this statement one finds that they really involve a rather different complex of ideas. Rural anarchism in France and Spain for example is a form of small-scale Communism, while anarcho-syndicalism in France and elsewhere more closely resembles the corporative state than any imaginative recovery of spontaneity in a rural setting.

The true romantic anarchism of the middle class is broadly of two kinds. There is the extreme liberalism of the *petit bourgeois* when his liberty is threatened during the later stages of capitalism. And there is the attempt to recover 'real' individual liberty within a community without any structure of authority. Some of the most interesting examples of the former may be found in America, but it is with the latter as it has proliferated in an English setting that we are primarily concerned. However, the former is important as an ideological source of the technique of civil disobedience.[9]

None of the varieties of anarchism had any necessary connection with pacifism. Proudhon, for example, wrote a celebrated defence of war.[10] The chief classic of anarcho-syndicalism was Sorel's *Reflections on Violence*. Bakunin postulated the need for total destruction before total reconstruction could be made possible. It was this type of anarchism which provided the stereotype of anarchist activity in the late nineteenth century and which may be found exemplified in Conrad's *The Secret Agent*. Even romantic anarchists did not adopt a pacifist approach. Neither William Morris nor Edward Carpenter were inclined to reject the possibility of violence.

At the same time romantic anarchists no longer identified themselves with the politics of liberal democracy, which they regarded as compromised and corrupted beyond redemption.[11] To that extent they were unwilling to involve themselves in wars instigated by liberal democratic politicians. Moreover, the anarchist community, once achieved, would be inevitably peaceful in attitude. Thus pacifism hovered on the fringe of anarchism even before the First World War, more particularly in the Brotherhood movement which was based on the ideals of Tolstoy. But it was only when the First World War and its aftermath had made the issue of violence crucial that anarchists tended to divide into those who rejected violence entirely and those who in effect rejected anarchism and accepted violence

[9] For a short account see C. A. Madison: 'Anarchism in the United States' (*Journal of the History of Ideas*, Vol. VI, No. 1, January 1945).

[10] *War and Peace* (1861).

[11] In recent years their political ventures include only such marginal interventions as Sir Richard Acland's Commonwealth Party and the Fellowship Party. For comparable attitudes towards political participation allied with a nostalgia for community see W. Z. Lacquer's: *Young Germany* (London, 1962).

on Marxist grounds for the revolutionary ends of the proletariat. Thus in so far as anarchism survived the inter-war
period it did so largely as a very important component within
the pacifist movement.

The central feature of romantic anarchism was nostalgia for
'community'. The intellectual and the Bohemian wished to be
immersed in the *gemeinschaft* of the small group. Yet they
remained individualists and the few artificial communities
which were actually created were subject to continuous fission.
Middleton Murry ruefully described the rebellious members
of his agricultural collective as the 'communiteers'. Each individual desired something different from the anarchist community and when this was not forthcoming the result was
disagreement and factioning. The history of almost all such
ventures is of high hopes, followed by disillusion within the
space of three or four years.[12]

The communitarian spirit was regressive rather than revolutionary, although it inspired a considerable amount of thinking
which constituted a prologue to sociology. Its main positive
offshoots have been the industrial village, the garden city and
the new town. The impulse can be traced back to Wordsworth
and Coleridge but perhaps the most immediate source was
Ruskin whose Guild of St. George is symptomatic of a persistent
strain of medievalism. William Morris himself was early
attracted to the Anglo-Catholic Movement and to the priesthood, while Edward Carpenter was curate for a period under
the Christian Socialist F. D. Maurice.

It is in Carpenter's *Civilization: Its Cause and Cure* (1889) that
one finds an archetypal source of the ideas which gave the
Labour Party a fatal attraction for all those whom George
Orwell labelled as fruit-juice drinkers, nudists, sandal-wearers,
sex-maniacs, and nature-cure quacks. Another archetypal
source may be located in Conrad Noel,[13] the Anglo-Catholic
priest who combined a colourful medievalism with radical
Socialism. Yet it is interesting that Noel was not a pacifist but
a believer in chivalry.

The affiliation of anarchism to the notion of 'moral force'
comes later. In the nineteen-thirties there appears an increasing

[12] See C. Gide: *Communist and Co-operative Colonies* (London, 1930).

[13] See L. R. Conrad Noel: *An Autobiography* ed. S. Darke (London, 1946).

interest in non-violence as a political tactic. The major influence here is Gandhi, who was in fact much influenced in his turn by Ruskin and Thoreau. It was the latter who provided Gandhi with the notion of non-violent resistance and civil disobedience. These ideas filtered back into Western culture through the example of the Indian leader, greatly assisted in their passage by antipathy to British imperialism.

The general preference for the guild, the communitarian, the Catholic and the rural was the counterpart of a fierce dislike of Protestantism, particularly of the Calvinist variety. Half-digested readings of R. H. Tawney led to an assimilation of Calvinism to capitalism and to a hatred of the rationalism characteristic of both. It appeared that all the ills of contemporary culture were due to a combination of Puritanism and capitalist enterprise. Capitalists had alienated the worker from his product and destroyed the aesthetic harmony of his environment. Their handmaids in so doing were the Puritans.[14]

The rejection of Protestantism is particularly evident in anarchist notions of progressive education. Education was to be based not on notions of training and discipline but on Actual Life. If Life could be reaffirmed and the free play of man's sensual nature restored then the neuroses of sin and guilt might vanish from consciousness. If the child were set within a natural environment then he might regain a lost harmony. In this way the psychological roots of war and aggression were capable of removal from the outset.

A movement which perfectly illustrates the current notions of progressive education within the context of anarchist ideas is 'The Order of Woodcraft Chivalry' founded by Ernest Westlake in 1916.[15] The membership of the Order was divided up into Witanas, Wayfarers, Waywardens, Pathfinders, Trackers, Woodlings, Elves and Babes. The Order published a magazine called the *Pine Cone* and met together annually in a 'Folkmoot'. The unit of organization was the Lodge.

[14] For a typical statement see Ethel Mannin: *Christianity or Chaos* (London, 1941). *Miss Mannin's Confessions and impressions* (London, 1930), is an important sourcebook for this period. It is interesting that Miss Mannin was appealing for arms for Spain in 1936, but by 1939 had become a pacifist. She eventually acquired some mild leanings towards Buddhism.

[15] *Woodcraft Chivalry. Aims, Ideals and Methods* in *The Woodcraft Way* Series No 3. published in 1927 (first published 1917). This is available in Friends' House Library, Euston Road.

Through woodcraft the evolutionary theory was applied to education. The aim of education was self-realization and this was achieved by the unfolding of the 'infolded God' within the individual, through response to the Eternal God enshrined in the Universe. The sequence of self-realization involved a recapitulation of the growth of the race, beginning with the palaeolithic stage. Natural history, gardening and handicrafts enabled education to be associated with activity, not with a process of intellectual abstraction. The result of this activity was chivalry, i.e. a form of 'strong yet gentle service' in which the meaning of life was learnt through co-operation. Capacity for aesthetic expression was to be engendered through ritual, drama and revelry practised around the ancient social symbol of the Fire. Balance and fullness were ensured by educating the sexes together.

The romantic anarchists shared their zeal for progressive education with the rationalistic anarchists, but otherwise the two forms of doctrine were sharply differentiated. Before going on to discuss the rationalists it may be useful to indicate one or two of the major differences.

The rationalists did not share the romantic interest in community. Their major concern was rather with the application of intelligence to the solution of social and political problems. This emphasis on rationality also rendered them singularly unresponsive to the mystical[16] element within romanticism. They opposed reason to mysticism, while the romantics countered by opposing the concrete to the abstract.

Thus the two branches of anarchism differed sharply in their attitude to Nazism. A few of the romantics with their mysticism of blood and intuition were capable of sympathizing with some aspects of Nazism, which Murry, for example, saw as more 'communal and creative' than liberal democracy.[17] But for the rationalists Nazism could never be anything more than an atavistic perversion.

[16] Of all mystics Blake is the most universally quoted amongst romantic anarchists, but Eckhart and Boehme are also influential. The tendencies to self-deification and antinomianism are particularly interesting. See, for example: *The Adelphi* Vol. II, No. 4, July 1931, pp. 286–8.

[17] *The Adelphi* gave some initial and qualified approval to Mosley's New Party at the time of its inception. (*The Adelphi*, Vol. III, No. 2, November 1931. 'Notes and Comments').

III. ANARCHS OF REASON

Bertrand Russell, one of the most eminent of rational anarchists, has claimed that he tries to analyse political situations as if they were problems in symbolic logic.[18] The claim is significant since it ignores the special character of political questions. Politics is not an exercise in logic but a practical empirical discipline, the nearest analogy to which is engineering. Even this analogy is misleading since politics involves choices and values and deals with the particular and the unique rather than the general.

The result of this rationalistic attitude untempered by empirical realities was what one might label a 'dissociation of intellect'. Intelligence appeared to have nothing to offer in terms of the next practicable step. Moreover, even the actual analyses were oddly selective considering the supposedly objective character of reason. In some cases the Allied Powers were discussed within a Marxist framework, while the Fascist Powers were discussed within a Freudian one. The psychology was in any case thin and brittle, presupposing simple reactions which were reversible just as simply, and making moral appeals in terms of consequences[19] which ignored the non-rational and the irrational elements in experience. Since they proved convincingly enough that men had behaved very badly in the recent past it seemed illogical for them to argue that all could now be different. It was equally illogical to combine a cynical realism in analysis with an extraordinary idealism in prescription.[20]

Rational anarchism is, in principle, political. It does not set out to reject liberal politics but endeavours to make them amenable to reason. This means that the rational anarchist is very rarely an absolute pacifist because his 'pacifism' is based on a calculation of consequences. Of course some rationalists, like Ponsonby, held that the consequences of war are always more deleterious than the consequences of peace. But most of them held that the consequences of war are nearly always

[18] In *We Did Not Fight* ed. Julian Bell (London, 1935), pp. 330 ff.

[19] One finds here an illustration of some of the consequences which follow when morality is based solely on consequences.

[20] In this respect A. A. Milne's *Peace with Honour* (London, 1934), is particularly interesting.

L

uniquely unfortunate. In certain extreme circumstances this might not be the case. Hence the possibility of violent reversals in their political attitude. It was because he estimated the consequences differently that Bertrand Russell was a 'pacifist' in 1936 and advised the Allied Powers not to be too squeamish about using the Bomb in 1947.

The rationalists provided acute analyses of political issues with a brilliance not shown by the romantic anarchists. The latter were more interested in general expositions of their position, but it is worth noting a relationship between the careful and specific considerations of the rationalists and the generalized emotional responses of the romantics. This relationship is very curious and is broadly indicated by the connection between the front page of the *New Statesman* and the back. The romantics reacted to the content of what men like Russell, Kingsley Martin and Noel Brailsford had to say on political issues largely in terms of symbolic stimuli. Provided certain key-words were present the romantics had little regard for the consistency of pronouncements by their cultic heroes.

It is now appropriate to illustrate some of the positions taken by certain exemplars of the rational position in the crucial period between 1936 and 1939. The aim in so doing is not, of course, to render them ridiculous : it is in fact far too easy to judge with all the clarity of hindsight when the situation at the time was agonisingly obscure and difficult. Nevertheless, the people concerned spoke with a characteristic confidence which never left them and with a lack of concern for brute fact and actual possibilities which is still nothing less than remarkable. This lack of concern does not appear in their analyses so much as in their prescriptions and it is the latter which are of particular interest. As for the analyses themselves they were often acutely formulated and stated in the lucid prose which seems to come naturally to 'rational' man. All four of the writers to be discussed, Brailsford, Russell, Kingsley Martin and Joad, were stylists of distinction.

The first two examples both date from 1936: Bertrand Russell's *Which Way to Peace?* and H. N. Brailsford's *Towards a New League*. We begin with the latter.

After a careful analysis of the history of the League Brailsford proceeds, in the third chapter of his pamphlet to *The Com-*

mentary. He points out that although the League had attracted a religious sanctity to itself this only gave the *status quo* a new rigidity. Otherwise the League was a 'functionless fifth wheel' to a history the springs of which lay in the peace settlement and in the instabilities of the capitalist system, with its concomitant psychology. The League had power only to create inertia: otherwise it did nothing to touch the causes of war to be found in population pressure, rivalry for markets and the drive towards exclusive fields for capital investment. This was because democratic public opinion has ceased to function over a large part of Europe and because diplomats were mere agents of combinations and competitions between sovereign Governments. It is in the hands of these Governments that the sanctions of the League reside so that the League can only act *with* the Great Powers, never against them. In other words, the League is an alliance of Britain and France who are the 'have' nations, and this vitiates the impartiality which should belong to an international organization.

However, it would seem alliances are inevitable, and the question therefore arises how to change the distribution of power in favour of the 'have-not' nations. One possibility is Federal Government, but a reform in the political order must be based on economic reform in order to be effective. Thus, besides Federal Government, there must be economic planning, responsible to a democratically elected legislature, which shall assure every nation full access to economic opportunities.

But what States are ready for Federal Government and for economic planning? Conceivably some States are, and it might be possible to form an Inner League of these. No nations would be excluded from the Inner League but some would exclude themselves. The Americas would be absent on account of the Monroe Doctrine. Germany, Italy, Poland, the Baltic and the Balkan States would be absent on account of their fanatical nationalism. Similarly Fascist Austria. Perhaps Russia, Spain and the Scandinavian nations might join.[21] France might be included while under 'Front Populaire' government, provided she were willing to face 'revision' and accept a new system of

[21] Yet the original League had been condemned for excluding some nations as moral pariahs! The selective moral indignation of the left is here particularly glaring.

common defence in place of her old alliances. Czechoslovakia was another possibility provided she rid herself of three million German subjects. As for ourselves this depended on whether by Britain one meant the capitalist empire or the generous island of the Peace Ballot.

This last question remained to be settled at the polls. Once the left had won the general election (in 1940) an alliance of mutual assistance could be made with France and Russia. This alliance would not, of course, be one of haves against have-nots, but it would renounce imperialism and prepare for peaceful change. There would then be no need to study how the Inner League might coerce its members because that problem only arose under conditions of national sovereignty. In any case loyalty could be secured by mutual benefits not by sanctions. The more men approached equality of benefits the more one could hope from reason.[22] Equality within and between nations is the basis of peace.

Brailsford's prescriptions are based on a clear commitment to the left, whereas those of Russell are concerned primarily with the consequences of war in terms of certain values. Bertrand Russell explicitly rejects the notion that all war is wicked: 'a small war for a great end may do more good than harm' (p. 151). He therefore concentrates on a comparison between the consequences of war and of pacifism.

In a war truth would be the first casualty: consider for example the Labour Party's aggressively one-sided attitude to Italy over the Abyssinian question, when in fact the issue concerned British imperial interests. A war would mean the end of judicial rationality: war-resisters might confidently anticipate execution. Britain would be ruled by a military dictatorship and the arts and sciences would collapse in a welter of superstition. The evidence for this was 'overwhelming'. If Britain were to arm then her Government would become more wicked, since wickedness depends on opportunity. Consequently the Empire would be even worse governed than hitherto.

On the other hand pacifism is common sense. It cannot be achieved through political parties or any 'difficult complicated or partial policy' (p. 221), but only by resolute belief and

[22] This particular argument comes from Brailsford's: *Why Capitalism Means War* (London, 1938), Chapter 8.

personal conviction. Pacifism must be complete otherwise it will be ineffective. The Danes for example have no arms and are even better off than ourselves. We should therefore emulate the Danes, hand over our colonies to an international authority and cede Jamaica to the United States. If Britain and France disarmed the Nazis would look ridiculous, and there would be 'a complete change in the character of the German Government . . .' (p. 142). 'To think otherwise is to attribute to original sin faults which are in fact attributable to the Treaty of Versailles' (p. 143). The only obstacles in our way are 'fear, pride and greed'! In any case if fear were our counsellor we would be ready for unilateral disarmament.

Russell discerned some further glimmerings of hope. Perhaps Germany would attack Russia first and, being satisfied, might then be disinclined to bother with Britain and France. Alternatively the United States might be aroused to prevent further German conquests.

Our second two examples date from 1938 and 1939 respectively. Firstly, we must be concerned with the policy of the Kingsley Martin's *New Statesman* relating to the crises over Czechoslovakia between May and October 1938. It will be remembered that the main body of League supporters and the official Labour Party wanted Britain to back Czechoslovakia. What the *New Statesman* wanted is less clear.

Kingsley Martin had supported the concept of collective security ever since Hitler's rise to power. At the same time he described himself as much influenced by current notions of war-resistance. His journal hinted periodically that if the British Government should fail to utilize the collective security system until it was no longer possible to halt Fascism without resort to a full-scale war then Socialists might have to fall back on war-resistance.

In May 1938 there appeared to be danger of war even over Czechoslovakia. Martin had previously indicated some unwillingness to preserve Czechoslovakia's existing frontiers and he now declared that no cause was worth a war which might nearly destroy civilization. In any case (June 4th) war was an inefficient means of combating ideas and the question therefore depended on stopping Fascism without resort to war.

In July the *New Statesman* admonished Citrine and the Labour

Party chairman James Walker for seeming to agree with Churchill's 'romantic nationalism'. On the other hand Neville Chamberlain was accused of really having no other policy but 'old-fashioned imperialism'. We were in fact returning to alliances and these would lead to war. Following Brailsford's recommendations the *New Statesman* suggested that democratic countries should unite economically and strategically, not with the idea of encircling Germany, but in order to build up an area of economic contentment. The German people should be told, over Hitler's head, that we were prepared to share imperial advantages with them. On July 23rd reasonable concessions to Germany were urged, together with a warning that war would follow if Hitler proceeded to extremes. Britain could not be a willing partner in the destruction of Czechoslovakia. On July 30th, however, the *New Statesman* approved the Runciman Mission.

On August 6th Critic commented on 'the old illusion that strong arms and collective opposition mean peace . . .' Two weeks later his journal was urging Britain to tell Germany that the warning against aggression given in May applied equally in August and September. However, by August 27th, when the crisis was accelerating, the *New Statesman* supported appeasement, anticipating *The Times* by ten days. If the Runciman Commission reported that an internal solution was impossible then the question of frontier revision must be immediately tackled. Russia was too far away to help and France would not honour her pledges. The real issue lay in Spain. Tough words to Mussolini and arms to Spain would 'strengthen hopes of peace in Central Europe'.

On September 17th, immediately following Chamberlain's meeting with Hitler in Berchtesgaden, the *New Statesman* rebuked the majority of the Press for welcoming the Premier's flight without being conscious that a new Hoare–Laval pact might result. It was resigned to a German settlement but wanted this backed by a joint guarantee of all the Powers to Czechoslovakia. However, on September 24th it derided the Anglo-French plan for a settlement with Germany, which had been substantially its own policy, and scoffed at the guarantees which it had suggested only the previous week. Chamberlain was an accomplice not a negotiator. It was a betrayal, a sell-out.

On October 1st, when the Munich conversations were not yet ended, the *New Statesman* dropped accusations that Chamberlain was betraying Czechoslovakia. Critic said that everybody knew war would solve nothing. One dared to hope for another respite and therefore another chance of avoiding the final catastrophe. However, once the respite was achieved the *New Statesman* (October 8th) declared that firmness on the part of Britain, France and Russia would have averted war with less devastating consequences to Czechoslovakia. It depicted Hitler as facing war-resistance at home, Mussolini as leading a reluctant nation and the British public as ready for war. However, only the previous week it had described the 'consternation' and 'nausea' of the British public over the possibility of war. By November 5th the *New Statesman* was saying of the September crisis: 'The Czechs have been betrayed.'

One turns finally to the prescriptions of Professor Joad as set out in *Why War?* published in 1939. C. E. M. Joad was a left-wing pacifist who based his position on considerations of rational prudence. He had at one time supported the League but had gradually come to recognize it as simply an instrument of Franco–British policy. At the same time he rejected Brailsford's notion of a group of Federalist Powers as being only a disguised version of alliances and balance of power. The present League was a trade union of burglars grown respectable (p. 177). Joad could only support a genuine League and so his prescriptions turned on the need to reform international organizations.

In Joad's view a reformed League would not consist of governmental nominees advocating national interests. It would consist of the nominees of peoples meeting in a Federal Parliament and elected without regard to national frontiers or national sovereignty. Individual states must give up the right to secede from the obligations of membership and to reject decisions with which they did not agree. In this way decisive action could replace interminable compromise and it would become possible to set up a Court of International Justice complete with an armed police force.

[23] Detailed documentation for this limited period is given in S. Davis, op. cit., on which this section relies. For the whole period one should consult E. Hyams: *The New Statesman: The First Fifty Years* (London, 1963). See also Conor Cruse O'Brien's indictment in the *New Statesman*, April 19, 1963 and Kingsley Martin's reply the following week.

Joad resembles Russell in his psychological analysis of the war mind. In fact, he tends explicitly to subordinate economic to psychological causes so that the demand for colonies is seen as basically a question of prestige not raw materials. The framework of explanation is a simple one of frustration and aggression. Versailles caught Germany in a net of frustrations from which are derived her present neuroses. If the Western Powers were to ally against her, this will only confirm the military despotism in power. On the other hand if grievances are removed justice and freedom will again assert themselves. The more Germany triumphs the less humiliated she will feel and her aggression will be that much lessened. So instead of giving way inch by inch in response to threats we should plan our concessions ahead to show that they are made in response to logic. In this way concessions will bring us credit. Moreover, there is the further advantage that small nations will no longer entertain 'unjustifiable expectations in regard to action to be taken by us on their behalf' (p. 192).

The economic causes are not neglected. Each colonial mandate should be shared by several countries, Germany among them. A World Conference should be called to deal with the inequitable distribution of territories and raw materials. The next step is to make the Empire a free trade area and announce that it will not be defended by force. The money so saved can be used to provide alternative employment to the arms industry and to establish an atmosphere of goodwill. If, in spite of these arrangements the dictators break their agreements then the moral opinion of the world will be against them. This moral opinion is more powerful than we think, particularly so in the United States, where it showed itself capable of transmutation into guns during the course of the Great War.

Disarmament is a gesture which breaks the vicious circle of hatred and suspicion. It must be complete, otherwise it ceases to be effective. To organize defence alone would be foolish. If we are defenceless then war is prevented at the outset. We may perhaps be invaded but at least we are not likely to be bombed.

IV. AN INTERPRETATION

It remains to attempt some interpretation of pacifism within the intellectual stratum of the middle class during the decade or so after 1928.

Two preliminary points need to be made in relation to the basic framework of the present study. In the first place, pacifism and Marxism occur within the same cultural milieu as two major responses to the same situation. Thus the association between pacifist withdrawal and revolutionary eschatology[24] noted in the course of comparative historical study is also found in the twentieth-century British situation. This is not to say of course that all or even most intellectuals were either pacifists or Marxists in the period between the wars. The point is that both these doctrines possessed a strong and growing attraction.

In the second place, the implications of study relative to previous periods suggest that sociological analysis should concern itself with the phenomena of *fresh* pacifism. The pacifism of the intellectuals is interesting because it is new. Pacifism can be ignored when it already possesses an institutional history, unless there is significant recruitment from outside to the institutions concerned. Thus the peace witness of the Society of Friends is interesting only as an example of institutional conservation, whereas outside recruitments to the Society are relevant in terms of contemporary motivations. In the same way certain institutional sources of the liberal pacific doctrine, like the Free Churches and the Labour Party, can be set on one side except in so far as middle-class intellectuals within those institutions develop in a strictly pacifist direction. Once one sets institutions aside, in particular proto-revolutionary sects like the Christadelphians, and post-revolutionary sects like the Society of Friends, then it is clear that pacifism in the period under review is particularly characteristic, with Marxism, of the intellectual stratum in the English middle class. The exceptions to this statement, more particularly in the ethnic minorities, have been discussed elsewhere.

Why did a pacifist movement emerge as a growing force round about 1928 and gain strong momentum in the years

---

[24] For the Marxist component see J. Symons: *The Thirties* (London, 1960) and N. Wood: *Communism and British Intellectuals* (London, 1959).

1933–5? Put quite simply the answer might be that there had after all been a war of appalling character in which part of a generation had been exterminated. As soon as the international scene began to darken in the late twenties one naturally finds the first signs of widespread disillusion. Then again in 1933, when the Disarmament Conference had failed and Hitler had come to power, the situation became more positively menacing. Quite clearly the more sensitive and alert members of the nation refused to countenance a repetition of the misused idealism, the lying propaganda and the wasteful obscenities of the First World War. They believed with deepening conviction that the older generation, politicians in particular, had let them down. Liberal democracy no longer seemed able to cope with its internal and external problems. Since 'politics' in the old sense had failed, sensitive men turned either to the apolitical doctrine of pacifism, or in the case of Marxism, to a political doctrine which promised to put an end to politics.

Such an analysis is less untrue than it is insufficient. It is important that it conforms to a normal feature in the genesis of sectarianism in so far as a gap yawned between expectations and actualities. Frustration depended in part on the level of anticipation. But it is not enough to observe that Parliamentary tycoons bamboozled the liberal intelligentsia with quite unreal expectations. The point is that they were *able* to do so. The optimism of the liberals was such that they were only capable of fighting such a war provided it seemed to be a means whereby all the Wellsian dreams of a new world order might be fulfilled. It was because optimism already existed that ideal expectations could be raised and it was under these circumstances that disillusion with the depression and the renewed prospect of war was so extreme.

Thus it is worth while examining the pre-existing liberal tradition because its emphases were easily capable under conditions of acute shock, of transmutation into pacifism and Marxism. A qualified optimism became a combination of fantastic optimism and fantastic pessimism such as is characteristic of the sectarian tendency. In the case of the Marxists they were as entirely pessimistic about the present as they were optimistic about the future.[25] The pacifist viewpoint was equally

[25] See D. G. MacRae: *Ideology and Society* (London, 1961), Chapter 16.

compounded of pessimism and optimism. Their analyses were as gloomy as their prescriptions were unreal. The transition from the one to the other is psychologically understandable but logically very curious, particularly so when it affected those whose training was logical and rational in character.

The liberal tradition provided a starting-point for both Marxism and pacifism in another sense. A central platform in its outlook of qualified optimism was the social efficacy of reason and morality. Provided truth was correctly expounded then men would respond in a recognition of their common interests. This view envisaged some dialectic between reason and the social reality. But as reason seemed to have failed the Marxists attempted to validate it in action while the pacifists believed that reason was its own validation. In other words, the pacifists thought it possible to preach a sermon to the world which would convert the stony heart of international diplomacy. If that failed then there was always martyrdom, but this martyrdom was still conceived optimistically. One might mount a cross but it was generally in sure and certain hope of resurrection. On the whole, however, there was no need to imagine too great a degree of unpleasantness. Provided one showed a willingness for martyrdom, a capacity for at least the gesture, then the world might be impressed and things need not perhaps be so very different after all. If the Germans were given cups of tea at Dover and the Japanese allowed into Australia all might be well.

The liberal background was relevant in other ways, notably as regards its positive content and its espousal of science. The positive content ensured that the intense activism of the thirties concerned the sort of concrete goals found in the Marxist programme. Similarly the alternative possibility of withdrawal always took place within a context of progressive ideas. In another situation, as for example in pre-revolutionary Russia one might find a much greater tendency to nihilism and total scepticism. The espousal of science was a particularly attractive element within Marxism. Not only was it congenial in claiming to apply science to human affairs but it offered a social world in which the status of scientists would be recognized. Compared with Marxism the pacifist creed had relatively little to offer. Conceivably those scientists who did adopt pacifist beliefs were the more inclined to Christianity.

If more scientists were attracted to Marxism than to pacifism the ideologues of the pacifist movement nevertheless used arguments derived from science. They were specially adept at employing a combination of evolutionary theory[26] with recent psychology. The latter was particularly important in providing a basis for the kind of progressive education which should eliminate the impulses to violence. Indeed the intellectual atmosphere of the inter-war period is as interesting a case of the ideological uses of science as it is of the ideological proclivities and interests of scientists. Just as it was possible for some nineteenth-century thinkers to extract optimistic implications from Darwin, so some twentieth-century thinkers were able to extract optimistic implications from Freud, though both might just as easily be regarded as providing more precise documentation of original sin.

As has been suggested both the liberals and the romantic anarchists faced a crisis of social identity which was deepened by the need to find an answer to the questions posed by internal and external violence. The crisis within the intellectual stratum corroborated the crisis in world affairs. Moreover, the central point at issue was one on which the middle-class conscience was already more sensitive than any other. Reason and Christianity were equally united that war, in principle, was wrong and stupid. The situation of intellectuals was thus one of extreme difficulty, and the apparent confidence of their varied responses may have been as much a reflection of the difficulty as it was due to intellectual arrogance.

There were two possibilities. They could accept the class war as a necessary purgation prior to universal peace. This option allowed them to achieve both social identity and community by submerging in the righteous violence of the proletariat. Or they could retain a separate identity and reject violence altogether. These were not the only options in fact available but this is the sort of dilemma which may have appeared to confront them.

It is at this point that Christopher Caudwell's analysis may have some relevance.[27] Caudwell himself chose the Marxist path and for him the *bourgeois* protagonists of pacifism simply

[26] Aldous Huxley and Gerald Heard for example.

[27] C. Caudwell: *Studies in a Dying Culture* (London, 1938), Chapter 5.

refused to admit the rightful violence of the proletariat or to face up to the violence of the capitalist system in which they were themselves inevitably implicated. When challenged to declare themselves by Armageddon they concentrated on saving their 'souls' (and their 'integrity') in typical Protestant-*bourgeois* manner.

Yet they were nevertheless accessories to violence. The economic and social relations in which they were involved were implicitly and potentially violent. The *bourgeois* State was itself an engine of violence. While the Marxists accepted their responsibility the pacifists turned to passive resistance as an apology for the old programme. With every other moral standard deserted (and in this Caudwell agreed with Orwell) they adopted pacifism as a last-ditch version of *bourgeois* morality. It was the politics of the rabbit faced by capitalist destiny.

Yet whichever path they took their individualism still retained its hold. They were poor bets even as recruits to Marxism, particularly when this represented little more than a youthful adolescent enthusiasm. The critical faculty remained with them, though dormant. The labile psychology of the intellectual always made him an object of suspicion within the Communist Party. If this labile psychology affected even a functioning institution like the Communist Party how much more did it affect the loose coteries of pacifism. The 'Peace Army' of trained yogi never materialized. The opportunity for corporate satyagraha never came. While many of the Marxists lasted until the Kruschev revelations and the Hungarian episode, the pacifists lasted hardly so long.

It was, in any case, very difficult to erect a functioning organization on the basis of a negative. Continued lectures on non-violence sustain about as much interest as continued cele-brations of how the proletariat won the revolution. Thus many pacifists left at the onset of war; others departed with the crisis of 1940. On the other hand the tendency to defect was counter-balanced by a continuous potential within the intellectual stratum to revert to similar attitudes. As within the Communist Party the turnover was high.

Many pacifists of the First World War now favoured fighting. Those archetypal figures of the thirties, Joad and Middleton Murry, perhaps best signalize the downward curve in pacifist psychology. Joad repudiated his pacifism and was received into the Church of England. Middleton Murry, having originally wanted to enter the Church as a pacifist literateur eventually found the 'body of Christ' in the ordinary stuff of undramatic Liberal democracy. By 1950 he was voting Conservative.

CHAPTER EIGHT

DISSENT AND ESTABLISHMENT

I. DISSENT AND THE PACIFIC DOCTRINE

THE most significant forms of denominational dissent have begun as *Ecclesiola in Ecclesia*. A group within the Church aspires to stricter standards than those achieved by the majority, and construes the moral permissiveness of the Church as involving an unnecessary degree of compromise with the world. In Catholic cultures such a group would form or join an order, but for Protestants the notion of the order is not only historically discredited but implies an acquiescence in the double standard. This standard implies that it is as appropriate for the Church to be permissive within her own sphere as it is appropriate for the monk to pursue perfection in accordance with his special vocation.

Protestantism rejects the conception of the dual standard. Admittedly it is only in principle that perfection is possible to all, and different levels of moral attainment will in fact remain as between man and man. But such an admission is not to be equated with ecclesiastical connivance at indifference, either to Christian morality or to Christian institutions.

The Protestant solution is to take the order out of the cloister and set it in the world. Whereas in Catholic cultures the average man is within the Church and the man of exceptional vocation within the order, in Protestant cultures all men are called to be tertiaries. The tertiary does not attempt a cloistered virtue but tries to make his everyday work a vocation. This may be regarded either as a secularization of the order or as a sanctification of the world. Both interpretations are correct since Protestantism is equally the most secular form of religion and the most religious form of secularism.

The world is an arena within which God may be glorified. The monk also knew this: to work is to pray. But for him the work of man constantly alternated with *Opus Dei*, the work of

163

God. The Puritan rejected this alternation because, to some extent, his work was his office. Whereas the ordered alternations of the monastic day marked a continuing division between spiritual and material, the ordered rationality of the Puritan's day indicated an attempt to redeem all time for spiritual purposes.

It was entirely proper for the early Puritans to be Calvinistic: once obliterate the distinction between spiritual and material and the great tensions of a rational theodicy cease to be applicable. The material order became, in a quite simple sense, the place within which God might be magnified and glorified in the course of man's spiritual pilgrimage. To earlier centuries it had appeared as though the world remained in some degree resistant to God. Puritanism overcame this resistance because it saw the condition of man and the world as given by divine ordinance and settled by an act of divine power and will. It was therefore appropriate for man, as His instrument to act and will unreservedly within it solely for the realization of His inscrutable purposes.

Taken in itself Calvinism may be both ecclesiastical and sectarian: there is no special connection with denominational religion. Indeed, the Church form of Calvinism, such as was established in Geneva and Scotland, produces a godly community in which new presbyter simply replaces old priest. However, should the godly community fail to establish this kind of organic connection with society as a whole then the alternative is dissenting separatism. Should a nation reject the reformed discipline the 'saints' cease to constitute a community and instead form an association for religious purposes. To the extent that this requires a change from involuntary to voluntary membership it is analogous to a development from status to contract. The formation of religious associations differs from sectarianism in that while sects tend to create new communities over against the Church community, the dissenting congregation remains, to use a Quaker phrase, 'still in the mixture'.

After 1647 the possibility of a Reformed Church in England on the Calvinist model became remote, and as it did so the dogmatic structure of Calvinism went into decay. The massive dogmatism of an ecclesiastical Calvinism ceased to be appropriate to the ideological requirements of a voluntary association on the denominational model. An overwhelming sense of the Divine Majesty slowly diminished into a vague Deism. As the experience basic to the theological structure of Calvinism was eroded there remained only a rationalistic deposit crystallized in a characteristic psychology. When the religious substance evaporated the rationalistic scaffolding remained as an attitude of mind.

At first an attempt was made to rebuild a religious foundation upon reason and nature. Science was called in to augment the role of scripture. But this attempt was associated only with a further weakening of the dissenting associations as they moved towards a deeper individualism from which the religious sense was largely absent. Ultimately even the rational Deity disappeared leaving behind the rational ethic. The reasonable religion of Unitarianism became the reasonable irreligion of the Ethical Society.

The progress (or regress) of Calvinism in England is one of the most striking instances of the type of development in which ideas gravitate towards their opposites. Calvinism began by ascribing all to grace and ended by ascribing all to nature. In the beginning it forgot the natural dignity of man and in the end it forgot his natural misery. The attempt to bring all men within the scope of a godly discipline became first a religious association and then a group of individuals with no religious awareness at all. The affirmation of the non-rational and the theological aspects of existence concluded in an earnest moralism which found theology incomprehensible.

A development of this kind obviously condemned the denominations to an increasing degree of social impotence. Granted the possibility of a rational ethic at the level of the individual, it could hardly form the viable basis of a group which aspired to be anything more than an incidental aggregate of individuals. The congregation was disintegrating into the aggregation. But genuine group purposes always transcend the provenance of a rational ethic and without being necessarily irrational must be based on non-rational premises. It was left for Methodism to restore the non-rational premises on which to erect a religious association.

Once again the origins of dissent began with *Ecclesiola in Ecclesia*. The Wesleys preached a Christianity in the Great

Tradition, combining strains from Calvin, Luther and the Caroline divines. In its initial stages the revival included a renewal of sacramental religion; but as expansion continued the social and theological differences widened. Gradually Methodism developed along denominational lines in the form of a new religious association, and as it did so the theological structure of the Wesleys followed that of Calvinism into decay. But while Calvinism developed towards an individualism of the reason, Methodism developed towards a highly subjective and individualistic sense of personal salvation. The remaining inheritance of Methodism now comprised an experimental religion derived from Luther allied to an emphasis on feeling analogous to the Romantic Revival.

Some comparisons are worth making between the direction of development in Methodism and in Calvinism. It has been argued that both began with internal movements for reform within the Church, rather than as sects. Both then developed into an associational type of religion which expressed an individualistic principle but which also controlled that individualism by subordinating it to the purposes of the religious group. This individualistic and associational type of religion inevitably experienced a diminution in the range of religious sensitivity, but whereas in Calvinism this involved a stress on reason, in Methodism it involved a stress on feeling. The latter was in an important degree a reaction against the former; nevertheless each, by virtue of individualism, formed a *praeparatio evangelii* for the pacific doctrine. Individualism, both by reason of the optimistic manner in which it is able to envisage the social problem and by reason of the commercial interests with which it became associated, is the natural basis for pacificism.

So far we have traced two developments in which a narrowing of theological range and richness to the requirements of religious individualism becomes the basis for optimism. The individualist is able to see the political problem as either soluble by reason or by a right attitude. Whereas the Enlightenment and the residue of Calvinism provided the one, Methodism and the Romantic Revival provided the other. While the old dissenters had obliterated the gap between what is and what ought to be by an act of will and then by a process of reason, the new nonconformists obliterated the gap by an emotional sense of salvation developing into an effusion of sentiment.[1] So doing they laid the twin bases of all that was most characteristic in Victorian Protestantism.

An emphasis on experience in religion originally signalized a recovery of the basic insights of the reformers. But the stress on feeling eventually led in directions which had less connection with classical Protestantism: emotion and sentiment. What for early Methodists had been a sense of assurance rooted in grace sometimes degenerated into a vague glow of diffuse religiosity. Evangelical assurance became humanitarian emotion.

For evangelicals the chief criterion of value tended to become the degree of religious fervour. Consequently spontaneity was valued at the expense of order. By the same token religious life became increasingly dependent on the expectation of recurrent revival supported by techniques of mass evangelism partly derived from America.[2] Great importance was attached to biblical fundamentalism and, in particular, to the exegesis of soteriological passages in the Pauline epistles. So far as politics were concerned evangelicals tended to be apolitical and deferential, or, at a higher social level, reformist in the Conservative tradition. In other words they were either what the modern sociologist terms 'deferentials', or paternalists in the manner of the so-called Clapham sect. It is worth adding that then (as now) both nonconformist and Anglican evangelicals maintained a pessimism about the redemption of the international order, unless perhaps the converted were widely elevated to positions of political authority.

By the middle of the nineteenth century, however, Methodism had taken up the traditional position of older dissenters in opposition to the political and religious establishment. The older dissenters had been supporters of the Whigs, the nonconformists supported the Liberals. At the same time the biblical foundation came under critical fire. Attacked in this way at base, evangelicalism evolved towards a humanitarianism vaguely rooted in the 'spirit of the gospels' and in an emasculated

[1] The emotionalism of evangelical nonconformity is crystallized in hymn-singing as well as in vigorous preaching. The Victorian admiration for Handel also had roots in the emotional needs of nonconformity.

[2] As suggested in Chapter 9 this type of religion stays within the Protestant tradition of denominational religion. It seems to me useful to regard both Pentecostalism and the Salvation Army as remaining within this tradition.

presentation of the Person of Christ which stressed the exemplary character of His life rather than the merits flowing from His death and passion.

Humanitarian sentiment both affected Methodism and partly derived from it. At its most attractive it produced a type of social idealism deeply concerned for the progressive establishment of the Kingdom of God. This social idealism we have already noticed in relation to late nineteenth-century Liberalism and the formation of the British Labour Party. In its least attractive form it produced forms of moralistic sentimentalism equally devoid of theological content or any serious apprehension of the real dimensions of the political problem. It is one of the unhappy paradoxes of Christian history that whereas the secular deposit of Calvinism was the South Place Ethical Society the secular deposit of Wesleyanism was Moral Rearmament and Dr. Frank Buchman.

The solution of political problems through individualistic humanitarianism naturally included the elimination of war. The humane individual concentrated his inevitably selective attention on the alleviation of suffering[3] rather than on planned social reconstruction, and since after 1870, war provided one of the sharpest examples of suffering it gradually tended to take highest priority in the march of progress. Some liberals not merely appeared to suggest that war was the principal evil but almost that it was the only evil. This does not mean that the religious and political liberals were pacifist : sentimental attitudes and sectarianism are in any case rarely associated. Pacifism existed only on the periphery : on the margin of religious dissent and of the liberal and Labour Parties. In general Protestant idealism rather coincided with the internationalism which reached its eventual apotheosis in the League of Nations Union.

Of course, the hopes of humanitarians included some degree of illusion. They were usually far from Utopian but they derived from an optimism that exaggerated genuine possibilities. This exaggeration and its evident failure to understand the contemporary world led to a partial recovery of the basic insights

[3] Selective partly in terms of his own interest. Apart from the rarer forms of individual moral sensitivity humanitarianism normally works within limits set by material interest.

of the Reformation. Lutheran and Calvinist positions were respectively restated by theologians who had undergone some apprenticeship in the Marxist ferment of the twentieth century, in particular Reinhold Niebuhr and Karl Barth. Amongst these there was a swing from pacifism to a sophisticated realism. The misery of man was now recognized as the necessary complement of his dignity. A sense of the Divine Majesty and Grace was therefore restored. Moreover, in the work of Niebuhr the traditional Lutheran awareness of the distinction between the City of Man and the City of God was recovered, without the inhabitants of the one in principle despairing of the inhabitants of the other.[4]

The foregoing account of the development of denominational religion has been necessary in order to provide a background for the growth of the pacific doctrine. An attempt has been made to illustrate the bases of sentimental and rational optimism in so far as these are rooted and reflected in a certain type of religion. However, something more now requires to be said concerning the social context within which religious and political pacificism arose. This context may profitably be considered from two points of view: in connection with the relation of a group to power and in connection with a group's economic interests.

With respect to power dissenters were excluded from actual political control, without at the same time encountering insurmountable difficulties in the acquisition of status and the exercise of pressures. To the extent that they were excluded they gained little experience of the limiting necessities of power; to

[4] See R. Niebuhr: *The Children of Light and the Children of Darkness* (London 1945), *Christian Realism and Political Problems* (London, 1954), and *Moral Man in Immoral Society* (New York, 1934).

It is perhaps worth remarking that in this country as well as in America the major intellectual critique of pacifism has been provided by Niebuhr. The theology of Niebuhr attempts to retain the dialectic tension between the perspectives of the Gospel and political reality, while continuing to exercise complete responsibility within that reality. To that extent it shows with the theology of Pascal an analysis of human limits, a tragic view of political action, and a sense of the paradoxes and ambiguities inherent in every possible type of decision. The achievement of Niebuhr has been to provide an understanding of political processes while both retaining a moral commitment and recognizing that the cause to which one is committed is also under judgement.

the extent that they were in a position to exercise successful pressures they were the less inclined to violence. In that they were disinclined to violence it was the more easy to grant concessions in response to pressure. As the ends of dissenters and nonconformists could be achieved without violence the whole method of armed force became unthinkable. Their view of the world could lay relatively little stress on the overt use of physical power.

Turning to the question of economic motivation, it is clear that such positions of dignity and relative wealth as were open to dissenters lay largely in the spheres of commerce and industry. Not indeed that the majority of them were wealthy merchants or industrialists, but such as achieved status tended to utilize this avenue of advance rather than others, while at a lower level many shared the general ethos of the trading community. This ethos expressed the traditional interest of trading communities in the maintenance of external and internal peace. In the earlier period one may perhaps note an emphasis on the latter and in the later period an emphasis on the former. The increasing attachment to external peace which grew up in the mid-nineteenth century derived from free trade and the obvious benefits which it brought to the 'workshop of the world'.

In this way dissenters moved within a current of social forces with little experience of power and clear material interests in peace. Paradoxically such was the implicit power of trade and such the paramount position of the United Kingdom in the world that a concern with overt force was in any case unnecessary. Moreover, reference has already been made to the implications of the individualism characterizing Protestant dissent and the trading community with respect to the moralization and rationalization of politics. Should policy remain unregenerate this might be regarded as simply due to a residual ignorance or a residual wickedness needing only moral suasion and more education for its elimination.

We can now make certain generalizations about the reactions of denominational bodies to the onset of war. In the first place, since the denomination is committed to the efficacy of the individual conscience or the individual reason it will accept divergent opinions within its organization in the liberal democratic manner. Differences will be regarded as capable of eventual harmonization by the progressive leadings of the spirit. In the second place, since dissenters are partly integrated into the social structure they will respond to major crises along the lines taken by society as a whole. If the nation finds itself at war the majority of dissenters will accept the necessity, albeit reluctantly. If the predominant mood of the nation is pacific, dissenters will be found amongst the protagonists of peace in disproportionate numbers. Finally since dissenting movements assimilate some social groupings which might in other circumstances and in different conditions adopt sectarianism, there is always the possibility of a sectarian response along the margin of the denominations.

These generalizations may be illustrated from historical material. It is possible to show that denominational bodies have never adopted an official policy of pacifism and also that tolerated minorities have appeared from time to time in support of the pacifist viewpoint.

We begin with a brief summary of the situation from the seventeenth to the nineteenth century, before considering the twentieth century in more detail. In the seventeenth century one finds the Baptists accepting the use of force involved in the Civil War. At the same time the question of peaceability frequently arose among them and a minority may have accepted the pacifism characterizing the Mennonite form of Anabaptism.[5] So far as the Congregationalists (or Independents) were concerned the Savoy Declaration of 1658 states their position on the use of force quite explicitly:

> It is lawful for Christians to accept and execute the office of a Magistrate, when called thereunto: in the management whereof, as they ought specially to maintain Justice and Peace according to the wholesome laws of each Commonwealth; so for that end they lawfully now under the New Testament wage war upon just and necessary occasion.[6]

One may assume that this attitude remained the position of

[5] L. Fargo Brown: *The Political Activities of Baptists and Fifth Monarchy Men* (Washington, 1912), p. 9.

[6] *The Savoy Declaration of Faith and Order 1658*, (London, 1959) ed. A. G. Matthews, Chapter 24 'Of the Court Magistrate', Section II, pp. 167–8.

dissenters throughout the period prior to the Methodist revival. The Methodist revival seems not to have altered this position in any respect. A few Methodists, notably John Nelson, took a pacifist stand, but there is nothing in the work of the Wesleys which condemns war in principle. Methodists served in the army during the Napoleonic Wars, and such objections to military life as occurred were solely based on the moral conditions which it fostered.

The peculiar attraction of the pacific doctrine for dissenters during the nineteenth century has already been noted. Herbert Spencer, himself of a dissenting background, comments approvingly on their peaceability as compared with the militarism of more priest-ridden Churches.[7] In the middle years of the century it was the Congregationalist Henry Richard who provided the most important leader for the peace society agitation. Few dissenters had any love for the jingoism of Palmerston; nor, for that matter, did they share Disraeli's concern for the preservation of the Ottoman Empire. However, with regard to the only two major wars of the time, the Crimean and the Boer Wars, they were divided.

Neither war represented an extreme threat to the national existence. The majority of the nation enthusiastically supported the Crimean War and carried many dissenters with them: nevertheless such opposition as existed tended to come from dissent, led by the Quaker John Bright. The Boer War again divided dissent just as it divided the Liberal Party. Hugh Price Hughes, the major influence in the Wesleyan Methodism of the time, had been previously associated with peace society meetings. At the same time he admired the radicalism of Chamberlain and eventually became a supporter of the war. By contrast the Baptist leader and liberal-socialist, Dr. John Clifford, came out in opposition. This disunity partly reflected the traditional dilemma of a liberalism which desired peace and which also feels impelled to attack illiberal régimes, amongst which it identified the Boer Republic.

[7] H. Spencer: *Principles of Sociology* Vol. II, Chapter 10, p. 785: 'The differentiation of these two functions of fighting enemies and propitiating deities . . . has gone furthest in those religious organizations which were separate from the State. Unlike the ministers of the Established Church, . . . dissenting ministers, derived from classes engaged in one or other form of industrial activities, are the least militant of religious functionaries.'

In the twentieth century denominational religion was confronted by total war. Prior to 1914 there had been considerable concern about the growing power of militarism, abroad and at home. The immediate reaction to the onset of the crisis was therefore in favour of neutrality, but the invasion of Belgium brought the vast majority into the ranks of those who supported entry at the side of France. Sir W. Robertson Nicoll, for example, carried on a vigorous pro-war propaganda through the *British Weekly* and even regarded Britain as a rod to chastise the international immorality of Germany. As amongst the trade unions so amongst the nonconformists there were grave misgivings over the possibility of conscription. These misgivings were signalized in the resignation of Sir John Simon from the Government. Moreover, as the scale, length and intensity of the war grew more evident, pacifist groups appeared in each of the denominations, particularly perhaps among those more alert and informed nonconformists who had been attracted to Christian Socialism prior to the war.

After the war the hopes of Free Churchmen, both pacifist and non-pacifist, centred almost exclusively on the League of Nations. At this juncture many pacifists felt that the League could be supported as the major agent of disarmament, and it was not until the thirties that some of them really faced the issue of sanctions. The Free Churches and the Established Church saw the principal key to the problem of war in controlled disarmament through the League. Indeed, Viscount Cecil saw the Free Churches as perhaps providing his most unswerving support. The Congregational Assembly and the Methodist Conference passed many resolutions in favour of collective security and all-round disarmament. The National Free Church Council organized support for the League. At the same time the interdenominational World Alliance for Promoting International Friendship through the Churches and the Fellowship of Reconciliation provided channels for understanding and mutual help. Conceivably bonds were forged between British and German Protestants to the relative exclusion of Catholic countries. Something of the internationalist sentiment and enthusiasm for the League may be gauged from the support which the Peace Ballot received in nonconformist Wales.

But at no time did the nonconformist bodies become pacifist.

From 1933 onwards the question of sanctions lay alongside the ideal of disarmament and at various junctures each denomination stated its considered view of the situation. In every discussion there emerged a pacifist minority and a non-pacifist majority, and the latter invariably conceded the right of the minority to its viewpoint. Thus in 1936 the Methodist Church explicitly accepted both positions as viable expressions of conscience.[8] In 1939 the Assembly of the Congregational Union commended both objectors and conscripts to the 'care of the Churches'.[9] In March 1933 the Baptist Union Council received a resolution from the Baptist Union of Wales requesting a clear lead against future participation in war. A strong committee was set up to consider 'The Attitude of the Baptist Denomination to War'. This report urged the surrender of a measure of national sovereignty to establish a really effective World Organization, but admitted hesitation in connection with 'the contention—endorsed by a majority of the committee —that a peaceful world cannot be secured apart from force organized in such a form and on such a scale as to be equal to the task of restraining disloyal and aggressive States'.[10]

When the Second World War began the Free Churches gave it their support, but this time there were few overtones of the Christian crusade, only acceptance of a grim moral and political necessity. However, the pacifism of a minority requires further consideration.

The first important name was that of S. E. Keeble, who was a socialist as well as a pacifist. It was under his influence that a Wesleyan Methodist Sociological Society was formed, later becoming the Wesleyan Methodist Union for Social Service. During the First World War Methodist socialists were divided, with Keeble taking the pacifist position and working for the U.D.C. and others, like J. E. Rattenbury, supporting the war effort. In October 1916 a small group formed the Wesleyan Methodist Peace Fellowship. It is interesting to note that the Union for Social Service came to an end in 1926 over the

[8] Declaration on the Church and Peace adopted by the Methodist Conference 1936.

[9] Quoted in R. Tudur Jones: *Congregationalism in England 1662–1962* (London, 1962), p. 416.

[10] Quoted in E. A. Payne: *The Baptist Union – A Short History* (London, 1958), p. 207.

question of war, some of its members maintaining that the foreign policy of the Labour Party was insufficiently distinguishable from that of the Conservatives.

Another important figure at this period was Arthur Salter, a prominent leader in the I.L.P. and a co-worker with Scott Lidgett in the Bermondsey Settlement. Salter was a doctor who came of a Brethren background and who adopted an absolute ethic on every issue. His uncompromising attitude towards the First World War was in some measure responsible for the pertinacity of the strict pacifists in the I.L.P., as distinct from the liberal pacifists and socialist quasi-pacifists. When the threat of war returned in the thirties he associated with Lansbury in conjunction with the International Fellowship of Reconciliation in efforts to organize influential opinion against war.

Henry Carter and Donald Soper both continued the pacifist tradition within Methodism. Carter came of a West Country background and was early interested in the holiness movement in Methodism. A very keen temperance advocate he became, in 1918, Connexional Secretary of the Temperance and Social Welfare Committee. A large number of resolutions came from his department to the Methodist Conference urging support for the League of Nations, particularly on the issue of disarmament. In 1933, when disarmament talks seemed to have finally failed he set out his full position as a complete pacifist. The Methodist Peace Fellowship, containing some 1,200 lay and 600 ministerial members, accepted him as its leader within the denomination. Carter was also very active in the formation of Christian pacifist Forestry and Land Units in 1940 and in refugee work. Donald Soper belonged to a younger generation than Carter. He succeeded to a radical tradition at the West London Mission and became a prominent sponsor of the P.P.U. Soper was both a theological liberal and a believer in the importance of the sacrament, although it seemed at times that his Christianity rested almost entirely on pacifist grounds.

Within Congregationalism Dr. W. E. Orchard provided a focus of pacifist opinion during the First World War. As minister of the famous Kings Weigh House Church in Mayfair he attempted to restore the sense of worship within the Free Churches, and eventually ended in the Church of Rome.

During the course of the war two other well-known Congregational ministers who embraced pacifism, Leyton Richards and Nathaniel Micklem, had to resign their charges. In May 1916 the Reverend F. H. Stead launched a League to Abolish War, a precursor of the Congregational Peace Crusade inaugurated after the war in 1926. Many Congregationalist students were influenced by pacifist ideas, particularly so at Mansfield College, Oxford, where C. J. Cadoux took a firm stand against the war. Cadoux served in the Friends Ambulance Unit and later became the most considerable of Congregationalist opponents of war. A distinguished church historian he adhered to an irenic theological liberalism.

Some of the difficulties in which pacifist dissenters found themselves may be illustrated from Leyton Richards's *Towards a Constructive Peace Policy for the Churches,* published in 1935. Richards argued that in a God-governed world any policy conflicting with His will as revealed in Christ is bound to miscarry. Calculation of probabilities was therefore out of the question. As a practical policy he advocated disarmament, arbitration and federalism within the framework of the League. However, he conceded that disarmament might require the existence of an international force, not for the purposes of war but in a preventive capacity. At the same time he remained an absolute pacifist: a Christian could not join this force but must take the risks involved in an unarmed international order. The international force was recommended solely as a *step* in the right direction. Thus while pacifists like Dr. MacGregor were concerned to reject the dual standard, one for the Christian as Christian and another for the Christian as citizen, Richards's proposals only succeeded in providing the dual standard with a fresh formulation.

Some comparison may be useful between the dissenting pacifists of the twentieth century and the humanitarians from whom they derived. Humanitarian and pacific liberals had stressed motive as important in achieving the good society and had therefore remained basically individualist. A right attitude was more important than doctrine. As has been argued in the chapter on the Labour Party this emphasis on the right attitude did not disappear but survived as a component element in the ethos of British Labour politics. Nevertheless the transition from liberal individualism to the Labour Party did involve some shift of emphasis. Liberals and socialists had both developed within a Protestantism which had lost its anchorage in the literal validity of the Bible and was seeking a new point of doctrinal attachment. But whereas the liberals and liberal-socialists tended to find the point of attachment in the *spirit* of the New Testament, those who became strict socialists found it in the *content* of the gospels. For them the gospels not only commended a principle of unlimited charity but provided a charter for the establishment of a new society. However, pacifist thinking during more recent years has perhaps tended less to stress either the spirit or the content of the gospels than to view the crucifixion as the perfect exemplification of sacrificial non-resistance followed by eventual triumph.

In a less sophisticated period the attempt to rest an extreme radicalism on the foundation documents of Judaeo-Christianity would almost certainly have included an aggressively eschatological as well as a pacifist emphasis. But for dissenters in the twentieth century, many of whom were middle class and university educated, the eschatology of scripture was ruled out as mythological. Moreover, not only had they been reared in a pacific tradition but their motivation was more one of sympathy than of acute frustration. Their socialism was therefore of a pacifist rather than an aggressive kind. To the extent that they desired an aggressive ideology they needed to reject the religious framework altogether and seek it in secular sources.

When the pacific doctrine became the pacifist dogma individualism gave way to a stress on community. The left-wing dissenters thus came to feel some affinity for the communitarianism of the Anglo-Catholics and of the liturgical revival. Like some Anglo-Catholics they posed the Church against the World, but for them the Church constituted the brotherhood rather than the institution. The actual institution, as T. S. Eliot noted, remained 'wrapt in the old miasmal mist', although they cherished the idea that if only it accepted pacifism a revival of influence would be the result. Nevertheless, having recovered a sense of community the brotherly values of the sacrament were a natural expression of that recovery. The emphasis of many dissenting pacifists on worship and liturgy is thus hardly surprising.

So it was that what had begun as the protest of the individual within the context of commercialism ended with a sacramental order of Socialist intellectuals. What had begun in a stress on the evil consequences of war ended in an absolute ethic which rejected consequences as irrelevant. Most surprising of all, it was asserted at the beginning of this chapter that the Protestant tradition began by rejecting the whole concept of the order, yet by the twentieth century it was precisely this concept that some of its more eminent representatives were most intent on reviving.

II. PEACE AND THE ANGLICAN CHURCH

The Church of England accepts the justice of war under appropriate circumstances.[11] According to Article 37, 'It is lawful for Christian men, at the command of the magistrates, to wear weapons and serve in the wars.' Such an acceptance of war is inevitable in a situation where the religious group is coextensive with the majority of the nation and where the national leaders are either dormant or practising adherents. Moreover, the broad concurrence of Anglican political attitudes and State policy is further ensured by the recruitment of bishops and higher clergy from the same social milieu as that of leaders in politics, business and the professions.

Thus the English Church has remained overwhelmingly opposed to pacifism and the highest positions in the Church are largely closed to those of a pacifist or radically left-wing persuasion. The two major exceptions between the wars were the pacifist Bishop of Birmingham, Dr. Barnes, and the Communist Dean of Canterbury, Dr. Hewlett Johnson, both of whom were appointed during the Labour Government of 1929 to 1931. The appropriate ecclesiastical rank for a priest of eminence who is also a pacifist would appear to be that of canon. Not only has the English Church opposed pacifism at the official level, but the pacifist minority within it is less

[11] The position of the Church of Scotland does not differ substantially from that of the Church of England. See, for example, the Report of a Special Committee approved by the General Assembly in May 1937. The United Free Church of Scotland is a body whose views appeared to resemble those of the English Free Churches in the degree of liberal concern shown in relation to the question of war. Special consideration is given to the United Free Church position in F. Manthey (Jr.) *Christians and War* (Ph. D. Thesis, Edinburgh, 1952).

acceptable and proportionately, as well as absolutely, much smaller than the pacifist minority within nonconformity.

The conservative attitude of the Established Church, as of all established churches, mainly derives from its position in English society. Comprehensive Churches possess a rich and continuing involvement in the mainstream of social life, which leads them to rely on traditional formulations of the political problem. These are more coherent and therefore less flexible than the biblical injunctions on which nonconformist positions are more exclusively based.

This is not to say that establishment, because it is inimical to pacifism, is necessarily inimical to social reforms. The establishment may be aligned with social forces which in particular circumstances have an interest in such reforms. The Anglican record in relation to the ten-hours bill and factory legislation, for example, is a fine one.[12] Nevertheless, to be established and to constitute a majority are limiting conditions on reformist tendencies. Where these conditions are absent, as in South Africa, the Anglican Church has been able to present a courageous opposition to Government policy. By the same token the Church of Rome is in a position to take up a progressive political attitude wherever it is in the type of minority which has few connections with the governing élite. But whereas reform is compatible with ecclesiastical organizations both when they represent majorities and even more so when they represent ethnic minorities excluded from power, pacifism still remains logically and sociologically impossible.[13]

Nevertheless, the Church of England recognizes pacifism as one alternative open to the conscience of Anglicans. This recognition is evidence of a residual sensitivity to the tension between Christianity and the institution of war which survives even the pressures of establishment. Even the most Erastian of establishments produces some Christian reservations concerning the ways of the world. Were England a theocratic State on the Islamic or Communist model, for example, the

[12] See W. T. Ward: *The Factory Movement* (London 1962), Chapter 16.

[13] The Roman Catholic Church may contain a pacifist or pacific minority in any society where it is largely identified with groups who are to some degree or other excluded. It is interesting to observe that in the United States a moderate amount of peace propaganda arose amongst Catholics, one motivation of which was the dislike of certain nationalities at being involved in a war on the side of Britain.

pacifist position could hardly be understood, much less tolerated. The existence of Article 37 is not simply evidence of ecclesiastical compromise but also proof that a question has been raised. The exemption of priests from compulsory military service is a further recognition of Christian reservations. Even in the atmosphere of bellicose nationalism aroused by the First World War the Anglican Church retained some awareness of these reservations. Thus when a conscientious objector was refused recognition on the ground that he was a member of the Church of England the Archbishop of Canterbury felt constrained to point out that there was no necessary inconsistency between Anglican profession and pacifist belief.[14]

Moreover, there is a wide range of opinion within the Church, even amongst those who in principle accept the possibility of a just war. In a situation of total war this range will hinge on the extent to which the national cause is identified with the cause of Christ and on the extent to which conscientious objection is regarded as a possible moral position. There will also be a division of opinion as to what weapons are necessary to the prosecution of the war as distinct from those weapons which simply involve horror for the sake of frightfulness. In this latter regard a notable protest against the methods of frightfulness employed by Bomber Command was registered by the Bishop of Chichester.

To the extent that Anglican leaders have felt compelled to identify the national cause with the cause of Christ it appears that 'vice' must pay its habitual homage to 'virtue'. Few prelates are prepared to follow a sometime Bishop of London in identifying the 'necessary' war as the 'just' war. Even fewer are prepared to follow G. B. Shaw in identifying an unjust war as a necessary one.[15] Those who most nearly see their own forces as soldiers of Christ do so because they can only accept war when Britain takes the role of a Sir Galahad unambiguously defending Christendom against the barbarians. Once this identification has been accomplished the pacifist position be-

[14] G. K. A. Bell: *Randall Davidson* (London, 1935), Vol. II, p. 818. Bell quotes a letter from the Archbishop to the Hon G. Collier dated April 4, 1916 in which he states that he has 'learned by experience that membership of a religious community is not found to be incompatible with even the most extreme vagaries of individual opinion'.

[15] G. B. Shaw: *Common Sense and the War* (London, 1914).

comes incomprehensible. Moreover, once so persuaded the Christian is likely to evidence a degree of bellicosity excelling that of his more secular brethren. The paradox of Christian militancy arises because some Christians, like some liberals, cannot engage in a war unless it is a crusade. The very fact that the New Testament so strongly recommends the peacemakers means that those who find themselves at war need to give their activities the fullest justification that religion can provide. If one believes that religion must enter into every action then a state of war requires explicit religious justification. Naturally this is most easily supplied amongst those Low Churchmen who uphold the traditional Erastianism of the English Church.

High Churchmen may be less prone to identify the aims of the Church as coextensive with those of the State and they are therefore less likely to see the war in simple terms of good and evil. The medieval element in English Catholicism may include an awareness of universal Christendom and a sense of community which is analogous to, and sometimes overlaps, socialist internationalism. An emphasis on the doctrine of the Incarnation, such as informed the Christian Social Union, only occasionally gives rise to pacifism, but it includes a strong awareness of the social problem. Charles Gore, for example, although he took unity over the First World War for granted, did not condemn conscientious objection in principle and warned against the dangers of an unrestrained militarism.[16] One finds William Temple displaying a like sensitivity during the Second World War in a protest against the notion that Britain was fighting for Christianity. We were, he said, fighting for a civilization which had been in contact with the Christian tradition, and which might become Christian in the future.[17]

Liberal Churchmanship is concerned to adjust Christianity to a scientific age and to achieve a progressive realization of the Kingdom of God on earth. The two foremost leaders of Anglican pacifism, Canon Raven and Bishop Barnes, were both of them theological liberals and practising scientists. The measured,

[16] Of course, an admiration for Catholicism or Catholic churchmanship can be associated with an appreciation of knightly virtue.

[17] *Towards a Christian Order* (London, 1944). A Symposium with Introduction by William Temple.

scholarly liberalism of Canon Raven may be contrasted with the more sentimental liberalism of (Canon) Dick Sheppard, Vicar of St. Martins-in-the-Fields, and founder of the Peace Pledge Union. The career of Dick Sheppard is important for the history of pacifism in the thirties, but it is not important as regards the position of the Anglican Church.[18]

In between the wars the Anglican Church gave support to the League of Nations. Two important conferences are worth mentioning as illustrating its position: C.O.P.E.C. and the Lambeth Conference, 1930. The C.O.P.E.C. Conference held at Birmingham in 1924 included the Established Church as one of its participant bodies. Twelve reports were issued, of which the eighth was devoted to the issue of war. The introduction to this report indicated a mixture of unanimity and conflict. All were unanimous (as had not been the case during the war) that the individual conscience must be the supreme authority. The chauvinistic attitude to war was rejected and was itself characterized as generally futile. But disagreement arose as to whether the principle of love *always* demanded non-resistance, particularly when the interests of third persons were at stake. Christians were pledged to decide whether their country had submitted its cause in good faith to an international court and had accepted the court's decision. If it had not then the appropriate course was conscientious objection. The stress lay on responsibility to support the League. The Lambeth Conference of the Anglican Communion in 1930 laid a similar stress to that of C.O.P.E.C. It emphasized individual conscience and it envisaged loyalty to the nation as subordinate to wider loyalties.[19]

[18] Plenty of information is available in R. Ellis Roberts' *H. R. L. Sheppard: Life and Letters* (London, 1942). See also Sybil Morrison: *I Renounce War* (London, 1962).

[19] Comprehensive material on the attitude of the Church of England is available in F. Manthey, op cit.

CHAPTER NINE

SECT, ORDER AND CULT

I. THE SECT

THE chief criterion by which a group is to be identified as a Christian sect is the extremism characterizing its rejection of contemporary society. This rejection, of contemporary society differs sharply from the rejection of the 'world' found in some Eastern religions. In so far as sects within the cultural area of Christianity reject the world as well as society they veer towards dualism, and should this tendency become complete then the association between passivity and activity disappears. The passive sect is left without its revolutionary counterpart.

It is, of course, important to recognize the persistent strain of dualism which has manifested itself in the history of Christianity alongside a more fundamental emphasis on the goodness of Creation. The influence of this dualist shadow behind the Christian substance can be traced in most forms of ecclesiastical Christianity as well as in Christian sectarianism. Nevertheless, the Judaic doctrine of Creation has generally succeeded in maintaining itself against dualist intrusions. The stress on natural theology in the Church and the sectarian emphasis on the idea of material restoration or renovation both indicate that matter is not viewed as inherently beyond redemption. Amongst the sects about to be discussed the Society of Friends provides the clearest example of a Christian sectarianism which, although it rejects society is nevertheless 'at one' with Creation.

I have argued that the extremism of the sect is evidenced in forms which are apparently entirely opposed: pacifism and aggression, perfectionism and amorality, autocracy and anarchy. *Les extrèmes se touchent.* Characteristics conspicuous by their absence are the delegated democracy of the denomination and the articulated compromises of the Church. From some view-points the sect is even further removed from the denomination than it is from the Church. The elements of pragmatism and continuous social adjustment found in the denomination are entirely foreign to sectarianism. Moreover, whereas a denomina-tion may see itself as a regiment in the army of Christ the sect generally views all other so-called Christians as crypto-Satanic. The denomination is aware of independent orders of truth and of alternative aspects of truth. In this respect even the Church seeks to comprehend a many-sidedness within itself. But the sect recognizes no valid alternatives or independent orders of truth outside the inclusiveness of its own vision. It recognizes neither incompleteness nor relativity. It has no uncertainty principle: the sectarian knows.

It follows that the sect has little use for the individual con-science. The point deserves special consideration because it is clearly very relevant to pacifism. In the minds of some people there is an inclination to regard every objector as a martyr for the Protestant conscience. Yet, the sectarian objector is not necessarily a person of generous impulses and high moral sensitivity for whom the obscene carnage of war is directly contrary to a religion based on love. He is not the kind of Protestant who is always questioning the way he should go. In fact he is not a Protestant at all, except in so far as he is equally not a Roman Catholic. It is grossly misleading to regard the sectarian as an extreme form of Protestant, particularly so in view of the fact that sectarianism historically preceded Pro-testantism by almost two millennia.

In the sect group-consciousness replaces the individual con-science. The sect is unanimous: even the Society of Friends insists on unanimity, and in its absence the logical consequence is breakage of fellowship. Once unanimity fails then the sect is likely to be sundered in two conflicting bodies. Whereas splits within denominations do not preclude close relationships and the likelihood of ultimate reunion, sectarian quarrels are inevitably absolute. The notion of discussion followed by an agreement to differ (so long as essentials are not at stake) is quite foreign to sectarianism. Members of sects may well be highly conscientious, but they are not men with a Protestant conscience. Both the polar extremes of sectarianism, autocracy and anarchy, logically require unanimity rather than individual decisions.

It follows that sects and denominations approach the question of conscientious objection raised by war and by conscription from a different angle. It was shown in Chapter Eight that the denomination will take note of a divergence and actively acknowledge the right of different members to come to varying conclusions, even though as a body it lends support to the war. Such an approach naturally regards the system of conscription with some reserve. The sect, however, seeks to discover the true 'line' with all due speed and then imposes a particular attitude on all members. Hence a Jehovah's Witness who enters the forces has abandoned his primary allegiance to Jehovah God and his loyalty to fellow Witnesses. Similarly a Christadelphian who accepts combatant military service has gravely strained the bonds of fellowship.

Even the Friends, with their tendencies to denominational Protestantism, reacted to the challenge of the First World War by meeting to discover the stand to be taken as a *group*. Those who, like some members of the Cadbury family, possessed consciences at variance with the majority, were felt to have strained fellowship and defaulted from their profession.[1] Within American Quakerism, during the nineteenth century, the most ruthless discipline operated against those who broke sectarian unanimity on the question of war.[2] A parallel case of the search for unanimity is provided by the controversy generated in the Communist Party in September and October 1939 over the 'line' to be adopted with respect to the Second World War. Once accepted, the 'correct' interpretation was binding on all members.

It may be that this characteristic of unanimity, which appears logically related either to authoritarianism or to almost total lack of authority, can be of use in the analysis of religious groups which in certain respects appear partly denominational and partly sectarian. An example of such a group is provided by the Elim Pentecostals. On the one hand the Adventism of the Pentecostals would seem to indicate a typically sectarian rejection of society, even though the stress on Adventism has in

[1] See R. Scott: *Elizabeth Cadbury* (London, 1955), Chapter 10.

[2] R. M. Jones: *Later Periods of Quakerism* (London, 1921), Vol. II, Chapter 18.

fact varied from time to time.[3] On the other hand the whole ethos of the movement is 'enthusiastic' in a manner closely resembling the revivalism of established denominations. Moreover, Pentecostals also resemble these denominations in having a separate pastorate and in a lack of stress on the importance of their institutional boundaries for the purposes of salvation.

Clearly any attempt at conceptual categories which leans towards the logical rather than the empirical type of construct will be confronted by mixed cases. At the same time one can justifiably attempt to assess the overall logic of any particular religious position, and in so doing the question of unanimity assumes considerable importance. Indeed it becomes quite crucial where the issue at stake is that of military service, since this symbolizes and focuses the relation of the religious group to the wider society. Thus in the case of the Pentecostals one finds that decisions with regard to conscientious objection are largely a matter for the individual, and that only a minority actually take the pacifist option.[4] Such an attitude is reasonably linked with the fact that Pentecostals are critical only of particular habits in the wider society rather than of its fundamental structure, and so builds up a cumulative impression that they belong, with such organizations as the Salvation Army, in the extreme evangelical wing of denominational Protestantism.

Post-Revolutionary and Proto-Revolutionary Sects

From the discussion of sectarianism in general we turn to the various groups within the scope of our definition, adopting the basic distinction set out in Section V of Chapter Four between those which are post-revolutionary and those which are proto-revolutionary. The former type constitute a distillation of revolutionary failure in which the Adventist myth has been largely spiritualized. The latter type have no actual experience of violent upheaval, and continue to anticipate a situation

[3] Of course some form of Adventism can be found in most Christian bodies. It is after all an article in the Nicene Creed. The sectarians are distinguished by the degree of prominence they give to the doctrine and by the immediacy of their expectation.

[4] B. R. Wilson: *Sects and Society* (London, 1961), pp. 88–9, discusses the question of Pentecostals and military service. An attitude similar to that of the Pentecostals is found in the Emmanuel Holiness Movement according to research done by T. R. Warburton.

where physical overthrow is appropriate either by God alone or by God with their assistance.

The kind of sect which spiritualizes the adventist myth has already been subject to examination since it includes those groups which are most famous historically: the Bohemian Brethren, the Mennonites and the Society of Friends. For these groups the myth was realized within a self-selecting community which maintained allegiance to such features of the original revolutionary programme as were viable in existing circumstances. In this way pacifism and the muted radicalism with which it was associated were both originally realistic. Quakers had every reason to be 'the quiet in the land' in 1660. They had looked for the restoration of all things and were confronted by the restoration of Charles II.

Thus pacifism begins as a realistic tactic at a specific juncture in revolutionary fortunes. It then becomes a permanent ideological fixture because it is encapsulated along with other elements of the belief system in an indissoluble union. The circumstances which gave pacifism relevance have passed but it is carried forward by other beliefs which possess a more continuous function. Like a dead body frozen in ice it will only disappear when the block melts as a whole. This is not to say, of course, that it loses all value. The Quaker witness against war has played an important part in sensitizing the human conscience to the issues involved and maintains a fruitful dialectic with unthinking acceptance of force and compulsion.

The chief technique by which a sect maintains the integrity of its belief system is the total environment. Whether a sect is completely authoritarian or almost completely lacking in a structure of authority it still aims to provide a total background for its members. Political as well as religious sects have frequently attempted to realize this aim. So far as the Society of Friends has been concerned the total environment has been reinforced by the doctrine of unanimity and (in the past) by rigorous discipline. This ensures that when a crisis like total war brings the traditional beliefs under renewed scrutiny the sect generally succeeds in maintaining its position.

One corollary of the above analysis is that psychologically as distinct from sociologically, pacifism is a phenomenon of one generation. Unless it is efficiently 'tied in' with beliefs which serve more continuously relevant needs it is remarkably evanescent. Thus a loosely organized movement like the Peace Pledge Union finds it difficult to survive the first generation of its existence. Indeed in the sphere of purely individual psychology pacifism rarely survives adolescence and early maturity.

While post-revolutionary sects incline to internal self-recruitment after their first phase of activity is past, the proto-revolutionary sects often continue to draw in recruits who are acutely hostile to the prevailing society over a long period. Their pacifism is thus more apparent than real. Two of the best-known examples of such sects are the Jehovah's Witnesses and the Christadelphians. They will be discussed together because they present interesting points of contrast and comparison.

The actual history and organization of both sects have been fully described in several important studies, but certain features are worth special mention. For example they both reject the distinction between ministry and laity which is found in all religious groups, ecclesiastical or denominational, which basically accept the social order. But whereas the Witnesses are absolutely autocratic the Christadelphians strive to keep organization to the barest minimum. Once again one has an illustration of polarization at extremes.

Another significant characteristic of Christadelphians and Witnesses is their verbalism. Like members of the Communist Party they are full of religious zeal but devoid of religious emotion. By comparison the denominations, and even the Churches, tend rather to rely on emotions, especially those aroused by music.[5] In the same connection the manner in which sects of this type conceive prayer and its appropriate content should be illuminating: some of the earlier sectarians (Ludovic Muggleton for example), rejected prayer altogether. It would appear that sectarians rarely experience religious tranquillity

[5] The question of music is an interesting one. It may be literally true that the man who has no music in himself is 'fit for treasons, stratagems and spoils'. Musical emotion has been historically so intertwined with religious emotion and, moreover, provides such an overwhelming sense of 'rightness' about the world that it could hardly fail to emasculate sectarianism. Even the introversionist sect remains very cautious about music, especially so when the members come together specifically for religious edification.

or devotional communion. The important point is that God
has a plan which it is their business to expound. Meanwhile
religious emotion is merely relaxing.

The plan is the apocalyptic myth and it is worth while
indicating the version of the myth accepted by the Witnesses
because it illustrates the continuing influence into modern
times of the three-stage division of history and also the persistent
margin of dualist religion mentioned at the commencement of
this chapter. As regards the tripartite division of history Witnesses conceive stage one as running from the Creation to the
Flood, stage two (under the limited control of Satan 'Prince of
this World') from the Flood to the Kingdom of God, while
stage three constitutes the fullness of time, when creation is
not only redeemed but restored. As regards dualism Witnesses
regard Satan as God's *other* son who was dislodged from heaven
only so recently as 1914. Mankind now awaits a repetition of
that event on some terrestrial battlefield.

Apart from Witnesses and Christadelphians, the major sects,
members of which have come before tribunals, comprise the
various branches of the Plymouth Brethren. The Brethren
illustrate the range and variety of possible combinations of
characteristics in the formation of religious groups. Most of
their characteristics link them to sectarianism as here defined,
but there are unmistakable elements which also link them to
denominational Protestantism. Furthermore, the fact that each
local meeting is autonomous does not render them susceptible
to generalization and summary.

It may be best to begin with a brief historical survey. The
Brethren developed originally in Ireland and the West of
England, drawing many recruits from the professions and from
people of aristocratic background. They included doctors,.
lawyers, officers, scholars and clergymen of the Church of
England and the Church of Ireland. It would appear some
Anglo-Indians and others concerned with colonial administration were also involved. Since the years around 1830 were a
period of crisis for the upper strata it seems reasonable to relate
the Brethren to this crisis.[6] If the connection is a genuine
one then they may be seen as an evangelical analogue to the

[6] See, for example, R. B. McDowell: *British Conservatism, 1831–94* (London,
1959), pp. 34–7.

alternative reaction which found expression in the ritualism of the Oxford Movement and of the Catholic Apostolic Church as founded by Edward Irving.

Although the Brethren were originally concerned to break down institutional barriers in a fashion characteristic of evangelicals they soon developed a capacity for separatism and schism almost unique in the history of Christianity. Schisms most frequently arose either with regard to the degree of separation from the world and-or over the propriety of eldership. The former issue gave rise to the major distinction amongst Brethren between those who are 'Open' and those who are 'Exclusive'. Of recent years the Brethren have grown in numbers and include many business men of substance as well as craftsmen and thrifty Scots fisher folk.

Doctrinally the Brethren are fundamentalist and it may be that their constant searching of the Scriptures, especially those written by St. Paul or imputed to him, has helped to exacerbate their capacity for fission. They entertain a lively anticipation of the Second Coming, and therefore regard secular politics and attempts at reform as misguided tinkering with a world under judgement. At the same time, in accordance with Pauline precept, and perhaps also in accordance with their initial social origins, they are subject to the powers that be, save for questions of conscience. In most spheres of activity Brethren are anxious to avoid being 'unequally yoked' with unbelievers, and their efforts to avoid secular contamination lead to a very severe insulation from modern means of communication. Most Brethren believe in a collective 'priesthood', although some have held to an eldership on the Presbyterian model. The overriding emphasis on St. Paul is further underlined by the subordination of women in the assembly.

The consequences of these varied sociological and theological strains for military service are interesting. Clearly the overall tendency is towards sectarianism in terms of the degree of protest against the world and it is not therefore surprising that a large proportion take the path of conscientious objection. Indeed it has almost become an accepted tradition amongst Exclusive Brethren that they enter the Non-Combatant Corps. Acceptance of non-combatant status provides them with a compromise between subjection to the powers that be and avoidance of the 'unequal yoke'. At the same time Exclusive and Open Brethren alike view conscientious objection as a matter for the individual conscience, so that it is possible for an Exclusive Brother to accept service without conditions and for an Open Brother to refuse service altogether. However, it is certainly the case that many more Open Brethren than Exclusive Brethren accept service without conditions and that professional soldiers are found only amongst the Open Brethren.[7] Indeed, the Open Brethren are considerably more inclined to engage in secular activities. They include for example at least two Members of Parliament.

Those Brethren, whether Open or Exclusive, who become conscientious objectors, cannot be said to do so on pacifist grounds. They would not hold that military service is morally abhorrent to human beings as such, but only that it is abhorrent to those whose prime loyalty must be the preaching of the gospel. It would be illogical for *them* to prematurely thrust into eternal damnation men whom they should strive to save. This apart they are quite clear that a nation must be defended and that it is the duty of its nationals to do so. Their position is therefore vocational and it provides a helpful transition to the next category of discussion: the order.

II. THE ORDER

The conceptual distinction between the sect and the order turns principally on the way in which the latter recognizes that its standards are not capable of being realized universally. The members of an order adopt what one might regard as a moral 'pluralism'. This relative recognition of the existing social structure indicates a much lower level of active hostility to the world or society than is characteristic of the sect. Hence there is no anticipation of a catastrophic end to contemporary society in the near future, but an emphasis on the realization of the Kingdom of God within the community itself. The order concentrates attention on the eternal as it is realized in every moment of the present. It is in the present that the self-selecting community either restores to perfection primitive ideals which

---

[7] In fact quite a number of military men have been Open Brethren, notably Sir William Dobbie, sometime military governor of Malta.

have been compromised and thrown down, or recreates the harmonies of nature.[8]

The order serves to canalize and sublimate tensions and tendencies which in other circumstances are capable of breaking out into the extremist phenomena of sectarianism. Thus if the order and the sect are studied dynamically and historically as well as in conceptual terms examples can be found of the order developing into the sect. The Spiritual Franciscans exemplify an order which developed a sectarian offshoot.

Even the denomination may partly acquire the characteristics of an order under particular historical exigencies, in spite of the fact that it begins by specifically rejecting pluralism and the dual standard. As the analysis in Chapter Seven tried to show the denomination initially rejects the dual standard and it does so without adopting the extremism of the sect. It achieves this middle way between the dual standard and extremism either by regarding the existing structure as given by arbitrary divine decision or by a belief in progress which enables it to accept recalcitrant elements because they are merely temporary. However, once the sense of the arbitrary is broken down and once historical experience like that of the two world wars impairs belief in progress then the religious mind is forced back towards some form of moral pluralism.

The pacifist movement in Britain and elsewhere has frequently given birth to communitarian experiments, particularly during wartime. These have generally been concerned either with forestry or with agriculture, and are perhaps best known through the efforts of Middleton Murry. A specifically Anglican example is provided by the Brotherhood of the Way. Two movements of particular interest are the Brüderhof and the Iona Community, since they are respectively outside and within the official Church.

The Brüderhof was founded by a Dr. E. Arnold, at Sannerz in 1920 and emigrated to England between 1936 and 1938. It explicitly rejects war together with many other State activities. Goods are shared in common and the community places a particular value on chastity. Woodwork, farming and various

---

[8] The search for natural harmonies belongs especially to the eighteenth century. In the nineteenth century the emphasis lay more on romantic medievalism and the recreation of communal, Catholic values.

craft activities are pursued, with particular emphasis on printing.

The Iona Community owes a great deal to the inspiration of the Reverend Sir George F. MacLeod who is a Socialist and the leading Presbyterian pacifist. It constitutes an imaginative offshoot of the work of the Church of Scotland. The members of the community and its associates are called upon both to live the gospel in the industrial and semi-secularized areas of Scotland, and to rebuild the ruined abbey of St. Columba on the island of Iona. In this way the life of the community and its building activities prepare the members for life in the modern secular, industrial situation. An outstanding feature of the Iona experiment has been its contribution to the ecumenical movement.

III. THE CULT

We turn now to a consideration of pacifism in relation to the 'cult', in particular those cults which have proliferated in Britain over the past three-quarters of a century.

Since the cultural context within which these groups appear is Judaeo-Christian it is necessary to point out that the major monotheistic religions, like Judaeo-Christianity and Islam, include an expression of the social totality. The sense of the objectivity of the divine which they celebrate is logically related to a fundamental group principle as well as to the dependence of all creation upon God. This means that monotheism has been rarely hospitable towards the more extreme forms of individualism, particularly as exemplified by the solitary mystic.

Christianity and individualism are compatible only in the denominational type of religion where individualism is sharply inhibited by group solidarity, even though the group concerned is not coextensive with the social totality. While it is true that the denomination may in one form or other diminish the objective reality of God to an abstraction of the individual reason or to an emotional sense of individual salvation, it never reduces the area of the divine simply to the self-exploration of the gifted individual. However, it is precisely this process of reduction which typifies the cult. The result is an emphasis on self-sufficiency which is logically associated with a hierarchy of spiritual conditions. Where religion is concerned with self-cultivation there can be no equality by virtue of God's unconditional grace.

Clearly many aspects of the modern situation present opportunities for a radically individualistic type of religion. Because the Church has striven to incarnate the divine through history and within society it is seen as compromised by innumerable social evils. Mysticism enables the individual to opt out of such evils. At the same time the mystic is not a member of a group suffering from oppression and is therefore not primarily interested in passing a sectarian judgement on society. He is more likely to be a creative personality, perhaps separated from forces of social integration, without suffering from class domination. It may be that he is subject to psychosomatic illness, valetudinarianism and various kinds of tension and psychic incapacity. In such a situation the cult offers peace, release and steady progress stage by stage towards spiritual maturity.

The fundamental criterion of the cult is therefore individualism. It is neither a worshipping community, like Church, order and denomination, nor is it the closely-knit separated band of the elect. The highest level of interpersonal action is a 'parallelism of spontaneities', more particularly of the kind involved in the common pursuit of psychological techniques or therapeutic discussion. The most characteristic form of face-to-face relationship is that of teacher (or *guru*) towards initiate, although in many cases communication is restricted to correspondence and the circulation of books. Thus a high degree of centralized organization may be associated with a very low degree of personal contact. The content of correspondence is more likely to be psychological advice than devotional reading.

However, individualism has many manifestations and the cult normally bifurcates in two broad directions. These need to be analysed because they are relevant to the way in which members of this type of group react to war. The first kind of cult lacks the mystical strain just discussed and is largely concerned with enabling the individual to fulfil the norms of his particular environment, by making him more self-assured, by increasing his intellectual power and by equipping him with manipulative techniques. It therefore meets the condition of those people who do not know how to maximize their opportunities.

The range of such groups will clearly vary from Pelmanism at one extreme, which is highly specific and almost totally manipulative, to scientology, which is not merely manipulative but also provides an apparatus of confession and interrogation derived from modern psychology, police methods, and the practice of the Catholic Church.[9] Also within this range lie those organizations, of which Christian Science is the best known, which offer release from bodily ills through a correct metaphysical and psychological approach. Quite plainly whether the main emphasis is on social manipulation or on psychological and bodily health, no norms will be generated which set the member in conflict with society. Thus when confronted by the challenge of war the member will react simply in conformity with social demands. His religion or psychological system will now assist him to adjust in his new role as soldier.

However, the second kind of cult is generally concerned with a programme of self-mastery and cultivation in terms of a condition of personal grace which may differ radically from the ideal of the wider society. While the manipulative type just discussed may be expected to have more appeal for the commercial middle class, the type based on mastery in terms of a condition of personal grace may rather appeal to professionals and academics. Because this latter type involves the possibility of a wide divergence from social norms it requires more extended discussion before its relation to pacifism can be elucidated.

Many mystical techniques are concerned with relaxation and with the negation of unruly sub-selves by the true self. In this connection relaxation is the basis of an attempt to achieve inner silence and attentive passivity through which the true self may be known. When the true self is known then the exterior compliances of everyday life are replaced by an inward

[9] The development of scientology is interesting because it illustrates how cults can broaden out the area of their concerns until they approximate to sects. There is now a tendency to regard those who have been processed by the methods of scientology as supermen who will take over the world.

spontaneity springing from genuine self-consciousness. It is from this emphasis on spontaneity that ambivalence towards violence and passivity derives. Absolute spontaneity logically involves the most extreme variations of consciousness between a sense of tranquillity in which the self is immersed in passive harmoniousness, and complete destructiveness as a symbol of irrational active power. Such an extreme variation may be regarded as analogous to the polarities noted in sectarianism.

Naturally, most forms of gnosis are concerned to reject the violent alternative. According to Ouspensky, violence must be replaced by understanding, which means placing oneself in the position of the other person. To be violent means a loss of one's temper: in real personal terms it achieves nothing. Nicoll expresses the situation as follows: 'A man cannot "do" unless he overcomes violence . . . "Doing" by means of violence is not "doing". All history, which is a history of crime, shows how violence cannot "do" in the work [i.e. the religious] sense. War follows war'.[10] Nicoll goes on to say that each personality is rooted in violence. In the course of making this point he resorts to an esoteric exegesis of the Bible entirely characteristic of the gnostic approach. One must know, not merely understand the Bible. In the gospels the Kingdom of God is described as suffering violence: this means that one must be violent against one's unruly selves in order to overcome the root of one's own violence. Only in this way is it possible to enter into the Kingdom of God, which is the circle of those attaining Conscious Humanity.

This type of religion often displays a sensitivity to individual psychology which is at least as profound as the formulations of Freud and his followers. But the cult lacks any sense of the problems lying at the centre of religious and political life. Harmony and the elimination of war is achieved simply by psychic identification at the appropriate level of Being. It follows that there is no external tragedy, only interior crucifixion. As in Christian Science, no God died at a particular historical time and place for the salvation of all men. The whole problem of the tragic character of social action and the need for unconditional grace which follows from human implication in

[10] H. M. D. Nicoll: *Pyschological Commentaries on Gurdieff and Ouspensky* (London, 1949), Vol. III, p. 1,213.

that tragedy is ignored. Interior crucifixion is in itself sufficient for inward and for outward peace.

The relation between this type of mystical religion and the questions raised by war may be illustrated from a pamphlet published by J. H. Cousins in 1914, entitled: *War: a Theosophical View*.[11] According to the viewpoint expressed here, there can be no inherent social problem and therefore no inherent social tragedy. Crucifixion is not a fundamental outrage, as it were an explosion at the heart of the moral universe which initially destroys any faith in an overall moral governance. Rather is it capable of being subsumed within moral categories. However, in order for this to be achieved the spiritual has to be divorced from the material and the particularity of the personal and of events within history has to be denied.

Thus for Cousins the seeming contradictions of experience are ultimately complementary. Indeed, sufferings such as are endured in wartime may be ennobling in that they assist in delivering the soul from personal passion and material things. Nations, like individuals, accumulate good or evil Karma, and war is simply an overt expression of this silent moral accumulation. In any case, life supremely *is*. It has no beginning and therefore cannot end, not having been given it cannot be taken away. No radical contradictions can exist, since individuals, nations and the universe itself lie within the same cosmic unity.

CONCLUDING NOTE

It may be useful to compare the terminological usage employed here with that of B. R. Wilson in his important article: 'An Analysis of Sect Development'.[12] Wilson's article provides a widely accepted formulation and since the multiplication of private vocabularies is not in itself desirable some reasons ought to be given for preferring alternative formulations. Of course,

[11] J. H. Cousins: *War: a Theosophical View* (London, 1914).

[12] B. R. Wilson: 'An Analysis of Sect Development' (*The American Sociological Review*, Vol. XXIV, No. 1, January 1959).

typological schema are not necessarily exclusive: they are more or less useful according to one's analytic purposes. Moreover, a comparison between typologies is often in itself a fruitful source of hypotheses.

The two typologies with which we are concerned represent different varieties of conceptual construction. The process of categorization may proceed according to the methods used by Weber or those used by Durkheim. The Weberian 'ideal type' of category selects a certain criterion or criteria as of fundamental importance and then works out the logical implications. It may be that the resulting formulation has no exact empirical counterpart: the usefulness of the construct lies in comparing empirical variations with logical implications. The 'ideal type' is thus a kind of sociological geometry.

Alternatively, one may adopt a more overtly empiricist approach and build up a construct on a basis of clusters of characteristics that appear to be related to each other. This method of formulating from a cluster of empirical characteristics involves a problem of selection followed by a process of abstraction which is not in fact so very different from the Weberian approach, but there is a greater emphasis on the empirical as compared with the logical mode of analysis. The danger of the empirical approach lies in a tendency to select criteria of marginal importance while the danger of the logical approach lies in a process of abstraction which is not sufficiently controlled by empirical material.

Wilson distinguishes four sub-types of sect: the Adventist, the Introversionist, the Conversionist and the Gnostic. The use of the word 'sect' in the foregoing material closely resembles the Adventist and the Introversionist categories as delineated by Wilson. The Adventist category roughly corresponds to the Active sect and the Introversionist category to the Passive sect. However, it is clear that there is some degree of overlap, in that, for example, some Passive sects are Adventist in ideology. This is, in itself, interesting, since the present analysis seems to indicate that where Passive sects are also Adventist they are proto-revolutionary in character, while a sect which is both Passive and Introversionist is post-revolutionary. If one wished to defend the emphasis on Active and Passive as compared with Adventist and Introversionist this could best be done in terms of a preference for criteria based on response rather than doctrine. At the same time it seems clear that criteria based on response and criteria based on doctrine are equally necessary, partly because it is important to observe where they parallel and where they cut across one another.

What Wilson has to say about the Adventist and Introversionist varieties of sect in some way reinforces the practice of employing the word sect solely with respect to these two types. He argues that they have a common aetiology rooted in an experience of prolonged frustration, which they do not share with the Conversionist and the Gnostic sects, and he notes that there is some evidence of an organic connection between them. Moreover, Wilson points out that Adventist and Introversionist sects are less liable to become denominations than other types of sect, which is consonant with the view expressed in the Appendix of this study that religious sects within my own restricted use of the word tend to remain sects or to die rather than to denominationalize.

The Conversionist sect as delineated by Wilson closely corresponds to what I have designated the denomination. It is therefore not surprising that he envisages the Conversionist sect as being much more likely to grow into a denomination than Adventist and Introversionist sects. He sets out the characteristic which when found in a Conversionist sect may lead one to anticipate denominationalization, and these in sum resemble the sort of organization which I regard as being a denomination *ab initio*. Such characteristics include crucial distinguishing marks like a democratic ethos, a separated ministry and a low degree of insulation from the world.[13] Indeed Wilson points out that this variety of 'sect' may even *begin* its life in a non-sectarian spirit. In other words his analysis is consonant with the contention set forth in Appendix I that some denominations are such from the outset. Thus the apparent differences of approach are in fact largely semantic.

The sub-type which Wilson labels the Gnostic sect closely corresponds to my usage of the word 'cult'. However, it seems

[13] His analysis in full is as follows. A sect becomes a denomination when it (1) has a democratic ethos, (2) treats subjective experience as a criterion, (3) reaccepts members on the expression of remorse, (4) lacks clarity as to its boundaries, (5) inherits a preaching order, (6) is ineffectually separated from the world, (7) is revivalistic.

to me that sect is an inappropriate word for groups which lack the basic fellowship principles of Christianity and in many forms are entirely assimilated to secular goals. The word sect used in a Christian context ought to indicate both a basic fellowship principle and the degree of radical rejection of society which its etymology implies.

CHAPTER TEN

PACIFISM, PASSIVITY AND THE PACIFIC DOCTRINE

ONE of the major tasks facing the sociologist who studies religion is the categorization of the varieties of religious response to the situations in which men find themselves. Such a task is not simply a matter of compiling a 'list' but includes the analysis of various possible combinations between different responses, the arrangement of responses in coherent affiliations, and the charting of typical sequences from one response to another. It is also necessary to assess which combinations, patterns and sequences have played a crucial role in history.

The present study has attempted to provide a small contribution to this immense intellectual enterprise by focusing attention on the particular response of withdrawal and by trying to analyse its relation to associated phenomena. This has involved a categorization of the types of withdrawal and quasi-withdrawal, an examination of the manner in which withdrawal is related to the major patterns of religious attitudes (as illustrated in the world religions), and an indication of the types of conditions in which withdrawal is a possible and a likely response. It remains now to bring together certain considerations which have been important throughout the study in summary form. This is perhaps best done by taking in turn the three basic kinds of doctrine: pacifism, passivity and pacificism.

I. PACIFISM

The pacifist sect arises in a context similar to that of the monastic order. They are stems from a common religious root and this root is some form or other of world rejection. Unless some degree of world rejection exists neither pacifism nor monasticism are logical possibilities.

Rejections of the world as Max Weber has shown in a classic essay, are of many kinds. According to which kind the character and extent of pacifism and monasticism will vary. For example, if the world is conceived in the dualist fashion as evil, or in the fashion of classical Buddhism as illusory, then pacifism and monasticism will be dominant themes in the complex of religious attitudes. If on the other hand the impulse to reject is subordinate to the belief that the material world is, in principle, the creation of a just God then pacifism and monasticism will tend to be less pervasive. A dialectic will be set up between the world as it is and the world as it ought to be, which enables the withdrawal involved in pacifism to be associated with a revolutionary assault on the *status quo*. Thus not only are pacifism and monasticism less dominant in Christianity than in dualism or Buddhism but pacifism is also related to revolution.

The two major religions which do not embody a rejection of the world are Confucianism and Islam. Neither Confucianism nor Islam entertains pacifist or monastic tendencies, except in so far as cultural contact has promoted serious divergences from their basic attitudes. Within Islam for example both Sufism and some forms of the Shi'ite 'heresy' represent important deviations from the central tendencies of the religion and they are thus able to entertain the possibility of pacifist developments. But, questions of cultural contact apart, it is important to note that certain differences exist between Confucianism and Islam which have significance with relation to war and to violence. In the former the world and society comprise an immanent harmony, while in the latter both nature and the human condition are given arbitrarily by the fiat of a transcendent Deity. It is this transcendent and active character of the Islamic Deity which gives the religion a military activism which is absent from Confucianism. The will of Allah may be imposed by the faithful through recourse to a Holy War. Such a Holy War needs to be further distinguished from the Christian Armageddon in that it is not conceived as a means of establishing a revolutionary realm of ideal justice. Its aims are relatively mundane. Thus while Islam accepts the Holy War it does not validate revolution. Revolution and withdrawal are equally absent from Islamic cultures.

So far consideration has been given to the existence and

extent of world rejection, or lack of such rejection, as this links up with the existence or non-existence of pacifism. It is also relevant to consider how this factor of world rejection affects the ways in which it is possible for a religion to develop. Broadly there are four ways in which religions may develop according to the degree of world rejection which they embody. Where rejection is total, as in Jainism or dualism, the pure religion cannot become the continuing faith of a majority within a given society. The only way in which it can secure a degree of acceptance which is at all widespread is by a division into two classes of adepts and probationers. These classes are analogous to the two- and three-fold classes in Christian sectarianism and the distinction between open and closed orders in Christian monasticism. Where, however, the rejection is severe but not total, as in Hinayana Buddhism it is possible for the religion to develop a second series of motifs capable of acceptance by the majority, leaving the original doctrine as the pure possession of an enlightened few. In religions where rejection is subordinate to a fundamental acceptance the original deposit of faith or Kerygma is susceptible to organic and continuous development. As this development proceeds the elements of rejection tend to become the special preserve of minorities, either sectarian or monastic. Finally where there is no rejection a religion develops by simple extensions, extrapolations and legalistic elaborations.

In other words, to the degree that the world is absolutely rejected a religion inevitably remains the belief of a minority while to the degree that the world is accepted religions have varying modes of adapting to the majority. To say that world rejection is the religious option of a minority is to say the same *a fortiori* for pacifism and monasticism. Pacifism is either the faith of a minority religion or the faith of a minority within a majority religion. It cannot be a majority faith because religion is not only an adjustment to the human condition but an expression of the political unit. There are certain limiting conditions pertaining to the political unit with respect to the use of force which make the attitudes of the pacifist sect or the monastic order politically impossible.

There are, however, certain conditions under which pacifist beliefs might temporarily become a majority faith within a society. This is where the group concerned forms a complete society in terms of awareness of membership but lacks political expression. Should a group come to possess such an awareness without any means of achieving political expression it may take the path of pacifist withdrawal. If it does so then there may also be a correlative tendency to adopt or emphasize a faith which differentiates it from the wider oppressive whole. For example the adoption of dualism in Bosnia, Bulgaria and Languedoc in the Middle Ages seems to have been partly related to the need for such differentiation.

It is also true that certain non-violent movements have attracted widespread support during the present century, but none of them have occurred where the groups concerned were integrated into a political State. Indeed, non-violent tactics were adopted precisely because such integration was denied. In the United States the emphasis on peaceful methods by coloured people (excluding the Black Muslims) symbolizes a wish to achieve their ends through means consonant with the wider system of values. In South Africa there is in addition a recognition of superior force. Non-violence in India largely constituted a tactic against British rule and did not survive independence in any significant way. Of course in each of these cases the religious background predisposed the movements concerned to the pacific alternative.

II. PASSIVITY

This type of withdrawal is sometimes associated with mysticism or aestheticism and has been given little emphasis in the foregoing discussions. The tendency to passivity derives from the radical individualism characteristic of mystic and aesthete.

So far as mysticism is concerned Troeltsch has emphasized the variety of expression it may achieve, from an asceticism which crushes all that is finite to a libertinism which treats everything as indifferent. Nevertheless there remains a general and persistent strain towards a minimization of fellowship, a hostility to institutions and an ahistorical outlook. The mystic seeks a spiritual freedom, either in its ascetic or libertarian form, which he regards as superior to the relative and contingent claims of social life. This pilgrimage towards the absolute easily replaces specific communal norms by a pure descriptive psychology. Clearly, a devaluation of the temporal and social can include passive indifference towards all the things for which men are normally willing to fight.

Aestheticism resembles mysticism in its devaluation of conventional norms and single-minded absorbtion. At the same time it is less concerned with the unheard music and the word which cannot be spoken than with music and words demanding expression. However, the emphasis on the immediacy of experience may prove as ahistorical as the mystic pursuit of the absolute. The creative process makes a claim upon the artist which transcends or even obliterates all particular loyalties. It is not his vocation to propagate a cause or to respond to calls demanding the expenditure of his energies in defence of society. In any case he may view destruction as diametrically opposed to creation. Admittedly only certain aesthetes will take up such a position, but it is one form which the sense of artistic vocation may take.

III. PACIFICISM

The individualism of mystic and aesthete is quite different in kind from the individualism of the western tradition as exemplified in liberal Protestantism and *bourgeois* idealism. It is this tradition which forms the basis of the pacific doctrine. Withdrawal is only involved here insofar as the real world of social processes is partly rejected in favour of a rationalistic and moral utopianism. The right reason and right feeling of the individual is envisaged as the main basis of social progress.

Liberalism is rooted in two major assumptions. The first is that truth and goodness only require correct exposition in order to be accepted. Thus the primary initiative is assigned to ideas and the central problem located in knowledge and education. The second assumption is that the interests of individuals, classes and nations are fundamentally complementary.

These assumptions have certain consequences. Should conflict persist in occurring in spite of the natural harmony of interests then it is necessary to locate the trouble in a cabalistic conspiracy. Two lines of action are then required. The harmony must be realized through the rationally based machinery of international law, and the cabalistic tendencies of the few must be countered by the government of the majority. Given that interests, rightly understood, are complementary, and that the majority are susceptible to such right understanding through political propaganda and the sermon, it follows that enlightened and democratic government is the prerequisite of peace. The only necessary war is one which ensures democratic government and the maintenance of international law.

Clearly such an analysis ignores the fact that interests are sometimes complementary and sometimes not, and may therefore obstruct as well as reinforce the peaceable dictates of abstract rationality. Moreover where interests are obstructive Pacific ideas cannot play the kind of decisive role which renders violence unnecessary. Ideas and sermons cannot eliminate basic conflicts though they may ameliorate them.

The defects of the pacific doctrine lie in the position and interests of the *bourgeoisie* at a particular stage in capitalist development. Peace enables trade to flourish and inhibits the victims of injustice from asserting their rights by violence. Because capital is international it dissolves particularistic ties and ignores the forces of social cohesion, thereby blinding its ideologues to the power of nationalism and religion as non-rational causes for which men are prepared to fight. The *bourgeois* is convinced by his peaceable self-portrait because his power is implicit and impersonal, whereas the power of the aristocracy had been overt and personal. Hence the myth of innocence. *Bourgeois* nations, like the United States and Britain, encouraged as they have been by the advantages of geographical isolation, tend to regard their foreign policies as exemplifying a special purity of motive and peaceability of intent.

Moreover, the concept of the complementary character of interests is based on an idealistic image of a market in which the participants are equals, be they classes or nations. But although those who benefited in the market, such as Britain and France in the mid-nineteenth century, might delude themselves as to its character, those who suffered from inequalities and disadvantages were less easily misled. A late-comer to industrialization and colonialization like Germany quickly recognized its interests as far from identical with those of its predecessors.

Thus while Britain, and to some extent France, were susceptible to the pacific doctrine, Germany was not. Indeed, as even the older nations felt the ill-effects as well as the advantages of free competition they too were less certain of the identity of interests.

Not that the tradition of *bourgeois* peaceability died out. The distaste for violence remained, but as traders recognized tha their rational interests pointed less clearly in the direction o, inevitable harmony, the propagators of peace tended to be found more frequently amongst the intelligentsia than the commercial classes. The intelligentsia, which was in any case partly motivated by the historic tension between money and intellect, eventually found it easy to adopt the Marxist analysis whereby war was the outcome solely of conflicting interests in the imperialistic phase of capitalism. Marxist intellectuals now cast the capitalist in the same role as *bourgeois* ideologues had cast the aristocracy. Their arguments implied that one need only eliminate the institutions of capitalism and peace would follow inevitably. On this analysis the only necessary war was the war to destroy capitalism or to assist in its destruction. All other wars, supposedly in the defence of democracy or international law were disguises for *bourgeois* interests. Thus the intelligentsia engaged in an analysis of war almost as far removed from reality as that of the nineteenth century Liberal.

This completes a summary of the major positions in relation to war which have been distinguished in the course of this study. Clearly, the previous pages are simply a prolegomena to the study of pacifism in which any number of subjects and issues have had to be set on one side. In particular, the detailed consideration of pacifist movements between the wars still remains to be done. Similarly movements in Eastern cultures require prolonged analysis. The argument as presented so far remains the sketch of a hypothesis for which possible illustrations have been provided in the margin rather than a series of propositions set up for systematic refutation and falsification in the approved Popperian manner. Nevertheless certain suggestions have been made and possible connections indicated and it is hoped that these may provide a starting-point for the careful and empirical study of the conditions and ways in which men and groups have aspired to peace.

APPENDIX

THE DENOMINATION

(Originally printed in *The British Journal of Sociology* Vol. XIII, No. 1, March 1962.)

THE discussion of the sociology of religion in those cultures rooted in the presuppositions of Christianity has been dominated by the typology of Church and sect proposed by Troeltsch. Comparatively little attention, however, has been given to cult, order and denomination. An attempt is here made to indicate how such neglect might be remedied with regard to the denomination, setting out certain claims it may have to be considered an independent sociological type. The analysis is inevitably an idealized abstraction and specifically emphasizes Arminian elements at the expense of Calvinist ones. Throughout the discussion the denomination is analysed by frequent comparison with Church and sect.[1] The concept of Church implied is broadly that of Troeltsch, but it is perhaps important to note that there is an implied reformulation of the concept of sect based on the notion of polarization at extremes.

Ever since Richard Niebuhr published *The Social Sources of Denominationalism* in 1929 there has been a tendency to regard the denomination as an advanced stage in the development of the sect.[2] Typically the sect is regarded as beginning its career with a group of the despised and rejected who in turn despise and reject 'the world'. With the arrival of the second generation, however, and in the absence of efficient built-in mechanisms designed to prevent it, there appears a tendency to compromise. On the one hand the sharpness of the motives activating the original founders has been dulled, while on the other hand the

---

[1] *See* J. Wach: *Types of Religious Experience* (London, 1951). Chapter 9 is entitled 'Church, Denomination, Sect'.

[2] H. R. Niebuhr: *The Social Sources of Denominationalism* (New York, 1929).

fruits of the economic spirit, so often associated with sectarian asceticism, have resulted in the laying-up of substantial treasures on earth as well as treasures in heaven. Some element of 'compromise' involving the relaxation of perfectionist rigour becomes increasingly attractive, especially to the more mobile members, and the sect, perhaps gaining in numerical quantity what it loses in terms of religiously defined quality, gravitates towards the status of a denomination.

Such an analysis both as regards the development of sects and as regards the genesis of denominations is not so much incorrect as atypical. It would apply, for instance, in a broad way, to such a religious body as the Society of Friends.[3] The Friends began in a chiliastic atmosphere with a stern rejection of the world and all its ways; with the course of time they came to distinguish themselves in business and in scientific pursuits and so eventually modified their position. But even as applied to the Society of Friends the conventional view of sectarian development is only partially accurate. Although Friends believed in a doctrine of the inner light which was peculiarly favourable to change, the process of becoming a denomination was slow and partial, partly on account of the complementary doctrine of unanimity.[4] The traditionalist element was always strong, while the contemporary pacifism of the large majority of Friends indicates that sectarian perfectionism has largely succeeded in maintaining itself in spite of the wealth and intellectual sophistication of some members. Moreover, such denominational tendencies as have appeared were in fact present in some degree from the beginning.

The particular insufficiencies of the conventional analysis with regard even to the Society of Friends indicate wherein lies it atypicality in general. They point towards the following complementary propositions: firstly that sects generally succeed in maintaining their sectarian character, and may even reinforce it, and secondly that denominations have normally possessed their denominational character from their very beginnings. With regard to the first proposition B. R. Wilson has

[3] H. S. Barbour: *The Early Quaker Outlook on the World and Society* (Unpublished Ph.D. Thesis, Yale). Obtainable Friends House, Euston Road.

[4] J. Sykes: *The Quakers* (London, 1960). Sykes's chapter on 'Quakers as Bourgeoisie' indicates that this period of wealth was in some ways a period of maximum withdrawal.

shown in his account of the Christadelphians that the advent of succeeding generations is by no means a crucial event in the life of a sect, and he has illustrated the way in which members of this body have largely maintained their rejection of 'the world'.[5] The Exclusive Brethren exemplify the reinforcement of sectarian attitudes, and only recently some half-dozen 'E.B.s' left the Universities of Oxford and Cambridge on grounds of principle. Differential social mobility, e.g. as between the fishermen of Peterhead and successful business men, makes little difference to their basic position. Such a process of maintenance depends partly on the efficiency of the built-in mechanisms of conservation and partly, perhaps, on the degree of inertia in society at large. It was with reference to the pullulating sectarianism of America in its era of dynamic and fluid expansion that the conventional analysis had its relevance. But in most 'normal' situations sects do not become denominations: they remain sects or they die.

With regard to the second proposition, the term 'denomination' refers in common parlance to the Methodists, the Congregationalists and the General Baptists. Common parlance should be respected. The Presbyterian Church of England and the Unitarians may be left on one side in the discussion which follows for sociological and historical reasons respectively. Perhaps the most striking aspect of the early history of these three representative denominations is a lack of the sectarian spirit: this is largely true even of the General Baptists. Dr. Horton Davies in his *The English Free Churches* rightly remarks that these bodies have not merely outgrown sectarianism but probably never experienced it.[6] Again, the article on Congregationalism in 'Hastings' points out that whereas the continental Anabaptists were variously characterized in their different branches by chiliastic notions, adult baptism, pacifism, and the denial of the right of Christians to be magistrates, all of which point in the sectarian direction, the English Congregationalists 'followed them in none of these things'. Similarly the English Baptists, although rejecting infant baptism, sharply differentiated themselves from continental Anabaptism. Certainly there existed a chiliastic fringe and a pacifist fringe during the Civil

[5] B. R. Wilson: *Sects and Society* (London, 1961).

[6] Horton Davies: *The English Free Churches* (London, 1952), p. 197.

War, and some Baptists associated themselves with the Fifth Monarchy Movement,[7] but this was a temporary digression, and a standard history of the Baptists comments that the majority of them 'held aloof'.[8] It may also be significant that while some Baptists were associated with the political democracy of the Levellers, none were associated with the Communism of the Diggers. The non-sectarian origins of Methodism are even clearer. The primary leadership of the movement was, of course, middle class, and the whole ethos of Methodism reflected that fact. Admittedly the ethical discipline of the early Methodist Societies within the English Church had a sectarian quality: but then so also has that of the Third Order of St. Dominic. The history of Methodism together with that of the Congregationalists and to some extent the Baptists begins in a 'Spiritual Brotherhood', or Holy Club' which in turn becomes *Ecclesiola in Ecclesia*, and finally a denomination, but at no point approximates to a sect.[9]

In thus criticizing the traditional categorization of religious groups one is, of course, assuming a fresh alignment of those categories. In arguing that Methodism was never really a sect one has somewhat pared back the meaning of that term. What follows is therefore an attempt to justify such a restriction of the characteristics which have hitherto been regarded as 'sectarian' in the course of asserting the right of the term 'denomination' to constitute a sociological type *sui generis*. Such a realignment as is now suggested has at least the advantage of bringing the theoretical meaning of the terms 'denomination' and 'sect closer to everyday usage (and so, perhaps, nearer to everyday

[7] See L. Fargo Brown: *The Political Activities of Baptists and Fifth Monarchy Men*, (Washington, 1912)

[8] A. C. Underwood: *A History of the English Baptists* (London, 1947), p. 84.

[9] See J. Wach: *The Sociology of Religion* (London, 1944), Chapter 5, Section II.

A good case can be made for regarding the denomination as the Protestant equivalent of the order. It may be viewed as a large organization of Protestant tertiaries, contrasting with the Catholic orders, which are small organizations of elites.

The Catholic orders canalize tensions along narrow channels, with a resulting high level of intensity. This gives them a likeness to sects, which carry similar tensions in an uncanalized, disintegrative form. Since the denominations funnel tensions through broad channels the level of intensity is relatively low, except in periods of social 'flood'. In such periods Catholic countries suffer sectarian inundations, whereas elsewhere the presence of denominational channels enables the bulk of the flow to be contained and directed.

social reality) as well as relating it more closely to the normative usages of theology.

One more preliminary word needs to be said with reference to the term 'cult', which is often used as a fourth typological category. It might be thought that any attempt to mark off the meaning of 'denomination' would do so in relation to 'cult' as well as to 'Church' and 'sect'. But quite apart from the difficulty of handling the consequent complications a comparison with 'cult' is omitted because, while cults undoubtedly exist within Christian cultures, they do not arise out of the initial sociological impulses of Christianity to the same degree as Church and sect. The latter can be discussed within Christian categories, but any attempt to define the meaning of cult only points to its marginally Christian character. The term cult requires a separate discussion since its peculiar characteristics do not merely separate it from other forms of Christianity but from Christianity as such. Church, denomination and sect embody tensions and goals directly implicit in Christianity but the cult is Christian only marginally, partially and incidentally. For example, the cult does not embody the tension with the 'the world' underlying the symbol of 'judgement', and does not point towards the 'Reign of God'.

Indeed, the rise of the cult is concomitant with the rise of forces making for dechristianization: the interdependent phenomena of impersonality, diminished fellowship and 'egocentricity' which characterize it are indicative of its sub-Christian status. Even the syncretistic aspect of the cult is not so much indicative of fresh religious impulses and of a desire to combine Christian insights with those of other religions as of a willingness to use the psychological techniques associated with Christianity and Buddhism for purely 'egocentric' purposes. Naturally the cult appeals to those sections of society, notably comfortable suburbia, whose way of life makes an ideology of mundane 'adjustment' more immediately meaningful than the specific goals and tensions of Christianity.[10]

[10] The mystical groups discussed by Troeltsch may also be regarded as cults, in that they too lack the fellowship principle of Christianity. Christian fellowship is attenuated both when a group concentrates almost exclusively on mundane adjustment (the horizontal reference, and also when a group is so *unconcerned* with such adjustment as to mystically devalue the historical, the temporal and the contingent (the vertical reference). Specifically Christian fellowship, of whatever kind, arises from the two frames of reference being held in tension.

In attempting to circumscribe the meaning of the term denomination not every feature mentioned will be unique. Some features will mark it off from the sect; other features will mark if off from the Church. It is the character of the combination which will be unique. Admittedly, any particular group which one might care to name would present a unique combination of churchly and sectarian characteristics, but in view of the fact that this particular combination is historically so important and in view of the fact that contained within it are unique *differentiae* of the first degree, it seems reasonable to argue that it constitutes a further class apart both from Church and from sect. The important point is that such a definition of the denomination as is now proposed should prove itself analytically useful. It seems to me that it does so because it avoids certain confusions as to the nature of the sect which arise from having only two ideal classifications, both of which tend to be overwise. That we should have allowed ourselves to analyse in these dichotomous terms seems to me to indicate the extent to which vulgar Marxism has penetrated the shape and style of our thinking. It will be advantageous if we begin the task of definition by a series of exploratory comments before attempting to reduce the matter to a precise formula.

In the first place and perhaps pre-eminently the denomination rejects the whole concept of *Extra Ecclesiam non salus* as defined in institutional terms. Typically the sect regards the whole of mankind outside its boundaries as a *massa damnata*. Within its fold are the sheep, while outside are the goats. The Church has a very similar attitude, except that the fold is a very large one, while the Shepherd employs a different method of recognition, based on an appropriation of the objective grace available in the sacraments. As Monsignor Knox wrote, perhaps with more clarity than charity: 'All the identification discs in heaven are marked R.C.' By contrast the denomination does not regard its own confessional borders as co-extensive with the boundaries of a New Israel, nor does it view itself as being in the possession of unique truth or unique authority. The Jehovah's Witnesses claim that they alone have the key; the Roman Catholics claim that they alone have the keys. The denomination merely claims that while there are doubtless many keys to many mansions it is at least in possession of one of them, and that anyone who thinks he has the sole means to open the heavenly door is plainly mistaken. The outlook of the denomination as an institution is therefore relatively tolerant, although its moral outlook may well acquire a censorious character, as Parnell found to his lasting cost.

To say so much is not to say that the denomination has no doctrinal standards, but it conceives the essence of the Church as being a unity of experience rather than a unity of organization. It is therefore possible to speak of inter-denominationalism, but hardly possible to speak of inter-sectarianism, or inter-ecclesiasticism. The idea of the Christadelphians, the Witnesses and the Exclusive Brethren engaging in full-co-operation pleases the imagination but hardly arouses expectation of fulfilment. This unity of experience to which the denomination appeals affects the form of its historical self-interpretation. Whereas the sect lacks such interpretation almost entirely and whereas the Church envisages an institutional succession extending through the episcopate back to the Apostle Peter, the denomination conceives of a unity of experience which largely ignores confessional frontiers. *Ubi Christus, ibi Ecclesia.* It is able to take this ground because while in a general way it accepts the Bible as authoritative, and while in non-scientific periods it has sometimes interpreted that authority mechanically and dogmatically, it holds to the idea of a central core of religious truth. Such a conception is as explicit in Oliver Cromwell as it is in Wesley. If you like, there is a citadel, and there are peripheral outworks which may be expended. Such a conception makes the denomination much more responsive to the climate of contemporary opinion than the sect, and, on the whole, more so than the Church. The question of divorce provides but one example.

Since this question of inter-denominationalism is of such importance one may perhaps be permitted on illustration. It is taken from Wesley's Journal for December 1st, 1767, which contains the following passage:

> Being alone in the coach, I was considering several points of importance: and thus much appeared as clear as the day: That a man may be saved who cannot express himself properly concerning imputed righteousness. Therefore to do this is not necessary salvation.

That a man may be saved who has not clear conceptions of it: (yea, that never heard the phrase). Therefore clear conceptions of it are not necessary to salvation; yea it is not necessary to salvation to use the phrase at all.

That a pious Churchman who has not clear conceptions even of justification by faith, may be saved; therefore clear conceptions even of this are not necessary to salvation.

That a Mystic who denies justification by faith (Mr. Law for instance), may be saved. But if so what becomes of 'Articulus stantis vel cadentis ecclesiae?' If so, is it not high time for us 'Projicere ampullas et sesquipedalia verba?' and to return to the plain word, 'He that feareth God and worketh righteousness, is accepted with him.'[11]

It was in these words that Lord Acton found implicit Methodism's eventual separation from the Church of England. Certainly it is true that such sentiments as these are not consonant with an ecclesiastical obedience. It is also true that a Catholicity of this kind is entirely distinct from the sectarian ethos.

In the sphere of organization the denomination tends to be pragmatic. Of course it is not completely pragmatic any more than it is completely free from special institutional claims. Moreover, to say that the tendency is pragmatic is not to say that the denomination is bereft of principles. The whole logic of the negative position it holds on the question of religious authority demands that its organization should be based on democratic principles. But there are no *particular* forms of organization which are regarded as being in the unique possession of a divine imprimatur. When Wesley ordained Coke and when he utilized and commissioned the laity he did so because he was, as Father Piette has rightly commented, a pragmatist before the term pragmatism was actually invented.[12] In this connection one must, of course, make proper allowance for the natural Protestant tendency to refer to the Bible as a source of authoritative organizational models, so that a particular form of Church government, whether it be by elders or deacons, whether it be independent, synodal or connectional will often be justified on the basis of biblical authority, more especially

[11] *Cambridge Modern History* (London, 1909), Vol. VI, pp. 85–6.

[12] M. Piette: *La Reaction Wesleyenne* (Brussels, 1927), p. 595. Quoted in E. R. Taylor: *Methodism and Politics, 1791–1851* (Cambridge, 1935), p. 33.

so in the seventeenth century. If we make this due allowance for the authoritative position of the Bible it becomes clear that pragmatism is no more than an implicit tendency, yet it remains true that no one form of organization is held to be an indispensable characteristic of any body claiming to be fully and truly Christian.

The underlying *principle* of organization, as distinct from particular forms is, of course, the priesthood of all believers. Authority is conceived as resting collectively in the whole religious body not in a separate order which is divinely commissioned to define religious truth. This collective authority may have an institutional focus, a conference or an assembly, but the basis remains representative of the Church as a whole.

So much differentiates the denomination from the Church, since in the Church the authority of the episcopal and priestly orders, or the authority of the Supreme Pontiff depends not on the collective voice of the Church but on a divinely instituted commission to teach. Such a position also differentiates the denomination from the sect. The sect often resembles the denomination in holding to the priesthood of all believers but when it does so the content of its interpretation is different. The sect may believe that because every man is a priest a separated ministry is superfluous or perverse. On the other hand, sectarian organization may be quasi-military. Either way it differs from the delegated democracy of the denomination. In fact this contradiction between utter lack of organization and military discipline illustrates the usual sectarian tendency (which we will have further occasion to note) to polarize at extremes. Whereas the denomination is characterized by moderation the sect is either Communist or anarchist, revolutionary or quietist, nudist or uniformed, ascetic or licentious, completely sacramental or non-sacramental, worshipping in a wild communal rant or, like the Seekers, in utter silence. Incidentally it is interesting to observe how these sectarian polarities appear in a muted and canalized form within the inclusive organization of the Church through the channels provided by the orders, for instance, the quasi-military rigidity of the Jesuits, the rejection of organization by the hermit, the elected silence of the Trappists.

In contrast to sectarian extremism in the sphere of organization the denomination may even appear to retain some of the
organizational forms and titles which belong to a Church, but
the content and understanding of these forms will be quite
different. The separated ministry is retained, but basically as
a matter of propriety and convenience. There may even be a
hierarchy of Bishops as in American Methodism, but these are
merely highly-placed administrators not the unique repositories
of a succession. There may be a ministry which alone has the
right to perform the sacraments, but, this is not because the
ministry possesses a character *'indelibilis'* which alone enables
it to do so, but because this is the particular function for which
the ministry has been set aside. It is an aspect of the division of
labour and in appropriate circumstances a layman may quite
legitimately celebrate. In such a position we observe the intrusion of utilitarian concepts into a realm which ecclesiastically
is dominated by non-rational sacred values.

As with the ministry so also with the sacraments themselves:
the forms may be retained but the content is different. Denominations often appear to have a very Catholic theory of
the sacraments, but the verbal similarities are misleading.
Doctrinal formulations may even refer to the 'real presence',
but this signifies the reality of the presence of God in the hearts
of the believers, not in the elements themselves. To the believer
this is a perfectly objective form of sacramental theory, but as
compared to the churchly theory, whether Roman, Orthodox,
Anglican or Lutheran, it is entirely subjective. This subjectivity
likewise exists in relation to the sacrament of infant baptism, in
which, if it is retained, the emphasis shifts from what is 'done'
for the child, to the dedication of the parents. Indeed such a
subjective approach affects the whole area of ritual practice: the
forms are everywhere instrumental rather than intrinsic. They
subserve religious values but they do not constitute part of
those values in their own right, except in so far as a certain sanctity attaches to them by association. What for the
Church of Rome is *Opus Dei* for denominational Protestants
is a form of words which happens to satisfy their religious
requirements.

But while Church and denomination differ from each other
in possessing respectively an objective and a subjective approach

to sacraments, the denomination is distinguished from the sect in that the sectarian tendency is to reject the sacramental idea completely. The fundamental idea of the sacrament, as it has developed in the Judaeo-Christian tradition, represents a fusion of the communal and brotherly values centred on the shared meal with the idea of sacrifice and with the idea of the holy: the sense of 'otherness', transcendence and sublimity which is religiously located in the Sanctuary. Now this fusion of humane and sacred values finds expression in a further idea: that the material world is potentially sacred and that this potentially sacred character is realized, symbolized and focused in the two elements central to human life, food and drink, and especially bread and wine. It is in connection with this relationship between the sacred and the material that the sectarian attitude is most clearly illustrated. The sect may regard all the material world as sacramental either on pantheistic or panentheistic grounds, or on the ground that God is about to restore all things to their original perfection, so rendering sacraments superfluous. Alternatively the sect may reject all commerce between the sacred and the material either because God is conceived as completely transcendent or because the material world is regarded (after the fashion of Gnostic dualism) as positively evil.

A further parallel illustration of radically different conceptions is found regarding marriage. To the Church marriage is an objective sacrament, to the denomination it is potentially sacramental, depending on the subjective attitudes of the participants, while to the sect it may either be regarded as an evil from the extreme ascetic viewpoint, as superfluous from the viewpoint of licence, or again as merely indifferent and contractual.

The denomination is most clearly distinguished from the sect and most nearly allied to the Church in the sphere of eschatology. From the point of view of developing a set of theological indices of sociological character eschatology is of prime importance. The sect having members who are largely alienated and rejected, frequently expects a divine reversal of its secular position or a total destruction of the corrupt material world in which members will be a select remnant miraculously transported to the New Jerusalem. As regards these eschatological events sectarians either wait passively, or actively prepare to engage in Armageddon when the trumpet shall sound. Meanwhile they refuse to consider any attempts to merely ameliorate present conditions and refuse to participate in wars for secular purposes. When the Divine Advent does not occur or when the holy war of Armageddon has failed in its object, the concept of the New Jerusalem is sometimes spiritualized and regarded as realized within the religious community, in which eventuality the idealism bound up inside the Adventist myth may realize itself in radical reforms on the secular plane. The Society of Friends is the most obvious example.

By contrast the denomination, which has a genuine stake in the present social order, retains the traditional eschatology of heaven and hell. This single fact places a sociological gulf between denomination and sect. With this criterion in mind it is quite clear that neither the Methodists, nor the Congregationalists nor the General Baptists (except momentarily and partially in one unique historical situation) were ever sectarian. In the modern situation even the traditional eschatology has largely given way to a form of universalism or to more subtle conceptions.

Another important, although neglected, theological index of sociological character, is found in the field of 'moral theory'. In this context 'moral theory' refers not to discussions about the nature of 'ought' and 'good' but to religious dynamics of faith and works. The meaning of 'works' is plain, but 'faith' is a term requiring some explanation. It does not connote assent to a series of credal propositions, as MacIver in his *Society* evidently supposes, but rather an attitude of mind.[13] The difference is that between '*fiducia*' (trust) and '*assensus*' (belief). Such an attitude refuses to 'justify' itself by attempting to assemble a formidable array of 'works' but, recognizing the ambiguity and corruptions of motive generally underlying such efforts, rests purely on the Divine Love and Compassion. Being thus free from anxiety and 'justified' in the sense that the publican was more 'justified' than the Pharisee, a man is thereby enabled to perform good acts as a *consequence* of love not in the course of an unnatural and impossible attempt to fulfil all the demands of the law. Such morality is free not con-

[13] R. M. MacIver: *Society* (London, 1955), p. 173.

strained: it flows from grace not the law. This approach may be regarded from the positive standpoint as a religious theory of the psychological dynamics of integration and of the good life.

In the Gospels themselves the relation between love and the law is presented in terms of high paradox. The law demands a righteousness which exceeds the righteousness of the Scribes and Pharisees yet grace and love extend to the worst of sinners. St. James develops the first arm of the paradox concerning the necessity of works, while St. Paul explores the meaning of justification by faith. Now it is characteristic of the Church either to scale this paradox down to manageable proportions, so that men are enjoined on the one hand to be reasonably decent and on the other hand offered forgiveness within limits and on conditions, or it attempts to mechanize the whole conception. The idea of the store of good works which the Church may dispense as coverage for the sins of her erring children, and the whole apparatus of confession and absolution, penances and indulgences, is part of the mechanization of the tension between love and the law. To further lower the tension the Church works out a series of compromises with the absolute demands of the moral law: such compromises and accommodations are necessitated by its inclusive sociological character. The result is the elaboration of the relative natural law, adapted to political necessities and practical possibilities.

The denomination, however, refuses to relax the tension between love and the law and proceeds to point up the relationship as conventionally conceived by the Church. It encourages perfection according to the law of Christ at least as an appropriate *aim* for the ordinary Christian and may sometimes allow love to overflow in 'enthusiasm'.[14] Nevertheless, it is sufficiently involved in the social nexus and its pressures to retain a balance between the two elements, so that while it is sometimes able to make a dynamic appeal to groups which might otherwise be revolutionarily 'inclined', it does not involve itself in the revolutionary and sectarian one-sidedness either of perfectionism or of licentious antinomianism.

---

[14] 'Enthusiasm' is sometimes regarded as indicating sectarianism. In fact 'enthusiasm' depends for its meaning on its sociological context, and cannot be used to indicate what that context is.

The sect, however, tends to take either one arm of the paradox or the other and to follow it through to a logical conclusion. Thus the sect may be absolutely perfectionist or entirely licentious: extremely ascetic or totally devoid of ethical notions. Whether it is one or the other and to what degree depends on its particular historical experience and on the other theological elements involved. A totally pantheistic sect will tend to be licentious, because the distinction between the holy God and nature has been blurred to vanishing-point, while the dualistic sect, which regards nature as contrary to God, will tend to be completely ascetic, even suicidal. Both the suicidal and the licentious tendencies arise from similar conditions of frustration, demoralization and sudden social change. A further reason why the denomination manages to avoid such extremes (which of course, have their secular analogues) is because it is fundamentally individualistic. Even if it presses perfectionist demands in some degree, the limit of their provenance tends to be the individual, or at most the family, and so revolutionary implications are avoided. In so far as the denomination conceives of social perfection it does so by beginning with the moralization of the individual will. This individualism is of such importance that it will be considered again in some concluding remarks.

The foregoing exploration of the meaning of the term 'denomination' can now be brought together in the form of a definition. The denomination does not claim that its institutional borders constitute the one ark of salvation. Its concept of unity is a unity of experience and its historical sense is likewise a unity of experience rather than an institutional succession. Its attitude to organization and to cultic forms tends to be pragmatic and instrumental, while its sacramental conceptions are subjective. This subjectivity is related to a fundamental individualism. In the field of eschatology its conceptions are traditional and in the field of moral theory its conception of the relation of faith to works is dynamic but balanced.

In coming to some concluding remarks it seems to me that one line of criticism might regard the incipiently pragmatic and utilitarian elements which we have noted in denominationalism as due to certain external influences related to secularization.

This may be partly true, but such elements also flow from the sociological character of the denomination, just as that character itself belongs to the type of society in which utilitarian ideas are immanent. Instrumental conceptions of organization and the denominational sociological type have historically reinforced one another, so that it is no accident that Britain and America, which have experienced the widest dissemination of denominationalism, have also nourished utilitarian and pragmatic attitudes respectively. One suspects that both phenomena arise in connection with an environment of cultural and economic individualism. That is to say, both are related to a type of society in which sacral and intrinsic values do not attach to communal and collective forms but only to the individual, so that these collective forms and arrangements are merely instrumental, and important only in so far as they subserve the individual.

It has been argued that this individualistic emphasis of the denomination is of first-rate importance. By individualism one does not necessarily mean an egocentric or anti-social attitude, though such may sometimes be involved, but a nominalistic rather than a realistic approach to the collective. One is here indicating individualism as a broad social tendency as well as a social philosophy possessed of both wider and narrower meanings. Similarly the collectivism, with which it is contrasted, is indicated as a social tendency as well as a social philosophy. On the one hand the individual is regarded as sacred and intrinsically valuable, and on the other hand intrinsic values are attached to the collective. Such a polarity between individualism and collectivism can be considered in relation to the polarity between conservation and change. The Church, the denomination, and the sect each stand in a specific relation to these twin polarities between individualism and collectivism and between conservation and change.

In connection with these relationships the denomination is individualistic while the Church is, on the whole, collectivist. The Church is, in principle, as at home in the unitary collective State as it was in the organicist State envisaged by Burke. The struggle in which certain Churches are engaged against contemporary Socialist States is basically on account of their totalitarianism in combination with atheism, not on account of their collectivism. The sect either drives the individualism of the denomination to the anarchist extreme or it drives the collectivism of the Church to the Communist extreme, although sectarian collectivism and ecclesiastical 'organicism' are, of course, phenomena radically different in kind. It pursues these extremes because it is sometimes reacting to great inequalities, sometimes to the brutal repression characteristic of collectivist régimes.

In relation to conservation and change the Church is naturally a force for conservation. This accounts for the occasional ambiguity of its relation to collectivism, since the society which it is conserving may in fact be an individualistic society. But in such a society the Church will in any case tend to be weak. The denomination, which is at home in an individualistic society, tends to be for or against change according as to whether the change promotes or threatens individual values. A denomination may provide some support for a Socialist Party to the extent that it promotes genuine individual values, and it will give to that party something of its own ethos. It is in this context that Morgan Phillips's remark about the British Labour Party owing more to Methodism than to Marx is a relevant half-truth. The general psychological direction of the sect, however, is towards revolutionary change, but in conditions of acute disappointment or when the forces ranged against are overwhelmingly formidable it may take a quietist and pacifist attitude.

On such an analysis as the foregoing one would expect the Church to be an institution covering all classes, although sometimes losing some members of the disinherited groups to the sects, whether religious, or (like the Communist Party) secular. These sects would be largely confined to the lower classes, although occasionally attracting alienated sections of the middle classes provided the ideological formulations appear sufficiently sophisticated. One thinks here of the attraction exercised by the mystique of left-wing sectarianism for alienated sections of the intelligentsia. The denomination is typically lower middle class (the position of Congregationalism in the U.S. being somewhat anomalous) with an appeal for the independently situated type of worker, the earnest self-improving artisan, and to the business man in so far as he is not swallowed up in the collectivism of late monopoly capitalism. The nonconformist shopkeeper is, of course, proverbial.[15]

The sociological idea of the denomination is the idea of Her Majesty's Opposition, of disagreement within consensus, except that the opposition is permanently out of office. As a social phenomenon the denomination is peculiarly characteristic of the United States and the British Commonwealth, and some of the *differentiae* of those societies, their Liberalism, their individualism, their pragmatism, their disunity within consensus, are at least related to the specific *differentiae* of denominationalism. One claims no more than a connection. As such the denomination flourishes in conditions and in countries where social change proceeds at a steady pace according to agreed criteria: in so far as acute social conflict exists men either embrace the ascetic rigours of the sect or turn to the sources of continuity and stability found within the Church.

---

[15] To use a metaphor of Professor Rupp, the denominations provide a social escalator, joining the upper working class to the lower middle class.

However, American Congregationalism, and Unitarianism, both in the U.S. and the U.K., are exceptional in that their membership has high social status. One may hazard the suggestion that denominational Christians have such high social status when a Church declines into a denomination, as did the Presbyterian Church of England in the seventeeth century. The process of Churches becoming denominations has been insufficiently studied. But in any case the numbers involved are small: say 2 million amongst some 50 million denominational Christians.

LIST OF SOURCES

2 : The Break with Nature

R. BENDIX: *Max Weber: an Intellectual Portrait* (London, 1960), Heinemann.

H. BERGSON: *Les Deux Sources de la Morale et de la Religion* (Paris, 1932), Alcan.

H. BUTTERFIELD: *Christianity and History* (London, 1949), G. Bell.

E. CASSIRER: *Essay on Man* (New Haven, 1945), Yale University Press.

C. DAWSON: *Religion and Culture* (London, 1948), Sheed and Ward.

H. J. FISHER: *Ahmadiyyah* (London, 1963), Oxford University Press.

H. FRANKFORT: *Kingship and the Gods* (Chicago, 1948), University of Chicago Press.

H. FRANKFORT: *The Intellectual Adventure of Ancient Man* (Chicago, 1946), University of Chicago Press.

C. W. MILLS and H. GERTH: *From Max Weber* (London, 1948), Routledge and Kegan Paul.

J. R. NOSS: *Man's Religions* (New York, 1946), Macmillan.

R. OTTO: *The Idea of the Holy* (London, 1923), Humphrey Milford.

A. R. RADCLIFFE-BROWN: *Structure and Function in Primitive Society* (London, 1952), Cohen and West.

E. TROELTSCH: *The Social Teachings of the Christian Churches* (London, 1931), Allen and Unwin.

J. WACH: *The Sociology of Religion* (Chicago, 1962), University of Chicago Press.

J. M. YINGER: *Religion, Society and the Individual* (New York, 1957), Macmillan.

3 : Catholic Compromise and Sectarian Rejection

R. BAINTON : *Christian Attitudes to War and Peace* (London, 1961), Hodder and Stoughton.

A. C. F. BEALES : *The Catholic Church and the International Order* (Harmondsworth, 1942), Penguin Books.

H. S. BENDER : *Conrad Grebel* c. *1498–1526* (Goschen, Indiana, 1950), Mennonite Historical Society.

G. BOAS : *Essays on Primitivism and Related Ideas in the Middle Ages* (Baltimore, 1948), Johns Hopkins Press.

R. BULTMANN : *Primitive Christianity* (Edinburgh, 1960), Collins.

C. J. CADOUX : *The Early Church and the World* (Edinburgh, 1925), T. and T. Clark.

C. J. CADOUX : *The Early Christian Attitude to War* (London, 1919), Headley Bros.

F. C. CONYBEARE : *Russian Dissenters* (Cambridge, Mass., 1917), Harvard University Press.

J. DUCHESNE-GUILLEMIN : *The Western Approach to Zoroaster* (Oxford, 1958), The Clarendon Press.

J. HECKER : *Religion and Communism* (London, 1933), Chapman and Hall.

F. HEER : *The Medieval World* (London, 1962), Weidenfeld and Nicolson.

J. E. HUTTON : *A History of the Moravian Church* (London, 1909), Moravian Publications Office.

M. KHADDURI : *The Law of War and Peace in Islam* (London, 1940) Luzac.

R. KNOX : *Enthusiasm* (Oxford, 1950), The Clarendon Press.

J. W. LIGHTLEY : *Jewish Sects and Parties in the Time of Jesus* (London, 1925), Epworth Press.

S. MOWINCKEL : *He that Cometh* (Oxford, 1956), Basil Blackwell.

M. NOTH : *The History of Israel* (London, 1958), A. and C. Black.

G. NUTTALL : *Christian Pacifism* (Oxford, 1958), Basil Blackwell.

W. O. E. OSTERLEY and T. ROBINSON : *A History of Israel*, 2 Vols. (Oxford, 1932), The Clarendon Press.

S. RUNCIMAN : *The Medieval Manichee* (Cambridge, 1947), Cambridge University Press.

K. SCHUBERT : *The Dead Sea Community* : (London, 1959), A. and C. Black.

A. H. SILVER: *History of Messianic Speculation in Israel* (Boston, 1959), Beacon Press.

F. STRATTMAN: *War and Christianity Today* (London, 1956), Blackfriars Publications.

F. STRATTMAN: *The Church and War* (London, 1929), Sheed and Ward.

W. D. WALLIS: *Messiahs* (Washington, 1943) American Council on Public Affairs.

H. J. WARNER: *The Albigensian Heresy*, 2 Vols. (London, 1922), S.P.C.K.

G. M. WILLIAMS: *The Radical Reformation* (London, 1962), Weidenfeld and Nicolson.

E. WILSON: *The Scrolls from the Dead Sea* (London, 1958), Collins.

R. C. ZAEHNER: *Mysticism Sacred and Profane* (London, 1961), Oxford University Press.

4 : A Pilot Study

W. H. G. ARMYTAGE: *Heavens Below* (London, 1961), Routledge and Kegan Paul.

H. N. BRAILSFORD: *The Levellers* (London, 1961), The Cresset Press.

H. N. BRAILSFORD: *Shelley, Godwin and their Circle* (London, 1936), Butterworth.

W. BRAITHWAITE: *The Beginnings of Quakerism* (Cambridge, 1955), Cambridge University Press.

L. FARGO BROWN: *The Political Activities of Baptists and Fifth Monarchy Men* (Washington, 1912), American Historical Association.

N. COHN: *The Pursuit of the Millennium* (London, 1957), Secker and Warburg.

J. FRANK: *The Levellers* (Cambridge, Mass, 1955), Harvard University Press.

G. P. GOOCH: *English Democratic Ideas in the Seventeenth Century* (2nd ed., Cambridge, 1927), Cambridge University Press.

W. HALLER: *The Rise of Puritanism*: (New York, 1938), Columbia University Press.

W. HALLER: *Liberty and Reformation in the Puritan Revolution* (New York, 1955), Columbia University Press.

c. HILL: *Puritanism and Revolution* (London, 1958), Secker and Warburg.

c. HILL: *The Century of Revolution* (Edinburgh, 1961), Nelson.

E. J. HOBSBAWM: *Primitive Rebels* (Manchester, 1959), Manchester University Press.

G. HUEHNS: *Antinomianism in English History* (London, 1951), The Cresset Press.

R. M. JONES: *Mysticism and Democracy in the English Commonwealth* (Cambridge, Mass., 1932), Harvard University Press.

K. MANNHEIM: *Ideology and Utopia* (London, 1936), Routledge and Kegan Paul.

H. R. NIEBUHR: *The Social Sources of Denominationalism* (New York, 1929), Henry Holt.

G. F. NUTTALL: *The Holy Spirit in Puritan Faith and Experience* (Oxford, 1946), Basil Blackwell.

I. PYZIUR: *The Doctrine of Anarchism of Michael A. Bakunin* (Milwaukee, 1955), Marquette University Press.

S. RANULF: *Moral Indignation and Middle-Class Psychology* (Copenhagen, 1938), Levin and Munksgaard.

G. SABINE (ed.): *The Works of Gerrard Winstanley* (Cornell, 1941), Cornell University Press.

G. SOREL: *Reflections of Violence* (London, 1925), Allen and Unwin.

J. SYKES: *The Quakers* (London, 1958), Allen and Wingate.

J. F. TALMON: *Political Messianism: The Romantic Phase* (London, 1960), Secker and Warburg.

P. M. WORSLEY: *The Trumpet Shall Sound* (London, 1957), MacGibbon and Kee.

5: Old and New Dissent: a Prologue

M. ANDERSON: *Noel Buxton: a Life* (London, 1952), Allen and Unwin.

N. ANGELL: *The Great Illusion* (London, 1910), Heinemann.

P. NOEL-BAKER and E. BAKER: *J. Allen Baker, M.P.* (London, 1927), The Swarthmore Press.

A. C. F. BEALES: *The History of Peace* (London, 1931), G. Bell.

H. N. BRAILSFORD: *The War of Steel and Gold* (London, 1914), G. Bell.

A. BULLOCK and M. SHOCK: *The Liberal Tradition* (London, 1956), A. and C. Black.

V. DE BUNSEN: *Charles Roden Buxton* (London, 1948), Allen and Unwin.

R. C. K. ENSOR: *England 1870–1914* (Oxford, 1936), The Clarendon Press.

H. EVANS: *Sir Randal Cremer* (London, 1909), Fisher Unwin.

G. P. GOOCH: *Life of Lord Courtney* (London, 1920), Macmillan.

E. HALEVY: *A History of the English People. Epilogue.* 2 Vols. (London, 1929 and 1934), Ernest Benn.

J. A. HOBSON: *Imperialism* (London, 1902), Allen and Unwin.

S. MACCOBY: *English Radicalism 1886–1914* (London, 1953), Allen and Unwin.

S. MACCOBY: *English Radicalism. The End?* (London, 1961), Allen and Unwin.

J. MORLEY: *Life of Gladstone.* 2 Vols. (London, 1908), Edward Lloyd.

C. PLAYNE: *The Pre-War Mind in Britain* (London, 1928), Allen and Unwin.

E. SILBERNER: *The Problem of War in Nineteenth Century Economic Thought* (Princeton, 1946), Princeton University Press.

H. SPENCER: *The Principles of Sociology*, Vol. II, Part V (New York, 1896), Appleton and Co.

A. J. P. TAYLOR: *The Trouble Makers* (London, 1957). Hamish Hamilton.

A. P. THORNTON: *The Imperial Idea and its Enemies* (London 1959), Macmillan.

K. WALTZ: *Man, the State and War* (New York, 1959), Columbia University Press.

B. WEBB: *Our Partnership* (London, 1948), Longmans, Green.

6: The Labour Party and the I.L.P.

C. R. ATTLEE: *As it Happened* (London, 1954), Heinemann.

P. J. NOEL-BAKER: *The Private Manufacture of Armaments*, Vol. I (London, 1936), Gollancz.

P. J. NOEL-BAKER, *et al*: *Challenge to Death* (London, 1934), Constable.

R. BASSETT: *Nineteen Thirty-One* (*London, 1958*), Macmillan.

R. BASSETT: *Democracy and Foreign Policy* (London, 1952), L.S.E. Publication.

G. M. BEATON: *Twenty Years' Work in the War Resisters' International* (Enfield, 1945). W.R.I.

B. BRAATOY: *Labour and War* (London, 1934), Allen and Unwin.

F. BROCKWAY: *Bermondsey Story* (London, 1949), Allen and Unwin.

F. BROCKWAY: *Inside the Left* (London, 1942), Allen and Unwin.

F. BROCKWAY: *Socialism over Sixty Years* (London, 1946), Allen and Unwin.

A. L. C. BULLOCK: *The Life and Times of Ernest Bevin*, Vol. I (London, 1960), Heinemann.

W. J. CHAMBERLAIN: *Fighting for Peace: the story of the war-resistance movement* (London, 1928), Heinemann.

C. A. CLINE: *Recruits to Labour* (New York, 1963), Syracuse University Press.

J. R. CLYNES: *Memoirs* (London, 1937), Hutchinson.

G. C. COULTON: *Pacifist Illusions: A Criticism of the Union of Democratic Control* (Cambridge, 1915), Bowes and Bowes.

G. D. CROSBY: *Disarmament and Peace in British Politics* (Cambridge, Mass., 1957), Harvard University Press.

C. CROSS: *The Fascists in Britain* (London, 1961) Barne and Rockliff.

H. DALTON: *The Fateful Years* (London, 1957), Frederick Muller.

E. F. M. DURBIN *et al*: *War and Democracy* (London, 1938), Routledge and Kegan Paul.

LORD ELTON: *The Life of James Ramsay MacDonald, 1866–1919* (London, 1939), Collins.

E. ESTORICK: *Stafford Cripps* (London, 1949), Heinemann

Fabian Lectures 1937: *Dare We Look Ahead?* (London 1938) Allen and Unwin.

K. FEILING: *Life of Neville Chamberlain* (London, 1946), Macmillan.

E. M. FORSTER: *Goldsworthy Lowes Dickinson* (Cambridge, 1934), Edward Arnold.

J. M. GAUS: *Great Britain: A Study in Civic Loyalty* (Chicago, 1929), University of Chicago Press.

G. P. GOOCH: *Studies in Diplomacy and Statecraft* (London, 1942), Longmans, Green.

List of Sources

J. W. GRAHAM: *Conscription and Conscience* (London, 1922), Allen and Unwin.

W. L. GUTTSMAN: *The British Political Élite* (London, 1963), MacGibbon and Kee.

LORD HALIFAX: *Fullness of Days* (London, 1957), Collins.

M. A. HAMILTON: *Arthur Henderson* (London, 1938), Heinemann.

H. J. HANHAM: *Elections and Party Management* (London, 1959), Longmans.

D. HAYES: *Challenge of Conscience* (London, 1949), Allen and Unwin.

F. W. HIRST: *The Consequences of the War to Great Britain* (London, 1934), Humphrey Milford.

P. V. KELLOGG and A. GLEASON: *British Labor and the War* (New York, 1919), Boni and Liveright.

J. KENT: *John Burns* (London, 1950), Williams and Norgate.

J. M. KEYNES: *The Economic Consequences of the Peace* (London, 1920), Macmillan.

D. KIRKWOOD: *My Life of Revolt* (London, 1935), Harrap.

M. M. KRUG: *Aneurin Bevan: Cautious Rebel* (New York—London, 1961), Thomas Yoselaff.

J. LEDERER (ed.): *The Versailles Settlement* (Boston, 1960), C. Heath.

H. B. LEES-SMITH (ed.): *The Encyclopedia of the Labour Movement* 2 Vols. (London, 1928), Caxton.

A. LIVINGSTONE: *The Peace Ballot: The Official History* (London, 1935), Gollancz.

R. B. MACALLUM: *Public Opinion and the Last Peace* (London, 1944), Oxford University Press.

J. MCNAIR: *James Maxton* (London, 1955), Allen and Unwin.

W. P. MADDOX: *Foreign Relations in British Labour Politics* (Cambridge, Mass., 1934), Harvard University Press.

K. MARTIN: *Harold Laski* (London, 1953), Gollancz.

E. G. MEEHAN: *The British Left Wing and Foreign Policy* (New Brunswick, 1960), Rutgers University Press.

R. MILIBAND: *Parliamentary Socialism* (London, 1961), Allen and Unwin.

LORD MORRISON: *Herbert Morrison* (London, 1960), Odhams.

C. L. MOWAT: *Britain Between the Wars* (London, 1955), Methuen.

L. NAMIER: *Europe in Decay: a Study in Disintegration, 1936–1940* (London, 1950), Macmillan.

LORD PARMOOR : *A Retrospect* (London, 1936), Heinemann.

H. PELLING : *The British Communist Party* (London, 1958), A. and C. Black.

R. POSTGATE : *George Lansbury* (London, 1951) Longmans, Green.

J. RAYMOND (ed.) : *The Baldwin Age* (London, 1960), Eyre and Spottiswoode.

A. L. ROWSE : *All Souls and Appeasement* (London, 1960), Macmillan.

P. SNOWDEN : *An Autobiography*, 2 Vols. (London, 1934), Ivor Nicholson and Watson.

W. STEWART : *J. Keir Hardie* (London, 1921), I.L.P. Publications.

H. M. SWANWICK : *Builders of Peace* (London, 1924), Swarthmore Press.

H. M. SWANWICK : *The Roots of Peace* (London, 1938), Jonathan Cape.

L. THOMPSON : *Robert Blatchford* (London, 1951), Gollancz.

University Group on Defence Policy : *The Role of the Peace Movements in the 1930's* (London, 1959), University Group on Defence Policy.

A. VAN DER SLICE : *International Labour, Diplomacy and Peace* (London, 1941), Oxford University Press.

C. V. WEDGWOOD : *The Last of the Radicals : Josiah Wedgwood, M.P.* (London, 1951), Jonathan Cape.

L. M. WEIR : *The Tragedy of Ramsay MacDonald* (London, 1939), Collins.

I. WILLIS : *How We Went into the War* (Manchester, 1918), National Labour Press.

I. WILLIS : *How We Got On With the War* (Manchester, 1920), National Labour Press.

I. WILLIS : *How We Came Out of the War* (London, 1921), International Bookshops Ltd.

H. R. WINKLER : *The League of Nations Movement in Great Britain, 1914–1919* (New Brunswick, 1952), Rutgers University Press.

L. WOOLF (ed.) : *The Intelligent Man's Way to Prevent War* (London, 1933), Gollancz.

G. M. YOUNG : *Stanley Baldwin* (London, 1952), Rupert Hart-Davis.

K. ZILLIACUS : *Inquest on Peace* (London, 1935), Gollancz.

7 : *Pacifism and the Intelligentsia*

R. ALDINGTON: *Death of a Hero* (London, 1929), Chatto and Windus.

R. ARON: *The Opium of the Intellectuals* (London, 1956), Secker and Warburg.

M. P. ASHLEY and C. T. SAUNDERS: *Red Oxford* (Oxford, 1930), The Holywell Press.

J. A. ATKINS: *Aldous Huxley : a Literary Study* (London, 1956), John Calder.

J. A. ATKINS: *George Orwell* (London, 1954), John Calder.

C. BELL: *Old Friends* (London, 1956), Chatto and Windus.

C. BELL: *Peace at Once* (Manchester, 1915) National Labour Press.

J. BELL (ed.): *We Did Not Fight* (London, 1935), Cobden-Sanderson.

H. N. BRAILSFORD: *Towards a New League* (London, 1936), *New Statesman* Pamphlet.

H. N. BRAILSFORD: *Why Capitalism Means War* (London, 1938), Gollancz.

V. BRITTAIN: *Testament of Youth* (London, 1933), Gollancz.

V. BRITTAIN: *Testament of Experience* (London, 1957), Gollancz.

V. BRITTAIN: *Testament of Friendship : The story of Winifred Holtby* (London, 1940), Macmillan.

E. CARPENTER: *Civilization : Its Cause and Cure* (London, 1889), Swan Sonnenschein.

C. CAUDWELL: *Studies in a Dying Culture* (London, 1938), The Bodley Head.

C. CAUDWELL: *Further Studies in a Dying Culture* (London, 1949), The Bodley Head.

L. FISCHER: *Mahatma Gandhi* (London, 1951), Jonathan Cape.

M. FOOT *et al*: *Young Oxford and War* (London, 1934), Selwyn and Blount.

E. M. FORESTER: *Two Cheers for Democracy* (London, 1951), Edward Arnold.

D. GARNETT: *The Golden Echo* (London, 1953), Chatto and Windus.

D. GARNETT: *Flowers of the Forest* (London, 1955), Chatto and Windus.

D. GARNETT: *The Familiar Faces* (London, 1962), Chatto and Windus.

C. GIDE: *Communist and Co-operative Colonies* (London, 1930), Harrap.

E. GILL: *Autobiography* (London, 1940), Jonathan Cape.

V. GOLLANCZ: *My Dear Timothy* (London, 1952), Gollancz.

V. GOLLANCZ: *More for Timothy* (London, 1953), Gollancz.

R. GRAVES and A. HODGE: *The Long Weekend* (London, 1940), Faber and Faber.

R. GRAVES: *Goodbye to All That* (London, 1929), Cassell.

R. B. GREGG: *The Power of Non-Violence* (London, 1934), J. B. Lippincott.

R. HARROD: *Life of John Maynard Keynes* (London, 1951), Macmillan.

S. HOBHOUSE: *Forty Years and an Epilogue* (London, 1951), James Clarke.

L. HOUSMAN (ed.): *What Can We Believe?* Letters exchanged with Dick Sheppard (London, 1939), Jonathan Cape.

A. HUXLEY: *Means and Ends* (London, 1937), Chatto and Windus.

A. HUXLEY (ed.): *An Encyclopedia of Pacifism* (London, 1937), Chatto and Windus.

E. HYAMS: *The New Statesman: the First Fifty Years* (London, 1963), Longmans.

W. R. INGE: *A Pacifist in Trouble* (London, 1939), Putnam.

W. R. INGE *et al*: *Causes of War* (London, 1935), Allen and Unwin.

J. HAMPDEN JACKSON: *Marx, Proudhon and European Socialism* (London, 1957). The English Universities Press.

C. E. M. JOAD: *The Book of Joad* (London, 1935), Faber and Faber.

C. E. M. JOAD: *Why War?* (Harmondsworth, 1939). Penguin Books.

A. CAMPBELL JOHNSON: *Peace Offering* (London, 1936), Methuen.

F. A. LEA: *The Life of John Middleton Murry* (London, 1959), Methuen.

C. DAY LEWIS: *The Buried Day* (London, 1960), Chatto and Windus.

J. LEWIS: *The Case Against Pacifism* (London, 1940), Allen and Unwin.

B. DE LIGT: *The Conquest of Violence* (London, 1937), Routledge and Kegan Paul.

S. M. LIPSET: *Political Man* (London, 1960), Heinemann.

R. MACAULAY *et al*: *Let Us Honour Peace* (London, 1937), Cobden-Sanderson.

E. MANNIN: *Confessions and Impressions* (London, 1930), Jarrolds.

E. MANNIN: *Privileged Spectator* (London, 1939), Jarrolds.

E. MANNIN: *Brief Voices* (London, 1959), Hutchinson.

A. A. MILNE: *It's Too Late Now* (London, 1939), Methuen.

A. A. MILNE: *Peace with Honour* (London, 1934), Methuen.

S. MORRISON: *I Renounce War* (London, 1962), The Sheppard Press.

A. L. MORTON: *The English Utopia* (London, 1952), Lawrence and Wishart.

G. MURRAY: *An Unfinished Autobiography* (London, 1960), Allen and Unwin.

J. M. MURRY: *The Pledge of Peace* (London, 1938), Michael Joseph.

B. NICHOLS: *Cry Havoc!* (London, 1933), Jonathan Cape.

L. R. CONRAD NOEL: *An Autobiography* (London, 1946), Dent.

M. PLOWMAN: *The Faith Called Pacifism* (London, 1936), Dent.

H. READ: *Poetry and Anarchism* (London, 1938), Faber and Faber.

H. READ: *The Politics of the Unpolitical* (London, 1943), Routledge and Kegan Paul.

E. M. REMARQUE: *All Quiet on the Western Front* (London, 1929), Putnam.

B. RUSSELL: *Which Way to Peace?* (London, 1936), Michael Joseph.

S. SASSOON: *Memoirs of an Infantry Officer* (London, 1930), Faber and Faber.

S. SASSOON: *Memoirs of a Fox-Hunting Man* (London, 1929), Faber and Faber.

S. SASSOON: *Siegfried's Journey 1916–1920* (London, 1945), Faber and Faber.

P. SELVER: *A. R. Orage and his circle* (London, 1959), Allen and Unwin.

R. C. SHERRIFF: *Journey's End* (London, 1929), Gollancz.

S. SPENDER: *World Within World* (London, 1951), Hamish Hamilton.

W. O. STAPLEDON: *Waking World* (London, 1934), Methuen.

J. SYMONS: *The Thirties* (London, 1960), The Cresset Press.

A. WOOD: *The Passionate Sceptic* (London, 1957), Allen and Unwin.

N. WOOD: *Communism and British Intellectuals* (London, 1959), Gollancz.

8: Dissent and the Establishment.

G. K. A. BELL: *Randall Davidsom*, 2 Vols. (London, 1935), Oxford University Press.

F. K. BROWN: *Fathers of the Victorians* (Cambridge, 1961), Cambridge University Press.

R. G. COWHERD: *The Politics and English Dissent* (London, 1959), Epworth Press.

H. DAVIES: *Worship and Theology in England* (Princeton, 1962), Princeton University Press.

M. EDWARDS: *Methodism and England* (London, 1943), Epworth Press.

J. FERGUSON (ed.): *Studies in Christian Social Commitment* (London, 1954), Independent Press.

A. FOX: *Dean Inge* (London, 1960), John Murray.

S. J. B. GROSER: *Politics and Persons* (London, 1949), S.C.M. Press.

P. HARTHILL (ed.): *Into the Way of Peace* (London, 1942), J. Clarke.

K. S. INGLIS: *Churches and the Working Classes in Victorian England* (London, 1963), Routledge and Kegan Paul.

F. A. IREMONGER: *William Temple* (London, 1948), Oxford University Press.

R. TUDUR JONES: *Congregationalism in England 1662–1962* (London, 1962), Independent Press.

A. D. LINDSAY: *Pacificism as a Principle and Pacificism as a Dogma* (London, 1939), S.C.M. Press.

A. LUNN: *Enigma. A Study of Moral Rearmament* (London, 1957), Longmans, Green.

G. H. C. MACGREGOR: *The New Testament basis of pacifism* (London, 1936), J. Clarke.

G. H. C. MACGREGOR: *The Relevance of the Impossible* (London, 1941), Fellowship of Reconciliation.

G. F. MACLEOD: *Only One Way Left* (Glasgow, 1956), Iona Community.

H. MARTIN: *The Christian as Soldier* (London, 1939), S.C.M. Press.

A. G. MATTHEWS (ed.): *The Savoy Declaration of Faith and Order, 1658* (London, 1959), Independent Press.

E. A. PAYNE: *The Baptist Union. A Short History* (London, 1958), The Carey Kingsgate Press.

C. RAVEN: *War and the Christian* (London, 1938), S.C.M. Press.

C. RAVEN: *The Theological Basis of Pacifism* (London, 1952), Fellowship of Reconciliation.

L. RICHARDS: *The Christian Contribution to Peace* (London, 1935), S.C.M. Press.

R. ELLIS ROBERTS: *H. R. L. Sheppard. Life and Letters* (London, 1942), John Murray.

E. ROUTLEY: *English Religious Dissent* (Cambridge, 1960), Cambridge University Press.

G. S. SPINKS: *Religion in Britain Since 1900* (London, 1952) Andrew Dakers.

L. STEVENSON: *Towards a Christian International* (London, 1941), International Fellowship of Reconciliation.

R. N. STROMBERG: *Religious Liberalism in Eighteenth-Century England* (London, 1954), Oxford University Press.

E. R. TAYLOR: *Methodism and Politics, 1791–1851* (Cambridge, 1935), Cambridge University Press.

A. C. UNDERWOOD: *History of the English Baptists* (London, 1947), Baptist Union Publications Department.

E. C. URWIN: *Henry Carter, C.B.E. A Memoir* (London, 1955), Epworth Press.

A. R. VIDLER: *The Church in an Age of Revolution* (Harmondsworth, 1961), Penguin Books.

R. F. WEARMOUTH: *Methodism and the Struggle of the Working Classes, 1850–1900* (Leicester, 1954), Edgar Backus.

R. F. WEARMOUTH: *The Social and Political Influence of Methodism in the Twentieth Century* (London, 1957), Epworth Press.

J. S. WHALE: *The Protestant Tradition* (Cambridge, 1955), Cambridge University Press.

9 : Sect, Order and Cult

G. S. ARUNDALE : *Peace and War in the Light of Theosophy* (Adyar, Madras, 1938), Theosophical Publishing House.

R. D. BOWMAN : *The Church of the Brethren and War* (Elgin, Illinois, 1944), The Brethren Press.

J. H. COUSINS : *War : a Theosophical View* (London, 1914), Theosophical Publishing Society.

M. S. CZATT : *The International Bible Students : Jehovah's Witnesses* (Scottdale, Pa., 1933), Mennonite Press.

H. DAVIES : *Christian Deviations* (London, 1954), S.C.M. Press.

E. GOSSE : *Father and Son* (London, 1958), Heinemann.

R. HUBBARD : *Scientology 8–8008* (Bedford, 1956), Foundry Press.

H. A. IRONSIDE : *The Development of the Brethren Movement* (Grand Rapids, Michigan, 1942), Zondervan Publishing House.

R. M. JONES : *The Faith and Practice of the Quakers* (London, 1927), Methuen.

R. M. JONES : *The Later Periods of Quakerism*, 2 Vols. (London, 1921), Macmillan.

W. Z. LACQUER : *Young Germany* (London, 1962), Routledge and Kegan Paul.

W. B. NEATBY : *A History of the Plymouth Brethren* (London, 1901), Hodder and Stoughton.

A. H. NETHERCOTT : *The First Five Lives of Annie Besant* (London, 1961), Rupert Hart-Davies.

H. M. D. NICOLL : *Psychological Commentaries on Gurdieff and Ouspensky*, 3 Vols. (London, 1949), Kitchen and Barratt.

R. PIKE : *Jehovah's Witnesses* (London, 1954), Watts.

E. J. PULSFORD : *Should Christians Fight?* (London, 1940), New Church and Missionary and Tract Society.

R. SCOTT : *Elizabeth Cadbury, 1858–1951* (London, 1955), Harrap.

H. SPEARMAN : *Modern Theosophy* (Adyar, Madras, 1954), Theosophical Publishing House.

H. H. STROUP : *The Jehovah's Witnesses* (New York, 1945), Columbia University Press.

T. S. VEITCH : *The Story of the Brethren Movement* (London, 1933), Pickering and Inglis.

B. R. WILSON : *Sects and Society* (London, 1961), Heinemann. Publications of the Aetherius Society.

List of Sources

Some References regarding Pacifism in the United States

C. A. BARKER : *Henry George* (New York, 1955), Oxford University Press.

M. E. CURTI : *Peace or War : The American Struggle, 1636–1936* (New York, 1936), W. W. Norton.

M. E. CURTI : *The American Peace Crusade, 1815–1860* (Durham N.C., 1929), Duke University Press.

M. E. CURTI : *Bryan and World Peace* (Smith College, Mass., 1930), Smith College, Mass.

R. HOFSTADTER : *The Age of Reform : From Bryan to F.D.R.* (New York, 1961), Knopf.

C. H. HOPKINS : *The Rise of the Social Gospel in American Protestantism, 1865–1915* (New Haven, 1940), Yale University Press.

J. NEAL HUGHLEY : *Trends in Protestant Social Idealism* (New York, 1948), King's Crown Press.

R. M. MILLER : *American Protestantism, Social Issues, 1919–1939* (Chapel Hill, 1958), University of California Press.

H. R. NIEBUHR : *The Kingdom of God in America* (Hamden, Conn., 1956), The Shoe String Press.

R. NIEBUHR : *The Irony of American History* (London, 1952), Nisbet.

M. Q. SIBLEY and P.E. JACOB : *Conscription of Conscience : the American State and the Conscientious Objector, 1940–1947* (Ithaca, 1952) Cornell University Press.

J. M. YINGER : *Religion in the Struggle for Power* (Durham N.C., 1946), Duke University Press.

Unclassified and General Sources

E. H. CARR : *The Twenty Years' Crisis, 1919–1939* (London, 1958), Macmillan.

E. G. GLOVER : *War, Sadism and Pacifism* (London, 1933), Allen and Unwin.

F. GROSS : *European Ideologies* (New York, 1948), Philosophical Library.

J. J. P. MACQUET : *The Sociology of Knowledge* (Boston, 1951), Beacon Press.

D. G. MACRAE : *Ideology and Society* (London, 1961), Heinemann.

List of Sources

K. MANNHEIM: *Essays on the Sociology of Knowledge* (London, 1952), Routledge and Kegan Paul.

K. MANNHEIM: *Essays on the Sociology of Culture* (London, 1956), Routledge and Kegan Paul.

R. NIEBUHR: *Nations and Empires* (London, 1960), Faber.

R. NEIBUHR: *The Godly and the Ungodly* (London, 1949), Faber.

R. NIEBUHR: *The Children of Light and the Children of Darkness* (London, 1945), Nisbet.

R. NIEBUHR: *Christian Realism and Political Problems* (London, 1954), Faber.

R. NIEBUHR: *An Interpretation of Christian Ethics* (London, 1948), S.C.M. Press.

R. NIEBUHR: *Moral Man in Immoral Society* (New York, 1934), Scribner.

W. STARK: *The Sociology of Knowledge* (London, 1958), Routledge and Kegan Paul.

Articles

W. A. COLE: 'The Quakers and the English Revolution' (*Past and Present*, November, 1956).

R. E. DOWSE: 'The Independent Labour Party and Foreign Policy, 1918–1923' (*International Review of Social History*, Vol. VII, Part I, 1962).

F. R. FLOURNOY: 'British Liberal Theories of International Relations, 1848–1898' (*Journal of the History of Ideas*, Vol. VII, No. 2, April 1946).

N. KEDDIE: 'Religion and Irreligion in Early Iranian Nationalism' (*Comparative Studies in Society and History*, Vol. IV, No. 3, April 1962).

B. JOHNSON: 'On Church and Sect' (*American Sociological Review* Vol. XXVIII, No. 4, August 1963).

J. R. LEVENSON: 'Confucian and Taiping "Heaven"' (*Comparative Studies in Society and History*, Vol. IV, No. 4, July 1962).

C. A. MADISON: 'Anarchism in the United States' (*Journal of the History of Ideas*, Vol. VI, No. 1, January 1945).

A. J. B. MARWICK: 'The Independent Labour Party in the Nineteen Twenties' (*Bulletin of the Institute of Historical Research*, Vol. XXXV, No. 91, 1960).

List of Sources

Y. TALMON: 'The Pursuit of the Millennium' (*European Journal of Sociology*, Vol. III, No. 1, 1962).

H. R. TREVOR-ROPER: *The Gentry 1540–1640* (Economic History Supplement No. 1, Cambridge University Press, London, 1953).

LIN TUNG-CHI: 'The Chinese Mind: Its Taoist Substratum' (*Journal of the History of Ideas*, Vol. VIII, No. 3, June 1947).

E. WERNER: 'Popular Ideologies in Late Medieval Europe' (*Comparative Studies in Society and History*, Vol. II, No. 3, April 1960).

B. R. WILSON: 'An Analysis of Sect Development' (*American Sociological Review*, Vol. XXIV, No. 1, January 1959).

H. R. WINKLER: 'The Emergence of a Labor Foreign Policy in Britain, 1918–1929' (*Journal of Modern History*, September 1956).

J. W. VANDER ZANDEN: 'The Non-Violent Resistance Movement against Segregation' (*American Journal of Sociology*, Vol. LXVIII, No. 5, March 1963).

Theses

R. L. ARMSBY: *The Early Quaker View of the State* (B.A., Birmingham, 1932).

H. S. BARBOUR: *The Early Quaker Outlook on 'the World' and 'Society'* (Ph.D. Thesis, Yale, 1952).

A. R. CHAMPION DE CRESPIGNY: *The Character and Conditions of Non-Violent Coercion as a Political Method* (Ph.D., London, 1963).

W. A. COLE: *The Quakers and Politics, 1652–1660* (Ph.D., Peterhouse, Cambridge, 1955).

S. DAVIS: *The Labour Party and Foreign Policy, 1933–1939.* (Ph.D., London, 1950).

E. FARRAR: *The Labour Party and International Organization* (Ph.D., London, 1952).

J. JUPP: *The Left in Britain* (M.Sc. Econ., London, 1956).

F. MANTHEY (Jr): *Christians and War* (Ph.D., Edinburgh, 1952).

A. J. B. MARWICK: *The Independent Labour Party (1918–1932)* (B. Litt., Oxford, 1960).

G. W. SHEPHERD: *Theory and Practice of Internationalism in the British Labour Party* (Ph.D., London, 1952).

E. STERNE: *The Opposition in the Liberal and Labour Parties to Liberal Foreign Policy 1906–1914* (M.A., Leeds, 1957).

M. I. THOMIS: *The Labour Movement in Great Britain and Conscription* (M.A., London, 1951).

P. S. WANDYCZ: *Liberal Internationalism: the Contribution of British and French Thought to the Theory of International Relations* (Ph.D., London, 1950).

INDEX

247

DATE DUE

26 '89